Overhauling Learning for Multilingual Students

An Approach for Achieving Pedagogical Justice

Jeff Zwiers

For information:

Corwin
A SAGE Company
2455 Teller Road
Thousand Oaks, California 91320
(800) 233-9936
www.corwin.com

SAGE Publications Ltd.
1 Oliver's Yard
55 City Road
London EC1Y 1SP
United Kingdom

SAGE Publications India Pvt. Ltd.
Unit No 323-333, Third Floor, F-Block
International Trade Tower Nehru Place
New Delhi 110 019
India

SAGE Publications Asia-Pacific Pte., Ltd.
18 Cross Street #10-10/11/12
China Square Central
Singapore 048423

Vice President and Editorial Director: Monica Eckman
Program Director and Publisher: Dan Alpert
Content Development Editor: Mia Rodriguez
Senior Editorial Assistant: Natalie Delpino
Editorial Intern: Lex Nunez
Production Editor: Vijayakumar
Copy Editor: Ritika Sharma
Typesetter: TNQ Tech Pvt. Ltd.
Proofreader: Girish Kumar Sharma
Indexer: TNQ Tech Pvt. Ltd.
Cover Designer: Gail Buschman
Marketing Manager: Melissa Duclos

Copyright © 2024 by Corwin Press, Inc.

All rights reserved. Except as permitted by U.S. copyright law, no part of this work may be reproduced or distributed in any form or by any means, or stored in a database or retrieval system, without permission in writing from the publisher.

When forms and sample documents appearing in this work are intended for reproduction, they will be marked as such. Reproduction of their use is authorized for educational use by educators, local school sites, and/or noncommercial or nonprofit entities that have purchased the book.

All third-party trademarks referenced or depicted herein are included solely for the purpose of illustration and are the property of their respective owners. Reference to these trademarks in no way indicates any relationship with, or endorsement by, the trademark owner.

Printed in the United States of America

Library of Congress Cataloging-in-Publication Data

Names: Zwiers, Jeff, author.

Title: Overhauling learning for multilingual students : an approach for achieving pedagogical justice / Jeff Zwiers.

Description: Thousand Oaks, California : Corwin Press, 2024. | Includes bibliographical references and index.

Identifiers: LCCN 2023054344 | ISBN 9781071921999 (paperback) | ISBN 9781071922026 (ebook) | ISBN 9781071922002 (epub) | ISBN 9781071922019 (epub)

Subjects: LCSH: Multilingual education–Aims and objectives. | Culturally relevant pedagogy. | Educational tests and measurements. | Curriculum planning.

Classification: LCC LC3715 .Z85 2024 | DDC 370.117/5–dc23/eng/20231206

LC record available at https://lccn.loc.gov/2023054344

This book is printed on acid-free paper.

24 25 26 27 28 10 9 8 7 6 5 4 3 2 1

DISCLAIMER: This book may direct you to access third-party content via web links, QR codes, or other scannable technologies, which are provided for your reference by the author(s). Corwin makes no guarantee that such third-party content will be available for your use and encourages you to review the terms and conditions of such third-party content. Corwin takes no responsibility and assumes no liability for your use of any third-party content, nor does Corwin approve, sponsor, endorse, verify, or certify such third-party content.

Contents

About the Author vii

Acknowledgments ix

Publisher's Acknowledgments xi

Introduction 1

Chapter 1. Pedagogical Justice 7

Chapter 2. What Students Learn and How They Grow 43

Chapter 3. Assessment 79

Chapter 4. Pedagogy 117

Chapter 5. Instruction 149

Chapter 6. The System 185

Appendix A Summary Chart 225
Appendix B Examples of Overhauled Units 227

Appendix C Examples of Big Idea Statements	259
Appendix D Examples of Products, Projects, and Performances	269
Index	273

About the Author

Dr. Jeff Zwiers is a senior researcher in the Center to Support Excellence in Teaching within the Stanford University Graduate School of Education. He has taught all subjects bilingually in secondary and elementary settings. His research and work focus on collaborating and co-teaching with teachers to enhance all instruction for multilingual students. This includes teaching and learning with more authentic communication across the disciplines, with an emphasis on improving student–student interactions. Jeff has also written books and articles on literacy, conversation, and language development, along with children's books and language development curriculums.

Acknowledgments

The approach described in this book is built on the ideas of key thinkers in the past 100 years or so. These thinkers include John Dewey, Lev Vygotsky, Deborah Meier, Gloria Ladson-Billings, Lilia Bartolomé, Geneva Gay, Pedro Noguera, Maxine Greene, Linda Darling-Hammond, Paolo Freire, Linda Tuhiwai Smith, Mikhail Bakhtin, Sarah Michaels, and Grant Wiggins. Unfortunately, their profound ideas and insights have not been applied well enough to our educational systems and practices. My hope is that this book will communicate a message that amplifies and extends their voices while turning their ideas into reality.

I would also like to thank the many wonderful educators with whom I have worked over the years. Their dedication and commitment to effective instruction and multilingual students' overall growth has been a continued inspiration for this work.

And I would like to express deep appreciation for my wonderful family and their boundless patience during the writing of this book.

Publisher's Acknowledgments

Corwin gratefully acknowledges the contributions of the following reviewers:

Kelsey Dietrick
Special Education Teacher/Diagnostic Coordinator
Bristol Township School District
Levittown, PA

Christine Landwehrle
Assistant Superintendent
Amherst, Mont Vernon, and Souhegan Cooperative School Districts
Amherst, NH

Cassandra Meyer
Teacher
Madison Metropolitan School District
Madison, WI

Melissa Miller
Middle School Science Educator
Farmington Middle School
Farmington, AR

Renee Nealon
Elementary School Teacher
Petaluma City Schools
Petaluma, CA

Jonell Pacyga
Professor
University of Northwestern–St. Paul
St. Paul, MN

Introduction

The main problem addressed in this book is the mismatch between the instruction and assessment that millions of multilingual students* need in order to thrive and the instruction and assessment that they experience. While this mismatch exists for most students, it is even more harmful for multilingual students (Cunningham, 2019).

The current model of learning, which is grounded in the accumulation of a set of facts and skills, ignores and devalues the many assets that multilingual students bring with them to the learning table. These assets include a rich array of languages, cultural backgrounds, knowledge, talents, interests, and stories. Accumulation-focused learning tends to overload multilingual students with linguistically complex tasks in English, disconnected information to memorize, and semi- to nonengaging content (Darling-Hammond, 2007). As a result, many multilingual students lack feelings of agency, belonging in school, respect, and freedom to voice their ideas and opinions (Beyer, 2017).

---

*I use the term "multilingual students" in this book. Most multilingual students grew up speaking a language other than English. Many speak two or more non-English languages. Multilingual students have a wide range of diverse backgrounds. Many come from other countries, many migrate, many are refugees, and many have had gaps in their schooling. The suggestions in this book will also benefit students who speak variations of English that differ from the language of texts and tasks commonly used in school.

For decades, testing companies, curriculum companies, and policymakers have perpetuated the narrative that large multiple-choice tests in English are all that we need to scientifically show learning progress—and that schools must do all they can to help all students to improve their scores in the same way. Yet as Chapter 1 describes, this narrative heavily favors monolingual, middle-class, English-speaking students. Multilingual students, in contrast, are more likely to struggle, disengage, and drop out of school than their monolingual peers (Christle et al., 2007).

When a system supports the success and well-being of one group more than others, that system is unjust and requires change. This book focuses on changing school-based learning at the classroom level and at the system level in order to achieve *pedagogical justice*. Pedagogical justice means giving all students the appropriate support, resources, instruction, time, encouragement, relationships, opportunities, and choices to become the individuals they were meant to be. For multilingual students, in particular, it means providing learning experiences that value their backgrounds and languages—not in order to memorize facts and skills for tests, but to learn and grow and thrive.

Most teachers have a mix of monolingual and multilingual students in their classrooms. And most teachers do not have time or energy to differentiate their lessons among their students. Even in the cases where such lessons and activities are differentiated, multilingual students are often asked less interesting and less cognitively challenging questions. I therefore recommend reading the following chapters with an eye on overhauling instruction for *all* of your students. Along the way, you will find that your monolingual students will also benefit from these changes.

Also, read this book with an eye on the long term. This is not a one-month or even a one-year process. In most cases, it starts in a handful of classrooms and grows over time. Chapter 6 describes different starting points (e.g., unit, course, assessments, grade level, policy, etc.) where a district or school might begin.

Overhauling takes time, but the stakes are too high to keep spending precious time on minor reforms and short-lived initiatives aimed at bumping up test scores a few percentage points. This book instead argues for an approach that addresses a multitude of issues:

- Giving students high levels of voice and choice as they learn
- Changing how we assess student learning and growth

- Focusing more on communication, products, and performances than on percentiles and points
- Valuing the building of relationships, fostering student agency, and encouraging student creativity

Chapter 1 starts with six dimensions of pedagogical justice: student agency, engaging challenges, idea-building, meaningful interactions, critical and creative thinking, and assessment for learning. Chapter 2 digs into what students should be learning and how they should be growing. Chapter 3 then looks at ways to assess these things more effectively and more engagingly than points-focused tasks and tests. Chapter 4 presents an alternative model for instruction and assessment, which I call the Idea-Building Approach. Chapter 5 describes how to overhaul classroom instruction for idea-building, with an emphasis on unit and lesson design.

The bulk of this book (Chapters 2 through 5) focuses on changing instruction and assessment in ways that are especially beneficial for multilingual students. Hopefully, many teachers will apply the suggestions in their classrooms. But to achieve pedagogical justice, the entire school needs to be on board, which requires administrative and systemwide support. This is the focus of Chapter 6. Each chapter also offers short activities to encourage you to stop, reflect, apply, and build up your own ideas as you read.

This book builds upon the work in my last book, *The Communication Effect*, which focuses on enhancing instructional activities to increase the quantity and quality of language use in every lesson. This book focuses on the bigger picture of (a) seeing how learning is currently defined, measured, and realized in our schools and (b) outlining an alternative approach to learning in school, which focuses on building up ideas to foster pedagogical justice for multilingual students.

The audiences for this book are the teachers, instructional coaches, administrators, curriculum writers, and professional development providers who are willing and able to make major changes over the long haul and to help all students grow into the amazing individuals they were meant to be.

I have been teaching and working in K–12 classrooms for over three decades. I have worked closely with teachers to design instruction that fosters student engagement and rich interaction across grade levels and disciplines. Along the way, I have seen *many* different efforts to raise "achievement" (yearly test scores), especially the scores of multilingual students. Computer programs, special language courses, and reading interventions came in to save the day. Some even raised test scores, but they have failed and still fail to adequately serve multilingual students in meaningful ways. And many such interventions caused even more harm.

Every single student has the right to resources, opportunities, support, and the pedagogy that they need to learn and grow as much as possible in order to reach their full and varied potentials (Darling-Hammond, 1997). Yet the current model was never designed—or even adapted—to meet the needs of multilingual students. Unfortunately, it has been a "sink or swim" model from the beginning—and without a major overhaul, many multilingual students will continue to "sink."

As you read the following pages, remember that everything we do in school—each activity and assessment, each conversation and assignment—either moves our students (and us) toward pedagogical justice or away from it. This overhaul is long overdue and cannot wait. Students in our classrooms need it right now.

References

Beyer, L. N. (2017). *Social and emotional learning and traditionally underserved populations*. American Youth Policy Forum. https://www.aypf.org/resource/sel-special-populations/

Christle, C., Jolivette, K., & Nelson, C. (2007). School characteristics related to high school dropout rates. *Remedial and Special Education*, 28(6), 325–339.

Cunningham, J. (2019). Missing the mark: Standardized testing as epistemological erasure in U.S. schooling. *Power and Education*, 11(1), 111–120.

Darling-Hammond, L. (1997). *The right to learn: A blueprint for creating schools that work*. Jossey-Bass.

Darling-Hammond, L. (2007). Race, inequality and educational accountability: The irony of "No Child Left Behind." *Race, Ethnicity and Education*, 10(3), 245–260.

ACTIVITY I.1
Building up Ideas

The purpose of this book is to help you build up your key ideas for improving the education of multilingual students. Throughout the chapters, you can start new ideas and add to them as you read and engage in the activities. Here is a sample big idea that you can build up in the next three chapters. I include several sample building blocks that you can use or replace. Building blocks tend to consist of examples from the book or from your own life, along with definitions and clarifications. This is just one of several ideas you can build up. I provide one sample idea per chapter for your convenience.

IDEA STATEMENT: The current system fosters pedagogical injustices for multilingual students and needs a major overhaul.		
We need to overhaul what we teach students and what we expect them to learn.		We need to overhaul how we assess students.
	We need to replace accumulation-based curriculum and instruction with a focus on communication and idea-building.	

Pedagogical Justice 1

> Never doubt that a small group of thoughtful, committed citizens can change the world; indeed, it's the only thing that ever has.
>
> —Margaret Mead

The current approach to educating students in the United States hasn't been working for millions of multilingual students. Even though many students graduate, too many don't—not because of their intelligence, study habits, mindsets, or home languages, but because schooling, by and large, has failed to effectively serve them in key ways. Of those students who do graduate, many do not have the same opportunities and preparation needed for postsecondary education as their monolingual peers. And these are just the tip of the iceberg of injustices.

This chapter looks at what pedagogical justice for multilingual students is and isn't, with an emphasis on maintaining an evolving awareness of (a) its six key dimensions, (b) the pedagogical *injustices* that have grown and deepened in recent decades, and (c) the root causes of pedagogical injustices in schools. Subsequent chapters focus on how to overhaul key areas of education in order to achieve pedagogical justice for all students—and for multilingual students, in particular.

Dimensions of Pedagogical Justice

You don't hear the term *pedagogical justice* as often as you hear the terms *social justice, equity,* and *educational justice*, which tend to describe broader educational and societal challenges. Even *educational justice* tends more toward describing the problems of inequitable resources across districts and schools. I chose the term *pedagogical justice* to focus on how classroom instruction and assessment need to change in order to best serve multilingual students and prepare them for meaningful and successful lives.

Pedagogical justice, first of all, does not mean raising students' test scores. It means using our energies, resources, and time to their fullest in pursuit of helping all students reach their many potentials. These potentials tend to fall under the categories of content knowledge, language, literacy, collaboration, social skills, emotional maturity, initiative, civic engagement, service, art, music, drama, problem-solving, and creativity, to name a few.

When students spend time on something in class, they are not spending time on other things. If multilingual students spend time on test preparation, memorizing, and superficially *covering standards,* then their precious lesson time is not being used for learning deeper things and for growing personally.

Figure 1.1 shows six high-leverage and high-need dimensions that support pedagogical justice. Note that there still can be pedagogical justice with weak or missing dimensions, but it thrives when all are strong.

Students have the right to learning experiences that intentionally and effectively promote these six dimensions. They have the right to be in settings that (a) actively work to foster these six dimensions and (b) concurrently strive to eliminate the pedagogical injustices described later in the chapter.

The six dimensions in Figure 1.1 work together. If you have students who are engaged in the challenge of building up a novel idea,

Figure 1.1 Six Dimensions of Pedagogical Justice

Pedagogical Justice					
Agency and Voice	Engaging Challenges	Idea-Building	Meaningful Interactions	Assessment for Learning	Critical and Creative Thinking

interacting with others, and using critical and creative thinking, then their agency and confidence grow—and you get to authentically assess a variety of strengths and needs along the way (e.g., interests, social skills, content mastery, language development, etc.). Keep this mutual reinforcement in mind as you read this and other chapters in this book.

For each dimension that follows, read its description and put a sticky note at the point on the continuum where your school is at the present time. Later on, you can re-reflect and move the sticky note (ideally, to the right).

Agency and Voice

Agency means that students have a strong sense of self-efficacy and autonomy in learning and applying their learning (Vaughn, 2020). They think, "I can learn this, do this, build up ideas, make decisions, and solve problems." Agency means that students feel more like subjects than objects (see Freire, 1970). Students with a strong sense of agency feel that they can make a difference in the world (Bandura, 2001). Students feel that they are trusted to make meaningful decisions and be creative in their learning experiences.

Agency helps students to feel that they have some control over what and how they are learning and feel confident that they can learn anything put before them. They have some choice in the learning process, such as how they build up their ideas and share their learning with their teachers and peers. Agency tends to flourish from positive feedback from teachers and students, as well as being allowed to self-assess and revise their work (Jones, 2019).

Voice means that students have opportunities to share their thoughts and ideas in meaningful ways for meaningful purposes, including shaping what and how they are learning. Others in the learning community, including teachers, genuinely value what students have to say and contribute. As St. John and Briel (2017) argue,

Instead of a top-down, teacher-directed approach to learning, students play an active and equal role in planning, learning, and leading their classroom instruction as well as contributing to the development of school practices and policies. This significant

philosophical shift requires all stakeholders to embrace the belief that there is something to learn from every individual regardless of age, culture, socioeconomic status, or other qualifying factors. (p. 1)

Voice thrives in learning experiences in which students have authentic opportunities to articulate their opinions, ideas, questions, and challenges. In settings that value students' voices, not only do students value each other's voices, but they also value their own voices.

Why is this a dimension of pedagogical justice? Many students have been denied opportunities to develop their agency in schools, particularly students who are living in poverty and in homes where English is not the primary language (Flores & Rosa, 2015). Students in these settings are made to feel more like objects than subjects, meaning that they feel that others (and the system) are controlling and limiting their abilities, choices, and growth. They often feel that others aren't listening to them. For example, when students consistently score low on tests, even after studying for them, many feel that they are not smart, that they can't keep up, and that people aren't seeing who they are and what they have learned.

When students lack agency and voice, they tend to feel that they have little control or choice over what and how they are learning. They lack confidence that they can learn challenging material, and they feel constrained by learning lists of disconnected information and skills.

Now think about where your setting is on the Agency and Voice Continuum. Put a dated sticky note on it.

Agency and Voice Continuum					
Needs Work					Strong

Engaging Challenges

Student engagement, according to the Glossary of Education Reform (2016), "refers to the degree of attention, curiosity, interest, optimism, and passion that students show when they are learning or being taught, which extends to the level of motivation they have to learn and progress in their education." If the task is engaging, interest in it (i.e., not for points) motivates them to keep working hard.

Challenge means that students have an appropriately (not too much and not too little) rigorous task or goal to accomplish. If it's appropriately challenging, it pushes students beyond their current levels. This aligns with Vygotsky's Zone of Proximal Development (Vygotsky, 1978), in which a learner is neither overwhelmed enough to give up nor bored by something already known or mastered.

Students can be engaged but not challenged and challenged but not engaged. We need to strive for both together. And yet, my observations and a handful of studies suggest that only about one in five lessons engage students in cognitively challenging learning (Mehta & Fine, 2019). It might be even less if you ask enough students.

A powerful type of engaging challenge is creating an authentic product or performance that encourages students to build up ideas and then communicate them to others (see Chapters 3 and 4). For instance, students might write a screenplay, create a museum exhibit, draft a business plan, write a short story, solve an environmental problem, or something along those lines—in fact, wouldn't *you* rather do these than take a test? Engaging challenges nurture students' excitement about learning and working on tasks, and students tend to put forth extra efforts to learn, create, and participate in classes.

Without engaging in challenges, students tend to be bored and/or not interested in learning, overwhelmed by tasks that are too difficult and not scaffolded, and often overwhelmed by the quantity of disconnected things to learn.

Why is this a dimension of pedagogical justice? It's flat out not fair to subject students to boring or overwhelming tasks—especially if we know they are boring or overwhelming. And because many tasks are in a non-native language for multilingual students, the tasks tend to be even more challenging. The tasks also tend to be full of questions, content, and cultural references that don't align well with the backgrounds and expectations of diverse students. Put yourself in their shoes: Would you want to do what you are asking them to do?

Now think about where your setting is on the Engaging Challenges Continuum. Put a dated sticky note on it.

Engaging Challenges Continuum						
Needs Work						Strong

Idea-Building

This book uses the term "idea-building" to describe the process of learning through the construction of concepts and claims. Related terms that are commonly used in research on learning include "schema," "understanding," "deep knowledge," "framework," and "network of understanding" (Nokes et al., 2010). The writings of many well-known educators and researchers in the last century (Dewey, Cazden, Mercer, Vygotsky, Darling-Hammond, Bruner, Gardner, Wiggins, and Greene) support the premise that students learn more effectively when they make connections and see how different pieces of information fit together to form a concept or claim.

Building up ideas means that students use language and thinking to help themselves and others construct key concepts and claims in their minds (see Chapter 2). This is the centerpiece of the approach described in Chapter 4 in which students engage in school activities such as thinking, talking, listening, and reading in order to construct and co-construct big ideas that last and continue to build in their minds over time. Instruction should clearly help students to build up robust ideas of value in a discipline, allowing students to be creative in their idea-building and communicating it to others, as well as encouraging students to push themselves and others to clarify and support as much as possible.

Why is this a dimension of pedagogical justice? Because in many settings, multilingual students have rare opportunities to construct and communicate important ideas in a discipline. They spend the bulk of their time memorizing disconnected information and practicing skills for assessment purposes. Instruction in such settings tends to not value the cultural and linguistic "building blocks" that multilingual students use to build up ideas.

Now think about where your setting is on the Idea-Building Continuum. Put a dated sticky note on it.

Idea-Building Continuum						
Needs Work						Strong

Meaningful Interactions

Meaningful interaction fosters powerful learning and pedagogical justice for a variety of reasons. Boyd and Rubin argue that "student talk supports inquiry, collaborative learning, high-level thinking, and making knowledge personally meaningful" (2006, p. 142). Meaningful interaction means that students have plenty of supported opportunities to talk about academic content with peers (Walqui & Heritage, 2018).

There should be both quantity *and* quality of talk. It should be engaging and productive, and it should help students build up ideas, make decisions, solve problems, and get things done. Meaningful interactions include short, medium, and long structured and unstructured dialogues, conversations, chats, and exchanges between two or more students in which students end up with clearer and stronger ideas than they started with.

Talk opportunities are supported when teachers, curriculums, and assessments intentionally help students to build up skills for productive talk with one another. For example, a teacher might model a conversation with a student, provide a visual organizer, and post *helpful* sentence frames for students to use in their interactions to exchange useful information.

Many multilingual students don't get enough practice engaging in meaningful listening, speaking, and conversing each day in school. You may be familiar with the practice of following a student throughout the day (or even one class period) to take notes on how often a student is given opportunities to talk in class. Most of these observations yield very low numbers of minutes (sometimes even counted in seconds) engaged in talk—and even less time engaged in *productive* talk. In a classic study of hundreds of classrooms, Nystrand (1997) observed that teachers asked most of the questions, questions weren't authentic, discussions averaged less than 50 seconds per class in the eighth grade and less than 15 seconds in the ninth grade, and small-group work ranged from 30 seconds a day in eighth grade to two minutes a day in ninth grade. The quantity of classroom talk has improved in many settings since 1997, but not enough.

Consider the difference between a student who uses even two sentences versus one sentence in the majority of pair-shares over the course of 12 years in school. Most of the time, if a student uses a second or even a third sentence, the utterance tends to be more meaningful—the student *wants* to communicate, strengthen, or clarify the idea—which in turn helps solidify language and content learning.

That is the quantity challenge. The quality challenge is making talk *meaningful*, which itself has a range of meanings. For the purposes of pedagogical justice, we can focus on meanings related to idea-building, making decisions and choosing sides in arguments, amplifying students' voices, and developing relationships. In meaningful talk, students value the contributions of others, co-construct concepts and claims, push themselves and others to clarify terms, and support ideas as much as possible. These are described in more detail in the following chapters.

Why is this a dimension of pedagogical justice? When instruction doesn't trust or motivate multilingual students to talk with each other, usually their interactions are focused on giving and getting the "right" answers. And after the right answer is given, there isn't much more to discuss (Nichols, 2006). Multilingual students have few opportunities to talk with others at length about academic topics. And the talk they do engage in is often quick and/or overly scripted (e.g., using memorized frames and dialogues).

Now think about where your setting is on the Meaningful Interactions Continuum. Put a dated sticky note on it.

Meaningful Interactions Continuum						
Needs Work						Strong

Assessment *for* Learning

Assessment for learning means assessment that helps to maximize present and future learning for a student (Gottlieb & Honigsfeld, 2019). It overlaps quite a bit with the term "authentic assessment," which means assessing all the important areas of academic learning and social growth (Wiggins, 1990). It also includes formative assessment practices in which teachers continuously observe what students are doing and saying, give feedback, and make adjustments to instruction in real time.

Students have the right to show their learning and development in different ways—not just with multiple-choice tests. It's not fair to subject students to boring and overwhelming assessments. And yet, ask most students about most assessments and very few of their faces will light up. They are seldom given choices in how they are assessed. But when we give more options, allowing students to choose how they want to show their learning, we get more positive responses.

Students have the right to redo and revise their assessed work, which is another thing that bubble-in tests don't offer (Darling-Hammond et al., 1995). The real world is full of "revisable assessments" in which you work on something over time, get feedback, improve it, and resubmit it. Revising allows students to self-monitor and reflect as they work on meaningful tasks. When students are excited to learn and work on relevant learning tasks, they will put forth extra efforts to learn and create. They will self-monitor and reflect on their learning and growth, especially when encouraged and allowed to revise and redo their work.

Why is this a dimension of pedagogical justice? Because assessment *for* learning is what multilingual students need the most and get the least. Most assessment is assessment *of* learning, which tends to focus on the past, what has been learned, and (more often) what hasn't been learned (e.g., deficits). Assessment for learning, especially as described in this book (Chapter 3), focuses on the quality of students' construction of concepts and claims. This includes the use of valuable "personal building blocks" (assets) from their own backgrounds and lived experiences.

Now think about where your setting is on the Assessment for Learning Continuum. Put a dated sticky note on it.

Assessment for Learning Continuum							
Needs Work							Strong

Critical and Creative Thinking

Critical thinking includes using cognitive skills to accomplish complex purposes. These include seeing different perspectives, building up both sides of an argument, supporting claims with evidence, making logical conclusions from available facts, and solving problems (Willingham, 2007). These skills also include discerning credibility, evaluating evidence, applying, analyzing, synthesizing, and interpreting (Paul & Elder, 2008). There are many lists and wheels and pyramids of thinking skills out there. They can get a bit cumbersome, so I recommend working with colleagues to come up with a handful of important skills that students will need and use most in school and beyond.

Creative thinking means coming up with novel ways to solve problems, overcome challenges, and communicate important messages to others. It is the process of coming up with a *new* and *useful* idea (Sternberg, 1999). This idea usually takes the form of a theory, process, idea, or product that meets some need (solving a problem, improving something, etc.). "New" means that the creative idea hasn't existed before in the given setting.

Creative thinking often involves several stages, such as immersion, incubation, brainstorming, discerning, deciding, and acting (Csikszentmihalyi, 1996). So how often do we encourage and allow students to engage in these stages of creative thinking? In my observations of classrooms, this is rare. Why? It takes time, you don't know what will result, and the result won't likely be on a state test.

Why is this a dimension of pedagogical justice? If we fill students' lessons with rote learning activities that don't foster critical or creative thinking, students' thinking stagnates or worse. According to Paul and Elder (2014, p. 19), "Much of our thinking, left to itself, is biased, distorted, partial, uninformed or down-right prejudiced." Unfortunately, tragic and unfair stories in the news abound of people lacking critical and creative thinking. The world needs people with these skills.

Yet such skills, especially creative thinking skills, are not often emphasized because they are difficult to test—especially through multiple-choice testing methods. Accurate assessment of such skills tends to require full sentences and a wide range of nuanced responses that computerized scoring can't handle. Thus, the students who tend to score low on multiple-choice tests and are labeled "behind" or "below grade level" get heavier doses of test preparation. Some educators think that multilingual students are not "ready" for critical and creative thinking because of their language proficiency, test scores, and grades. They are wrong. Every student can and does critically and creatively think, and every student has the right to be *challenged and interested* in engaging in such thinking (which too many curricular programs do not do well enough).

We must also remember that all human thinking is highly sculpted by what we do. The mind is shaped by whatever it spends time on. So, spending lots of class time giving short answers to questions, filling in blanks, minimally sharing for points, writing just to satisfy a rubric, and skimming texts to answer comprehension questions molds a student's thinking. On the other hand, spending class time collaboratively arguing about important questions in a subject, building up key claims and concepts, answering essential questions, writing to communicate ideas to others, and creating works of literature and art shapes students' minds differently. We need to analyze lessons and assessments and keep asking, "Do these activities inspire students to think critically, respect and connect with others, construct unique and valuable disciplinary concepts, and cultivate students' agency and identities?" We must continually consider the types of thinking that we want our students' minds to be shaped by over time—and how well our instructional and assessment practices foster such thinking.

Why is this a dimension of pedagogical justice? Multilingual students in many classrooms aren't given tasks that push them to use higher-order skills or be creative during learning. The tasks (e.g., worksheets) do not motivate them enough to put forth extra efforts to think and create. And if we are displacing the development of key thinking skills in life with memorizing temporary facts, learning grammar and vocabulary for test purposes, and practicing multiple-choice skills, then we are preventing students from reaching their full potentials. This displacement is widespread yet subtle. Many curriculums and teachers don't even realize it. Afterall, teachers and students stay busy, and each class period is filled to the brim. Yet if you observe enough classrooms with multilingual students and you look for time spent on developing their critical and creative thinking, you won't see enough (Bouygues, 2022).

Now think about where your setting is on the Critical and Creative Thinking Continuum. Put a dated sticky note on it.

Critical & Creative Thinking Continuum						
Needs Work						Strong

Now look back at the six dimensions and pick one or two to work on in the next year. The following chapters will help.

Pedagogical Injustices

In this section, we take a closer look at some of the many *injustices* that students have had to endure because school systems have (a) not been aware of them, (b) not tried to address them, and/or (c) not focused enough on strengthening the six dimensions of pedagogical justice.

Because you are reading this book, you are likely more aware than most people of the pedagogical injustices that multilingual students have had to endure and overcome. Yet many people, even longtime educators, still do not understand the degree to which commonly accepted approaches to learning have fostered these injustices. They lack awareness of the strength and depth of the root causes of these injustices as well as the strength and depth of their detrimental effects on students—especially multilingual students.

Districts and schools engage in countless data walks, data dives, and data meetings to analyze how and why students aren't doing well on yearly tests. They tend to be highly aware of gaps in test scores, particularly between different groups of students. Test scores are communicated in a variety of bright colors, columns, pie charts, and media, most often showing that multilingual students aren't "achieving" or "performing" at the same rate as English-only peers. However, the energy and time spent on analyzing and addressing low scores takes away from noticing more important and insidious injustices that multilingual students face. Test-score awareness is not the awareness that we need. Instead, we must widen our lenses and open our eyes to the many lasting and harmful injustices that persist—ironically and egregiously—as a result of the focus on test scores!

Many argue that test-score gaps are a pedagogical injustice or even the main injustice. They are wrong. The injustices are the ramifications of what we do in the classroom to multilingual students before and after the tests. These ramifications, which often come in the form of curriculums, assessments, and practices, often become the injustices described in the following sections.

Here are some of the worst injustices.

Placement

Students who score low on major tests often receive labels and interventions that send them the message that they are not smart, not academic, burdens on the system, hard to teach, will never belong in AP classes, and so on. Entire schools and districts are shamed by this process. If students score low, they are labeled as needing extra help, or "intervention." Intervention programs tend to focus on test-score improvement, which tends to be even more boring and demotivating for students *and* teachers.

Multilingual students are often less likely to be placed in electives, advanced courses, and postsecondary education programs (Mitchell, 2016). This often results from being placed in intervention programs such as remedial, academic literacy, English language development (ELD), and test-prep courses. Students' schedules often become "tracks," based on their proficiency in English and the courses they take.

In some cases, entire school schedules and curriculums look like test-prep interventions. Instead of taking interesting electives, students are often placed in various reading and language classes that are designed to help them do well on tests. These extra accumulation-based classrooms tend to whittle away students' agency, active learning, creativity, and hope. Students are often treated generically, as buckets to fill, because the end result is emptying their learning into a static and irrelevant test. I have seen too many classrooms full of multilingual students quietly answering questions for a computer program marketed as an all-in-one reading comprehension and language development "solution."

Belonging

Multilingual students are more likely to feel like they don't belong in school than monolingual speakers (Cha et al., 2017). This is especially true if they are not feeling success, not building relationships, not understanding the teacher, not understanding the assessments, and so on. Many are refugees or have experienced trauma in their lives, and they are not used to sitting for hours on end, listening to a teacher, and following directions for activities they have never seen before. They are often very reluctant to participate in classroom discussions for a variety of reasons, a big one being that they will make a mistake—linguistic or content-related—and be laughed at. Many students' feelings of nonbelonging increase over the years. Most do make friends in school, which helps, but too many do not to fully engage in classroom activities, take on leadership roles, or put forth extra efforts on assignments.

Lack of Motivation

Schools hope that by extrinsically motivating students to accumulate facts and skills with the reward of higher grades—along with punishment for low grades—they will increase the school's test scores. And they hope that students will *learn* as a result.

And yet, many students aren't interested in just accumulating large sets of disconnected content and practicing the skills for taking tests for getting points. These students find ways to just get by and stay off the radar. But year after year, the lack of interest and disengaged learning adds up. A great many multilingual students feel this way, and they are often even further behind in the test-prep game because their language and content knowledge do not overlap as much with the language and content valued in U.S. schools and their assessments.

Many students aren't even motivated by grades. They don't see the extra work between a *C* and an *A* to be worth it. Or they simply don't want to "play the game" and go through school's not-so-engaging hoops. These students are bright, talented, creative, and bursting with potential. But we don't notice or cultivate these traits. Instead, through test-score labeling and shaming, test-score-focused learning tends to whittle away their pride, agency, voice, and motivation to learn year after year.

Many students are not motivated by taking tests or seeing final test scores. This is especially true when taking the yearly "high-stakes" tests in one's non-home language. The stakes are not really that high for students, so many don't try very hard, and the scores often reflect this. I am actually surprised that so many students try to do well on them. There is very little in it for them. The tests are both boring and stressful at the same time. It takes extra thinking and extra work, with plenty of stress from having time limits. And when they have little idea how to answer, it is demoralizing. Many get frustrated during the tests, thinking that they will let down themselves, their families, and their teachers.

Mindsets About Learning

The most damaging yet least visible pedagogical injustices are in the minds of students. They include negative self-talk, lack of agency, low confidence, and low persistence both in school and in learning outside of school. They include the widening of gaps between how students think of themselves as learners and how they should think of themselves. Imagine going to a school that offered all instruction in a language you don't know very well and then gave you monthly tests in that language. Each year they tell you to get your scores up, set goals for your test scores, and study harder. They put you in intervention classes that focus on more memorizing disconnected facts and skills. Each year you feel less like a student and less connected to other students, the school, and learning.

Test-prep teaching also shapes a student's mindset of what it means to learn. Over the years, multiple-choice assessment and instruction asks students to reduce learning down to memorizing things, getting right answers for points, and then moving on. Not only does this affect students' K–12 experiences, but it also shapes their beliefs about what learning means their entire lives.

Many curriculums have pages and pages of test-like activities and worksheets that can and do fill up precious lesson time. Not surprisingly, instruction that prepares students for boring tests tends to be boring for students and boring for teachers. Memorizing facts and practicing skills is not very engaging, especially if the end goal is taking a long test with a bunch of random texts. In test-focused teaching, students see learning as accumulation. This is a highly limiting mindset because learning is so much more. Knowledge—if it is to stick, grow, and be useful—needs to be used, not just memorized and counted up. We must continue to ask ourselves, "Do we really want our children just to think of learning as getting better at piling up facts and choosing right answers, or do we want them to think of learning as building up ideas, solving important problems, and thinking critically?"

Separation

Another injustice, whether intentional or not, is that the current system, with all its high and mighty talk of "closing achievement gaps," actually *separates* students. First, students are separated by their test scores and other data into labeled categories, tiers, and intervention levels. Then many are separated into various tracked programs and schedules. Multilingual students can get stuck in these tracks for years, separated from monolingual peers.

Bourdieu (1986) argued that students bring with them ways of thinking about learning and the world, which he called cultural capital. He also argued that the school system tends to separate possessors of inherited cultural capital from those who don't have it. The system, therefore, maintains social differences. Cultural capital—along with academic, linguistic, and social capital—is the knowledge, experiences, and skills passed down from family and community that provide advantages in a given system (e.g., testing and test-based instruction). Assessments, in particular, tend to have a narrow spectrum of the types of capitals that they value for showing academic learning.

But even worse, students are separated from themselves—from their identities, cultures, languages, aspirations, gifts, and self-confidence. The end result for many students is that they are separated from reaching their many potentials and from future opportunities that depend on reaching those potentials.

In many ways, the focus on narrowing the in-school "achievement" (based on test scores) gap is actually widening the real-world achievement (learning important things and doing well in life) gap. Even when test scores improve and the test-score differences narrow, the rift between where students are and their potentials often increases. "To pay for" a few more points on tests and make the school look good, students spend large amounts of learning energy focused on disconnected facts and low-level skills. Then after seeing success in scores, schools continue to mold and trim students into good test-takers who work to raise their scores up to levels on par with averages of monolingual students. The school might look good in public records and "data dives," but students spend loads of precious class time doing things that don't matter much, don't interest them, and don't last. Wasting students' time and hindering their potentials is injustice.

ACTIVITY 1.1
Indicators of Pedagogical Injustices

To achieve pedagogical justice, it is vital to understand and be aware of the many pedagogical *injustices* that hinder student development. Activity 1.1, for example, helps you to uncover potential pedagogical injustices in your setting. It is also meant to help you get a sense of how relevant the ideas in the following chapters are for you.

The following questions are indicators of pedagogical injustices that are common in schools around the country and world. If the answer in your setting is "Yes" or "Somewhat," put a checkmark next to the question (*Note:* You can also use a rating system such as 0–3). And if you don't know the answers to any of these, work with colleagues find ways to answer them.

____ Is a higher percentage of a certain group of students (e.g., students who speak one or more languages in addition to English) not doing as well in school as another group of students (e.g., monolingual English speakers)?

____ Are multilingual students often told that they are "behind in school" based on their test scores?

____ Do multilingual students to feel that school just isn't for them? Do they think it's not worth it to try very hard, that it's better to just "play school," or it's easier to just get by doing the bare minimum?

____ Do multilingual students feel culturally disconnected from curriculums, instruction, or assessments? Do they feel that school is boring?

____ Does your school or district take pride in being data-driven, creating a range of color-coded spreadsheets that show the test-score growth and deficits of various subgroups?

____ Are the voices, interests, insights, and so on from multilingual students drowned out by the voices and preferences of adults, standards, yearly multiple-choice tests, and the curriculums based on them?

____ Do students spend more time and energy on memorizing information and practicing skills than using them to build up ideas of their own?

____ Do multilingual students engage in learning activities that lack critical and creative thinking?

____ Do students spend large percentages of lesson time listening to the teacher, doing individual work, and not interacting with peers?

Even one of the above indicators of pedagogical injustices can significantly limit the learning and growth of students. One of the goals of this book is to help you and your setting become even more aware of the many subtle and not-so-subtle injustices that your multilingual students face.

The Main Cause of Pedagogical Injustices

As you can see in Figure 1.2, pedagogical injustices in school tend to stem from a main cause: accumulation-based learning.

Accumulation-based learning requires students to memorize and pile up a loosely connected assortment of facts, concepts, and skills in order to get points, grades, and test scores.

Accumulation-based learning has had many names over the years. For example, Freire's banking model (1970) brings to mind teachers depositing information of their choosing into little piggie banks inside students' heads—information that students later "withdraw" for tests. Similarly, when teachers transmit knowledge to students, it is often called *transmission* learning (Slavin, 2012). Picture a radio station broadcasting to students. Later on, the information is then meant to be transmitted back to teachers and others on assessments.

In what is often called the *factory model* of schooling (Sleeter, 2015), schools act a bit like factories. Picture students of all different interests, talents, and backgrounds going into a factory (a school) and coming out the other side looking, thinking, and talking the same—that is, if they don't get rejected somewhere along the line.

And in the *teacher-centered classroom*, we can picture the teacher, like the hub in the middle of a wheel, being the giver and tester of all knowledge. The teacher asks a question, a few hands go up, one student is called on, the student gives a short answer to the teacher, the teacher gives feedback, and the pattern continues (for more on this pattern, look up IRF [initiation-response-feedback] and IRE [initiation-response-evaluation]).

Figure 1.2 The Main Cause of Pedagogical Injustices

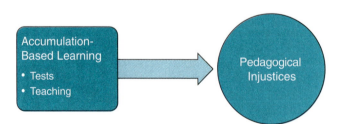

Other terms often associated with accumulation-based learning are "drill and kill," "passive learning," "recitation," "fidelity," "one-size-fits-all," "spray and pray," "gluing apples to the tree," "accountability," "direct instruction," "test and threaten," "data-driven," and "follow the pacing guide." There are more, but you get the gist.

Before moving on, I want to acknowledge that not all instruction is shaped by accumulation-based learning. Instruction is very diverse, and there are many schools and teachers who are engaging students in powerful learning. But in the majority of classrooms across the United States (and world), countless hours of teaching are still largely shaped by the accumulation-based approach represented in Figure 1.3.

Starting at the far right of Figure 1.3, you see that accumulation-based learning is mostly driven by extrinsic rewards (e.g., points and grades) and standardized tests. Students tend to care more about the grades, and schools care more about the test scores. Curriculums and learning activities tend to be focused on helping students get better at choosing correct answers on classroom and interim assessments, which tend to emulate the larger year-end state tests. If students don't score well on these assessments, teachers often provide additional activities to help students improve their grades and their chances of getting more right answers on the state tests.

Much of the ELA (English language arts) and math curriculums, professional development, instructional coaching, strategy development, improvement cycles, PLCs (professional learning communities), and teacher resources have been pushing students toward

Figure 1.3 Accumulation-Based Learning Approach

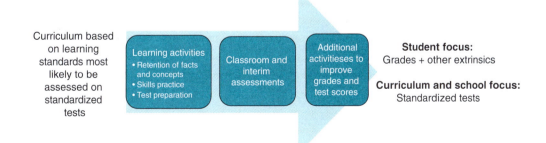

being able to score well on multiple-choice tests and scored writing assessments. The highest-stakes (for schools, that is) tests tend to assess language arts and math, but other subject areas also lean toward multiple-choice based learning in their assessments. The exceptions are art, music, drama, physical education, and technology—which many students find to be the most engaging classes.

There are two core components of accumulation-based learning that help to feed pedagogical injustices and sabotage high-quality learning for multilingual students: tests and teaching.

Tests

Schools are mandated to use multiple-choice tests because they are seen as cheap and efficient ways to assess large groups of students and compare how they do on the same(ish) test questions. Here are some of the major concerns regarding the use of such tests to assess students and schools. As you read through each of these concerns, consider how it can contribute to pedagogical injustices faced by multilingual students.

Tricks without treats. Students often feel like they are being tricked by test-writers into choosing wrong answers—which is actually true. Test-writers write distractors to be as attractive as possible (like fishing lures) to get students to choose them. Test-writers also use vocabulary, colloquial expressions, and grammar that cater to native speakers of English (Abedi et al., 2004; Menken, 2006). Many items even seem to be worded to confuse and fool students, who would likely answer more items correctly if they were worded more clearly. In other words, they might have learned the content or skills, but the language of the test items hinders authentic assessment (Abedi, 2003). Finally, many items are not focused on key content because, if the topic is important, it tends to be taught and learned by most students, which is something that bell-curve-based tests don't want. If everyone learns it and scores well on an item, it is usually thrown out (Popham, 1999). This is the best way to get a wide spread of scores on items.

Lack of choice. Tests, despite being "multiple-choice," offer very little choice for students in how they might want to show what they have learned. They never get the chance to explain why they chose an answer, right or wrong. Most of the important things we do in life are not quick, multiple-choice decisions. We need to build ideas over time, foster relationships, compare apples and oranges, stick to a topic, read long texts, think critically for a purpose, write to real audiences, and the like. The purpose of reading each short text on tests is to answer the questions, nothing more. There is little to no building of concepts or claims on such tests. This lack of choice of how to build then transfers over into curriculums, learning activities, and even teacher and student philosophies of learning.

Disconnectedness. A basic analysis of the items on the tests quickly shows how disconnected the test-writers are from the rich lives, thoughts, and communication styles of real students in a variety of communities across the country. The tests are written by adults within the walls of some distant testing company. I remember taking what were called Iowa Tests each year in school. I grew up in Washington state. Did the students in Iowa take Washington tests? In addition, the tests' short texts jump wildly from topic to topic. Students might read a fable, then a text on coin collecting, then a text on plate tectonics, then a story about Abraham Lincoln, followed by the topic of ant colonies, and so on. There are very few settings in the real world where one needs to quickly jump around so much from topic to topic.

Validity. State tests claim to show progress in learning state standards. The content in the items, especially in ELA, often doesn't match what students learn in school (Popham, 1999). Students who acquired the knowledge and language at home have an advantage. The tests provide lengthy color-coded reports of the numbers of questions that students missed and the areas that they need to work on. Such reports give the illusion of an accurate and complete assessment of learning. This, of course, is based on the assumption that all students being compared had the same amount of motivation, energy, and language abilities. Even if the tests are perfectly valid for every single student, does it matter? Do we get information—in a timely manner—that is so insightfully valuable to teachers that they can improve learning and growth? Are the scores so valuable in shaping instruction that it is worth the shaming, stigma, stress, boring lessons, and so on, that students have to endure? The most valid information comes directly from a student's teachers and daily student work.

Item bias. Research on test items has shown that the tests are often culturally and linguistically biased (Bach, 2020). Students who have learned a standard (e.g., in ELA or math) often choose the wrong answer because of the complicated way the question and/or answer choices were worded. I have analyzed many items and found myself saying "Why didn't they just use simpler language like ... ?" After a while, I start asking questions like, "Are you really wanting to test learning of standards or just use confusing language to create a nice bell curve for each item and the test?" Second, tests often test language rather than content. Whether by design or accident, more complex uses of grammar and vocabulary in an item make it more difficult. Students get dinged for not knowing content that they actually might know when, in fact, it was the wording that tripped them up.

Negative impact. A significant body of research suggests that high-stakes testing negatively impacts student learning (Amrein & Berliner, 2003; Del Carmen Unda & Lizárraga-Dueñas, 2021; Nichols et al., 2012). Some studies found that, on average, the more pressure students felt to perform on tests, the less intrinsically motivated and less likely to become self-directed learners they became. Other studies have shown that high-stakes testing tends to have large *negative* impacts for students from nondominant cultural and linguistic backgrounds (Horn, 2003; Pierre, 2016; Zabala, 2007). Many students who struggle with or fail tests end up dropping out of school and/or landing in prison (Del Carmen Unda & Lizárraga-Dueñas, 2021).

Teaching

Accumulation-based teaching is shaped by multiple-choice and short-answer testing. As you read through each of these concerns related to teaching, consider how it can contribute to pedagogical injustices for multilingual students.

Quality of learning. Accumulation-based learning tends to lower the overall quality of learning, even for students who are motivated by points and like the content. It's too hard to memorize all the disconnected facts and skills presented in the standards and curriculums—especially in a second language. It's even harder to retain all the standards months and years after being tested on them. Over time, this inundation can lead to a lot of learned helplessness (e.g., "With so much to learn, why try hard?"), which significantly reduces learning.

Little wiggle room. Most of accumulation-based teaching tries to cover a broad range of standards, facts, and isolated skills that can be tested with multiple-choice items. Commonly used commercial curriculums try to make sure every straw in every standard is learned (covered) by the end of April. Students are often overwhelmed, quickly moving from topic to topic, without much wiggle room for students falling behind in this approach. The pacing guides influence the pacing rather than student learning and growth (David, 2008).

"Neat and clean" learning. Accumulation-based classrooms tend to prefer learning that is "neat and clean," which means dicing up information and skills into pieces, putting them into lessons, and then checking them off as students answer questions correctly. For example, if a student gets three questions right on a quiz, a teacher or a machine will tell you that the student "learned" a standard, and it's time to move on.

Lack of interaction. Accumulation-based teaching also tends to lack opportunities for rich student interaction. When students are expected to be receptacles and memorizers of disconnected facts and skills, they don't need to talk much. They might share short answers in a pair-share, but the interaction ends fairly quickly, with a bare minimum of language use. Multilingual learners, in particular, suffer in such settings because they are not benefiting from rich and extended interactions with peers. Such interactions would help them develop language, content, relationships, confidence, and agency. But instead, they are stuck answering a wide range of questions that are meant to quiz them rather than help them co-construct ideas.

Root Causes

Accumulation-based learning did not just appear from thin air, nor is it sustained in a vacuum. It has root causes. I list five here, but you might find more in your setting. All of the root causes, as you can see in Figure 1.4, are rooted in the mind. The root causes tend to fester in people's minds and in different layers of the system. They start with adults who form opinions and make decisions about what and how to learn (e.g., legislators, administrators, and teachers). These thoughts, many of which are harmful, often worm their way into students' minds (e.g., I'm not trustworthy, learning is countable, I'm not as human as monolingual English speakers, I'm just here to receive someone else's ideas, I'm not a good student, etc.).

As you read these root causes and engage in the activities, reflect on what they are and how prevalent they are in your setting.

Figure 1.4 Root Causes of Accumulation-Based Learning and Pedagogical Injustices

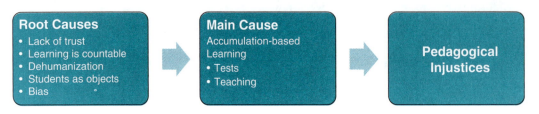

Root Cause: Lack of Trust

A major root cause of accumulation-based learning is a lack of trust in educators and students. The underlying thinking (usually from legislators and noneducators) is, "Teachers and/or students are lazy or ineffective and therefore we must keep them *accountable* through statewide tests that show us how effective they are by comparing students across the state. Those test scores will show us all we need to know to make decisions about which schools and students to punish, reform, or reward."

Not only is such thinking wrong; it is harmful. Lack of trust is never good for relationships. In this case, the relationships are between the community, district leaders, teachers, and students. When low test scores show up (usually months later), the blame game begins: Parents and community blame district leaders and teachers, district leaders blame teachers and students, and students don't blame anyone because the scores don't matter to them. When teachers, in particular, don't feel trusted, they feel that parents and community (and district leaders, sometimes) don't have faith in them to be professional, creatively apply their knowledge of pedagogy, and do their best for each student. Lack of trust makes students feel that adults don't have faith in them to take initiative, build up ideas, work together, be creative, learn from mistakes, and make decisions.

The vast majority of schools and teachers don't need to be held accountable. They are doing great work beyond the limitations of the highly problematic pedagogy of accumulation-based learning. Most teachers know that learning is not accurately represented by yearly multiple-choice test scores and that they shouldn't spend all of their class time helping students become better test-takers. What if we asked teachers and students what they would like to focus on (and not use the term "accountable" at all)? Maybe we would hear responses such as robust learning of content concepts and idea-building skills, kindness, patience, agency, collaboration, clarity, reasoning, creativity, and so on. We look more closely at these in Chapter 2 and at ways to see these types of learning and growth in Chapter 3.

Lastly, students don't need to be "held accountable" with yearly tests. If you took the tests away, students wouldn't suddenly stop coming to school, stop engaging in learning activities, or stop doing homework. They would actually get several weeks of learning back and likely become even more engaged because their teachers would have the freedom to focus on relevant and deep learning experiences and assessments.

Root Cause: Learning Is Countable

If you think learning is mostly countable, then accumulation-based teaching is the answer. It is a tempting approach to embrace. It is highly visible. Curriculums do all that they can to fit in a wide range of activities and questions to help students memorize facts and skills for benchmark and year-end tests. There is lots of enticing "alignment" with the tests. And yet, there is seldom enough connection to students' lives, choices, interests, or ways of communicating. In too many classrooms, students see learning as a daily barrage of practice activities for points.

Countable learning has never worked well for most multilingual students. More so than their monolingual peers, multilingual students depend on rich interactions and purposeful learning to motivate them to work hard despite the challenges of learning in their non-native language. Under the guise of "closing achievement gaps" (i.e., narrowing test-score differences), many students are being corralled into stagnant learning spaces where short answers rule.

Even calls for accountability, equity, and equitable practices tend to promote surface-level treatments if the ultimate desired outcomes are mostly measured by multiple-choice tests. Students become so focused on getting lots of right answers (and doing so with the least amount of thinking) that they don't develop abilities to construct robust understandings, use higher-order thinking skills, and clarify their amazing thoughts.

Granted, some learning is countable. Quiz me on my times tables (up to 12 times 12, that is) or the names of different types of rocks, state capitals, or spelling words and count up how many I get right. Many countable facts and skills can be useful for idea-building—if and when they are actually used for building ideas (see Chapter 4).

This book argues that we need to go well beyond memorization and count-them-up learning. Most *important* areas of learning and growth in life are not countable or easily comparable using numbers. What score(s) would you give the Eiffel Tower? Newton's Laws? Toni Morrison's *Beloved*? The theory of relativity? Democracy? The *Mona Lisa*? These products and the ideas within them are priceless and powerful without grades or points. And each one of our students is capable of similar ideas and products as well.

Root Cause: Dehumanization of Students

Another emerging term related to this work is "humanizing." It applies to pedagogy, learning, interactions, and assessment. It has a range of definitions, many of which are a mixture of key aspects stemming from constructivist, assets-based, and culturally responsive approaches. At its core, humanizing focuses on valuing all students as humans who are bursting with knowledge, hopes, destinies, talents, interests, potentials, and identities (Carter Andrews & Castillo, 2016). Humanizing is needed because of the many dehumanizing and inequitable aspects of accumulation-based instruction and assessment. Such learning, particularly at the school and district levels, tends to value students and teachers based on test scores. And it devalues anything that is not on tests, such as interests, social skills, physical abilities, artistic talents, creative writing, drama abilities, and critical thinking skills.

Many adults who make educational decisions don't treat students as young people who are fully human (Reich & Mehta, 2021). The system subtly chips away at their humanity by telling them that they don't fit in, they can't handle grade level learning, and such. As Lilia Bartolomé argues, "Therefore, any discussion having to do with the improvement of subordinated students' academic standing is incomplete if it does not address those discriminatory school practices that lead to dehumanization" (Bartolomé, 1994, p. 175).

One way of dehumanizing students is to treat them as objects. In many settings, multilingual students are seen as rough objects to be polished, shaped, and molded by the schooling and testing processes. Objects don't choose (what and how to learn), don't talk, and don't think. We focus on filling the object with large quantities of facts and skills that we can quickly measure with test questions, much like depositing and withdrawing money from a bank (Freire, 1970). The role of these objects, ultimately, is to make our school look good (test-score-wise) and not deviate from the multiyear plan laid out for them.

This view of students as objects clearly promotes accumulation-based learning and assessment. And even though all students are seen as objects in accumulation-based pedagogy, multilingual students are often even more objectified. They are often lumped into the "English learner" category with extra needs and low test scores, all of which are considered problems that make the school look bad.

Root Cause: Bias

Bias is the unfair tendency to prefer one thing, idea, or person over others, often based on prejudice, surface features, and distorted reasoning. In education, such bias often takes the form of deficit-based views of multilingual students and having low expectations for what they can learn (Warren, 2014). In a biased system, because of students' skin colors, accents, primary languages, and/or cultural backgrounds, many are considered less likely to succeed in school, be able to think critically, and do well in life.

One type of biased thinking is the belief that students are not capable of constructing ideas, learning complex concepts, and higher-order cognition. This is a major reason for the existence of so many lists of standards, multiple-choice tests, and the factory-like model of learning that hasn't changed all that much in the last 100 years. There are even many people out there who don't want students to think deeply and excel in school, especially not multilingual students. Accumulation-based teaching, in a nutshell, has become an effective way to "control" the thinking of young people and keep marginalized students in the margins.

Bias takes other harmful forms in school, such as bias that favors decontextualized content and language. This bias comes from people who don't understand that language and content are most effectively learned *in context* (National Research Council, 2000). Accumulation-based learning, for example, requires a large amount of decontextualized, unrelated, and underrecycled language. Because of the need to use many disconnected texts to cover and "check off" standards, students can get overwhelmed by the barrage of new and disjointed content and its language. Things pass by so quickly that there is little recycling or "rooting" of key words and phrases in the brain. When students reach their "my-brain-is-full" frustration level, their learning slows down. Multilingual students tend to reach this frustration point sooner, on average, than monolingual English-speaking students.

Education also tends to be biased toward the use of numerical data (e.g., test scores), which can be crunched and displayed in many different ways. I have been at meetings where teachers were told that their students' scores indicated the need to improve reading comprehension, word knowledge, and grammatical conventions. In one meeting, a teacher said, "I am not that surprised by any of this—because I spend all day with my students—but I can surprise you with the many additional things that they can do."

Other common biases in schools include biases toward the following:

- Silent and individual reading and writing over collaboration and student talk
- Memorization instead of idea-building
- Using "correct" English in complete sentences right away and placing more importance on correctness than communication
- Assessing with multiple-choice items and very short answers
- Traditional" teaching and thinking that major changes will be too drastic, too risky, or too much work
- Reading and math
- Valuing only "mainstream" American monolingual language use and culture(s) and assimilating students into them

There are more, but for now, take a moment to think about how such biases might play a role in promoting accumulation-based learning and pedagogical injustices in your setting.

Root Cause: Ignorance

There are two meanings of ignorance to address, both of which overlap with and contribute to the other four root causes. The first means to ignore. This includes turning a blind eye to all the evidence of the pedagogical injustices that affect multilingual students' learning and lives. This evidence includes decades of data on how poorly the testing practices and test-based curriculums are serving our multilingual students (Au, 2020; Solórzano, 2019). It includes ignoring the suggestions and wisdom of educational experts and research. It includes ignoring the gut feelings that we are just not doing the right things for our students in school.

The other type of ignorance is not knowing. This includes not knowing students, what they know, how they learn, what they want to learn, and so on. It includes not knowing that there are other types of learning that are more effective than accumulation and transmission. Many people who make major decisions in education (e.g., boards, policymakers, curriculum writers, and administrators) do not know enough about learning and about students, especially multilingual students. They have not looked at enough research, have not talked to enough students, or engaged in enough ongoing reflection on how diverse students in their settings learn and grow. Many have spent too little time in the classroom, and many base their knowledge on their own limited schooling experiences many years ago. Some try to disguise their ignorance by relying on numbers and "common sense," thinking that education "isn't rocket science."

Ignorance tends to point people (e.g., policymakers, school boards, educators, parents) in the direction of the low-hanging fruit, which is the familiar "answers for points; more points is good" approach. But our students deserve better than low-hanging fruit. They deserve all the fruit—and the entire tree.

> How do these root causes promote accumulation-based instruction in your setting?

ACTIVITY 1.2
Recognizing Injustices in Your Setting

One of the goals of this book is to help you and your setting become even more aware of the many subtle and not-so-subtle injustices that your multilingual students face. Copy or create this chart and then work with one or more other educators to fill it in. Notice that it is based on Figure 1.4. Add to the chart over time as you hone your abilities to see and hear injustices around you.

Examples of Root Causes of Injustices in Your Setting
• Lack of trust:
• Learning is countable:
• Students as objects:
• Bias:
• Ignorance:
In your setting, what are signs of pedagogical injustices?
What are three of the most prevalent pedagogical injustices in your setting? What is evidence of them?   1.   2.   3.
How do the injustices affect your students?

Keeping the Purpose of Education in Mind

We must always keep in mind the purpose of education, which is to do as much as it can to help all students reach their many potentials. These potentials are varied, including abilities to communicate effectively, use creativity, solve major problems, build up complex ideas, collaborate, develop deep relationships, empathize, appreciate other perspectives, grow, and care.

Depriving students of the opportunities to reach their potentials is pedagogical injustice. This is what's happening to millions of multilingual students within the prevalent model of pedagogy: accumulation-based learning. If you asked 300 of the most prominent and accomplished academics to design an effective approach for learning in our schools, what would they recommend? Would it be what we have now—or something very different? It likely wouldn't be what we have now.

When we have a system that, decade after decade, disengages, marginalizes, and shames large numbers of brilliant students who have similar intelligences, desires to learn, and creativities—but differ in language and cultural backgrounds—then the system must be overhauled. Being multilingual affords many advantages in life; we cannot continue to let our school system turn it into a liability.

But challenging the status quo, especially in our current sociopolitical environment, is difficult. And it's uncomfortable to feel the tension between having to work within the confines of a harmful system and the desire to do the right thing by our students. Yet some of the most important and liberating change movements across human history started with teachers in the trenches.

The remaining chapters outline a major overhaul of accumulation-based learning. The changes are grounded in the six dimensions of pedagogical justice and in the research on educating multilingual students, language development, identity, and reducing pedagogical injustices.

Meaningful learning can and does happen without focusing on test scores. In a properly overhauled system, students can score several "levels" below grade level *every year* and still have great lives. They can reach their potentials, consider themselves to be confident learners, and be successful in a wide range of endeavors. In fact, some students with nonstellar scores do even better in life because their schools did not waste copious amounts of lesson time and energy focused on test preparation.

The overhauled learning in this book is much messier and more complex than accumulation-based learning. It happens over time. It grows. It goes somewhere. It spirals. It builds. It adapts. It inspires. And hopefully, the following chapters will inspire you to join our small group of thoughtful and committed citizens who will change the world of education for our students.

CHAPTER IDEA

Here is one idea that you can build up from this chapter. If another idea was sparked for you, feel free to build it instead. Remember to add personal examples, definitions, questions, and insights as building blocks along with new blocks gathered from this chapter. Some sample blocks are provided.

IDEA STATEMENT: There is ongoing tension between the dimensions of pedagogical justice and the root causes of pedagogical injustices in our system.		
	We need to be aware of the injustices faced by multilingual students.	
How can we strengthen the dimensions of pedagogical justice in our setting?	A major root cause in our setting is that many educators think that learning is countable.	
Being multilingual has many advantages.		

References

Abedi, J. (2003). *Impact of student language background on content-based performance: Analysis of extant data.* National Center for Research on Evaluation, Standards, and Student Testing, Graduate School of Education & Information Studies, University of California.

Abedi, J., Hofstetter, C. H., & Lord, C. (2004). Assessment accommodations for English language learners: Implications for policy-based empirical research. *Review of Educational Research*, 74(1), 1–28.

Amrein, A. L., & Berliner, D. C. (2003). The effects of high-stakes testing on student motivation and learning. *Educational Leadership*, 60(5), 32–38.

Au, W. (2020). *High-stakes testing, standardization, and inequality in the United States*. In *Oxford research encyclopedia of education*. Oxford University Press.

Bach, A. J. (2020). High-stakes, standardized testing and emergent bilingual students in Texas: A call for action. *Texas Journal of Literacy Education*, 8, 18–37.

Bandura, A. (2001). Social cognitive theory: An agentic perspective. *Annual Review of Psychology*, 52, 1–26. doi:10.1146/annurev.psych.52.1.1

Bartolomé, L. (1994). Beyond the methods fetish: Toward a humanizing pedagogy. *Harvard Educational Review*, 64(2), 173–195.

Bourdieu, P. (1986). The forms of capital. In J. G. Richardson (Ed.), *Handbook of theory and research for the sociology of education* (pp. 241–258). Greenwood Press.

Bouygues, H. (2022). *Teaching critical thinking in K–12: When there's a will but not always a way*. Reboot. https://reboot-foundation.org/wp-content/uploads/2022/07/Reboot-White-Paper_NAEP-5.pdf

Boyd, M., & Rubin, D. (2006). How contingent questioning promotes extended student talk: A function of display questions. *Journal of Literacy Research*, 28(2), 141–169.

Carter Andrews, D. J., & Castillo, B. M. (2016). Humanizing pedagogy for examinations of race and culture in teacher education. In F. Tuitt, C. Haynes, & S. Stewart (Eds.), *Race, equity and higher education: The continued search for critical and inclusive pedagogies around the globe* (pp. 112–128). Stylus.

Csikszentmihalyi, M. (1996). *Creativity: Flow and the psychology of discovery and invention*. HarperCollins.

Cha Y.-K., Ham S.-H., & Yang K.-E. (2017). Multicultural education policy in the global institutional context. In Y.-K. Cha, J. Gundara, S.-H. Ham, & M. Lee (Eds.), *Multicultural education in global perspectives* (pp. 11–21). Springer Nature.

Darling-Hammond, L., Ancess, J., & Falk, B. (1995). *Authentic assessment in action: Studies of schools and students at work*. Teachers College Press.

David, J. (2008). What research says about pacing guides. *ASCD*.

Del Carmen Unda, M., & Lizárraga-Dueñas, L. (2021). The testing industrial complex: Texas and beyond. *Texas Education Review*, 9(2), 31–42.

Flores, N., & Rosa, J. D. (2015). Undoing appropriateness: Raciolinguistic ideologies and language diversity in education. *Harvard Educational Review*, 85(2), 149–171. https://doi.org/10.17763/0017-8055.85.2.149

Freire, P. (1970). *Pedagogy of the oppressed*. Seabury Press.

Glossary of Education Reform. (2016). Student engagement. https://www.edglossary.org/student-engagement/. Accessed on March 29, 2023.

Gottlieb, M., & Honigsfeld, A. (2019). From assessment of learning to learning for and as learning. In *Breaking down the wall: Essential shifts for English learners' success*. Corwin.

Horn, C. (2003). High-stakes testing and students: Stopping or perpetuating a cycle of failure? *Theory into Practice*, 42(1), 30–41.

Jones, B. (2019). *Nine things you can due to support student agency with formative assessment*. WestEd.

Mehta, J., & Fine, S. (2019). *In search of deeper learning: The quest to remake the American high school*. Harvard University Press.

Menken, K. (2006). Teaching to the test: How No Child Left behind impacts language policy, curriculum, and instruction for English language learners. *Bilingual Research Journal*, 30(2), 521–546.

Mitchell, C. (2016). Study: Current, former ELLs take fewer advanced, college-prep classes. *Education Week*. https://www.edweek.org/teaching-learning/study-current-former-ells-take-fewer-advanced-college-prep-classes/2016/11. Accessed on April 18, 2023.

National Research Council. (2000). *How people learn: Brain, mind, experience, and school: Expanded edition*. The National Academies Press.

Nichols, M. (2006). *Comprehension through conversation: The power of purposeful talk in the reading workshop*. Heinemann.

Nichols, S., Glass, G., & Berliner, D. (2012). High-stakes testing and student achievement: Updated analyses with NAEP data. *Education Policy Analysis Archives*, 20(20).

Nokes, T. J., Schunn, C. D., & Chi, M. T. (2010). Problem solving and human expertise. *International Encyclopedia of Education*, 5, 265–272.

Nystrand, M. (1997). *Opening dialogue: Understanding the dynamics of language and learning*. Teachers College Press.

Paul, R., & Elder, L. (2008). *A guide for educators to critical thinking competency standards*. Foundation for Critical Thinking.

Paul, R., & Elder, L. (2014). *Critical thinking: Tools for taking charge of your professional and personal life* (2nd ed.). Pearson Education.

Pierre, T. (2016). *The impact of high-stakes testing on low-income students and students of color*. Masters Dissertation. State University of New York, Empire State College. ProQuest Dissertations & Theses Global.

Popham, J. (1999). Why standardized tests don't measure educational quality. *ASCD*, 56(6). https://www.ascd.org/el/articles/why-standardized-tests-dont-measure-educational-quality.

Reich, J., & Mehta J. (2021). Healing, community, and humanity: How students and teachers want to reinvent schools post-COVID. https://edarxiv.org/nd52b

Slavin R. E. (2012). *Educational psychology: Theory and practice*. Pearson.

Sleeter, C. (2015). Multicultural education vs. factory model schooling. In H. P. Baptiste, A. Ryan, B. Arajuo, & R. Duhon-Sells (Eds.), *Multicultural education: A renewed paradigm of transformation and call to action* (pp. 115–136). Caddo Gap Press.

Solórzano, R. (2019). *High-stakes testing and educational inequality in K–12 schools*. Oxford University Press. https://doi.org/10.1093/acrefore/9780190264093.013.938.

St. John, K., & Briel, L. (April 2017). *Student voice: A growing movement within education that benefits students and teachers*. VCU Center on Transition Innovations.

Sternberg, R. J. (Ed.). (1999). *Handbook of creativity*. Cambridge University Press.

Vaughn, M. (2020). What is student agency and why is it needed now more than ever? *Theory into Practice*, 59(2), 109–118. https://doi.org/10.1080/00405841.2019.1702393

Vygotsky, L. S. (1978). *Mind in society: The development of higher psychological processes*. Harvard University Press.

Walqui, A., & Heritage, M. (2018). Meaningful classroom talk: Supporting English learners' oral language development. *American Educator*, 42(3), 18–23.

Warren, M. R. (2014). Transforming public education: The need for an educational justice movement. *New England Journal of Public Policy*, 26(1), Article 11. https://scholarworks.umb.edu/nejpp/vol26/iss1/11

Wiggins, G. (1990). The case for authentic assessment. *Practical Assessment, Research and Evaluation*, 2, Article 2.

Willingham, D. T. (2007). Critical thinking: Why is it so hard to teach? *American Educator*, 31, 8–19. http://www.aft.org/sites/default/files/periodicals/Crit_Thinking.pdf

Zabala, D. (2007). *State high school exit exams: Gaps persist in high school exit exam pass rates—Policy brief 3*. Center on Education Policy.

What Students Learn and How They Grow 2

Each student is bursting with gifts for the world.

Parents, legislators, educators, employers, teachers, and students all have different visions and hopes for what students should learn and how they should grow. At present, all states and most of their schools use lengthy lists of standards that are separated by grade level and discipline. Each standard usually applies to every student equally (i.e., "one standard fits all") such that there isn't much of a continuum of learning (you either learn it or you don't). Lists of standards lean much more heavily on academic learning, especially of facts and skills, than on personal growth.

We start this chapter with the *who* of learning (our students), then a bit of the *why* of learning, then move into the *what* of learning (content), and end with *how* students can and should grow in five different categories.

Students Are Different

Every student in every school is different, with different backgrounds, strengths, interests, talents, and needs. Each student will learn differently and end up with different ideas, skills, and personalities each year of school and beyond. Each student will communicate and grow differently.

Each student has a different path and destiny. We should never want students to end up the same! They should leave each school year with more developed and cultivated differences. This is vital for them—and vital for the world. Educators and education influencers at all levels (K–12) must understand this—it is a vital part of this overhaul work and for addressing pedagogical injustices.

Yet the current, traditional, factory-like accumulation-based approach of schooling seeks the opposite. It seeks to ignore, chip away at, and even discourage differences that don't fit students into the molds of efficient test takers. Rather than narrowing so-called "achievement gaps," it tends to narrow down who students are and who they will become. In contrast, we should want our students to reach their many potentials, grow their many talents, and become the amazing individuals they were born to be. In other words, we cannot just value the differences that students bring to school; we must also value the differences that students develop and "take away" as a result of schooling.

Most of you agree with the last two paragraphs. It's not a question of whether we should value student differences. The question is, given the many constraints (e.g., standards, tests, and curriculums) placed on school systems and teachers, *how can we put our efforts where our values are*? We start answering this question in this chapter, but the answer will build as you work through subsequent chapters.

Why Do Humans Learn?

We seldom sit around trying to answer the question, Why do humans learn? We are more focused on the *what* and *how* of learning, along with a lot of *how we know* students are learning. But a solid answer to this *why* question gives us insights for coming up with the *whats* in the next section. I lump most purposes for learning knowledge, language, and skills under five overlapping categories.

To get things done. This includes most of the basic and daily tasks that we need to do to do life: ask for directions, use a phone, make meals, fix toys, buy groceries, pay bills, accomplish tasks for work, overcome challenges, and the like.

To foster relationships. This includes all that we learn in order to be good family members, friends, co-workers, and citizens, along with how to strengthen relationships with others over time. It includes learning how to empathize, forgive, be patient, listen, care, and commit.

To build up solutions, concepts, and claims. This includes the knowledge and skills that we learn in order to accomplish tasks in a discipline. It includes building up solutions to complex problems and building up two sides of an issue to decide which side is stronger (a.k.a., argumentation).

To grow. This includes the learning that we do to grow into good and happy humans. It includes the knowledge and skills we are interested in developing, as well as things we feel obligated to work on because we want to be better people. It includes growing in our multilingual and multicultural identities.

To satisfy our curiosity and need for meaning. Humans are driven by a natural curiosity to understand and make meaning of our worlds. This includes the many philosophical "meaning of life" questions that we ask throughout the course of our lives, along with the innate wonderings we have about how things work, why things happen, and what's next.

These aren't the only reasons for learning, but they cover a lot of ground, especially in school. These are the main purposes emphasized in this book's overhaul work.

What Should Students Learn?

What should students learn? This question cannot be answered by looking at the front material of a curriculum guide or at best-selling books listing all of the knowledge that students are lacking. Such lists can provide some guidance, but they fall well short of providing all the key things that each of *your* multilingual students should learn to have great lives. They don't know your students, and they tend to emphasize "learning" that is highly testable and countable. (*Note*: Even though I refer to the term "standards" in this book, it helps to use terms for what students learn that don't imply that they either learned it or not. All students learn content and skills on a continuum, with differing levels of intensity, and they show this learning in a wide range of ways.)

The *what* of learning matters a lot for pedagogical justice because what multilingual students are taught (and not taught) has played a huge role in the pedagogical injustices described in the previous chapter. Many of the commonly listed standards and the language used to teach and assess them are rooted in dominant, English-only, middle-class values, languages, and culture. For example, there are many standards worded like this: *Demonstrate strong command of the conventions of standard English grammar and usage when speaking or writing.* You will not likely find many standards that value the development and use of non-English languages. Nor will you find many standards that value growth in multilingual and multicultural identities and practices. Nor will you find many that value the use of varied languages and communication strategies such as translanguaging and translation.

This doesn't mean that we toss out all the standards and start over. Many of them are things that students should learn. For example, we do want students to eventually develop a "strong command" of different ways of using English, including what is often called "standard English," in order to communicate in a variety of situations with a variety of others. At the same time, we must continue to analyze standards for biased language and focuses that skew toward English-only practices and cultural assimilation. A priority should be to help students use and develop all of their communication resources (languages, art, movement, etc.) to build and share their ideas with the world.

We should therefore edit standards (like the "strong command" ones) as well as add standards for the multilingual and multicultural development growth of students. I suggest working with others in your setting to (a) analyze the goals and standards used by other districts and multilingual education organizations (NABE, ATDLE, CABE, etc.) and (b) draft a short set of goals or standards that focus on areas such as developing students' abilities to use their entire linguistic repertoire for academic tasks and assessment, interpret and construct multilingual and multicultural texts, and cultivate their multilingual and multicultural identities.

Keep your draft multilingual-multicultural standards in mind as you adapt and emphasize the more commonly used standards in your curriculums. Often, the lists get so long that we only have time to briefly "cover" them. Instead, this chapter suggests using a short "list" of meaty things that fit together well enough to engage students *and* stick in their minds.

Yes, the following things are difficult to assess. But for now, don't worry about their testability. Just think about the future and well-being of each student. If you have kids at home, think about them. Would you like them to learn these things, regardless of their testability?

The following list isn't complete. It is only meant to get you started in thinking differently about the *what* of learning in your setting and how emphasizing these things can foster pedagogical justice for multilingual students.

Big Ideas

Research on experts in various fields tends to show that they organize knowledge around important ideas that guide their thinking about topics and problems (National Research Council, 2000). Each discipline (and life itself) has a wide range of key concepts and claims that can be classified as big ideas (Zwiers, 2019b). What makes an idea big?

An idea is "big" if it helps us make sense of lots of otherwise meaningless, isolated, inert, or confusing facts. A big idea is a way of usefully seeing connections, not just another piece of knowledge. It is more like a lens for better looking than something additionally seen; more like a theme than the facts of the story—A true idea doesn't end thought, it activates it. It has the power to raise questions and generate learning.

(Wiggins, 2010, p. 1)

Concept-based ideas tend to be complex processes, cycles, theories, and systems that are important in a discipline (Mitchell et al., 2017). They usually have multiple parts (examples, definitions, and sub-ideas) that fit together somehow. Concept-based big ideas tend to be less arguable and less prone to differing opinions than claim-based big ideas.

Sample concept-based big ideas include the following: *Animals adapt to survive. Authors use figurative language to show rather than tell. Greed is a major force in history. The sun is the origin of most types of energy. The quadratic formula is derived from completing the square.*

Claim-based big ideas are more arguable, require evidence to support them, and usually have counterclaims. Some examples of claims include the following: *We need school uniforms. Social media is harmful. We need to ban all uses of plastic. The main theme of the story is hope. Freedom requires sacrifice. Graffiti is art. We shouldn't judge a book by its cover. We need to start the school day one hour later.*

I always put idea statements into a single sentence, which is much like a thesis statement for an essay or a topic sentence for a paragraph. I tend to use a visual like Figure 2.1 to help students construct ideas. But you can also use a semantic map, an outline, actual wood or plastic blocks, or something similar. Many more idea statement examples are found in Appendix C.

Students could memorize idea statements and even memorize supporting and clarifying sentences (e.g., a whole paragraph or even an essay), but this "learning" is not as lasting or meaningful as when students build up the ideas and put them in their own words. In short, we should not treat ideas as something that *we* teach. Rather, our teaching should consist of providing resources, knowledge, encouragement, modeling, and scaffolding for the idea-building processes.

To build up ideas, students need to use knowledge "building blocks" (Ausubel, 2000). There are two main types of building blocks. One type is support blocks, which tend to consist of evidence, details, facts, anecdotes, and examples. The other type is clarify blocks, which include definitions, visuals, and paraphrases.

For example, Student A is building up an idea, "Some bees 'dance' to communicate directions and distances to other bees." She watches a short video and reads an article with diagrams on bee movements. These sources provide scientific definitions, examples, facts, and questions that help her strengthen and clarify her ideas. She also adds vital personal knowledge and experiences to the idea (watching bees at the park). Her idea might look something like the one in Figure 2.1. Then she tells a partner her idea and its building blocks, which helps the partner build up a similar idea in her mind.

Figure 2.1 Sample Idea-Building Visual

Some bees "dance" to communicate direction and distance to other bees.		
Diagram of movements and what they mean	How do they learn to do this?	Watched bees in the park
"Dance" means to walk in circles	Saves time and energy	Example from video

You have likely read many abstract and theory-based texts in which you said to the author, "Give examples of what you just described!" or "What does that mean?" This is how we strengthen and clarify big ideas.

A big idea builds as students add building blocks that support it and clarify terms within it. Overlap of clarifying and supporting is common; a person might use an example to clarify a term or idea. You can also have students put "heavier" or "stronger" evidence and examples in larger blocks. This helps students improve their evaluation skills. Under the idea in Figure 2.1, for example, the student put the diagram of movements in a large block because of its importance in supporting the idea.

Idea-building also aligns with other common pedagogical concepts such as building and using schema, "chunking," mental representations, and essential understandings. Nokes et al. (2010), for example, argue that experts and successful students organize and categorize what they are learning into knowledge structures (schemas, chunks, solutions, and ideas), which help them construct mental representations of problems and challenges as well as provide a framework for remembering new information in the discipline.

We want all of our students to develop as much expertise as they can across content areas, which comes from idea-building, not just memorizing. For multilingual learners in particular, who are frequently denied opportunities to engage in deeper levels of learning, idea-building (see Chapter 4) can make students less passive and disengaged and more active and enthusiastic agents of their own learning.

Big-idea learning is very different from accumulation-based learning. As Wiggins (2010) puts it,

> *A big idea reaches out, it pushes against boundaries, it asks us to possibly rethink other things we thought we knew. It raises questions and problems—and thus, generates new ideas. We see new connections and we initiate inquiries to validate or critique the idea. A big idea activates thought and permits transfer—and thus creativity. (para. 29)*

This is the stuff of great learning and, for most of us, the reason why we went into teaching.

Figure 2.2 includes sample big-idea statements that span across grade levels and disciplines. Additional big-idea statements are in Appendix C.

Also, keep in mind that small- and medium-sized ideas can support bigger ideas. The entire dancing bee idea, for example, could be used to build up an even larger idea such as, "Living creatures have learned to communicate to survive." This is how knowledge tends to be structured, with categories and subcategories, ideas and subideas. Outlines and semantic maps show this structure fairly well.

Figure 2.2 Big-Idea Examples Across Disciplines and Grade Levels

	K–3	4–7	8–12
Science	Water moves in an endless cycle.	Earthquakes often happen when tectonic plates move.	Photosynthesis helps a plant use the sun's light to make energy.
Language arts	Stories can teach us how to be better people.	Metaphors help to show rather than tell.	Historical novels help us see how people lived and thought in the past.
Math	Subtraction means taking away one amount from another.	A line shows you a constant relationship between two variables in a situation.	The quadratic formula is derived from completing the square.
History	Rosa Parks was a hero.	Surplus food production was needed for civilizations to form.	The stirrup changed the course of history.
Social studies	A community is a group of people who take care of each other.	Utopia is impossible.	Democracy is fragile.
Visual and performing arts	We need to appreciate music from all cultures.	Some ideas are best communicated through art.	Impressionists revolutionized the art of painting.
Health/P.E.	You are what you eat.	Exercise has many benefits to one's health.	Mental stress can have deleterious effects on the body.

Building Up Competing Ideas: Argumentation

An important type of idea-building is argumentation. Argumentation involves building up two or more opposing claims and deciding which claim is the heaviest or strongest (Zwiers, 2019a). To do this, students mostly use support blocks (evidence, examples, and data), clarify blocks (definitions and reasoning), and thinking skills (evaluating and interpreting). This process can be represented by a visual such as this balance scale shown in Figure 2.3.

We want students to learn how to engage in objective *truth-seeking* argumentation as opposed to just *win-seeking* argumentation, which is what persuasion and debate tend to do. Truth-seeking means that the students, individually or with partners, strive to collaboratively build up both sides of the argument as objectively and strongly as they can (Zwiers, 2019a). They should "park" their initial opinions in the back of their heads and not hold back evidence from either side. They then work to clarify and support each side *as well as possible*, and then eventually they evaluate the supports (evidence and examples) to see which side weighs more.

Because they are e**valu**ating in this last stage—and students have different **values**—they might differ in their final choices. This is OK, as

Figure 2.3   Argument Balance Scale

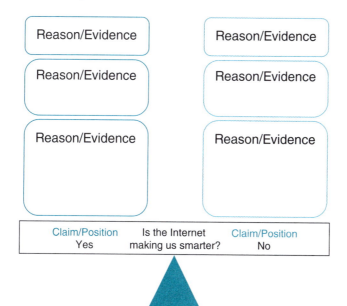

long as they can explain their value-based decisions. Over time, students learn that a *stronger* (heavier) side means the objective quality and credibility of evidence and support for a side is more convincing—and that it does not mean louder, angrier, or more persuasively eloquent (the world does not need any more decision-makers with these traits). Argumentation also offers a powerful opportunity to share and discuss students' different values, which tend to stem from their varied backgrounds.

Here are a few of the many argument-based topics that you might use. Just remind students to *build up both sides as strongly and clearly as possible* before deciding which side weighs more.

- Are we doomed to repeat the past when we don't learn from it?
- Should animals be used in medical experiments?
- Is social media harmful to society?
- Should we double the taxes on gasoline?
- Should we engage in stem cell research?
- Are dogs better pets than cats?
- Should we colonize space?

But even more important than deciding on a particular issue (e.g., cell phones in school or not), the bigger "meta-idea" that we want students to develop by using argumentation topics is this: People should collaboratively and objectively seek what is right when engaged in any argument or decision that we face in the future. The big-idea statement could be this: "When we need to decide between two sides of an argument or decision, we build up both sides as much as possible and use critical thinking to evaluate which side weighs more." I don't know about you, but I would love to see students build up this idea and put it into action in every decision they make, now and during their entire lives.

One of the big benefits of argumentation for students is that it builds up their agency and engagement in school (Meier, 2002). Why? One reason is that we trust students to choose a side, which may differ from our choices or that of other students. They are trusted to think, value, and choose, rather than just memorize. Students might not use grammatically perfect English or lots of "academic vocabulary." But they know that this doesn't matter because their goal is to make an important decision—not to be tested on how well they write, speak, or read. We encourage them to use their own values to evaluate the weight of evidence on each side. They learn that in important areas and arguments, there are not right and wrong answers but rather strong and weak ones, each depending on how clear and logical the reasoning is.

Activities for Crafting Big Ideas

The following activities can help you to come up with one or more big ideas for your setting. Ideas can come from you, students, curriculum guides, standards, essential questions, life, news, and texts that students are reading in and out of school. Ideas should (a) be valuable (worth precious school time), (b) be buildable (not just a basic fact or skill), and (c) push students to learn and grow. There are different options you can choose to come up with big ideas to build, listed in the following activities.

ACTIVITY 2.1
Start With an Essential Question

An essential question can help you frame the big idea a bit more quickly. It can also motivate students to construct an answer. But be careful. Just posing a big essential question doesn't guarantee that your students will be interested in answering it. You might love it, but students might not. I sometimes ask teachers, "Would the majority of your students get excited about this question?" If you think so, then stick with it for now and come up with a topic sentence or thesis statement (idea statement) that will be the beginning of an answer to the question. This is a first draft of a possible big idea that will guide learning in the unit. You can modify it as you look at content and skills to be learned and as you get to know what students know and can do with respect to it.

Figure 2.4 has some essential questions with corresponding idea-statement drafts. Fill in the last three rows with questions and ideas that your students will answer and build.

Figure 2.4 Generating Big-Idea Statements From Essential Questions

Essential Question	Big Idea Statement that Starts to Answer the EQ
Why were civilizations able to form?	People figured out better ways to farm, so they had extra food to trade and sell.
What is a ratio?	A ratio is a common relationship between pairs of numbers.
What is a major theme in *Holes*?	An important theme in *Holes* is that friendship can help you through life's difficulties.
How can the water you drink be billions of years old?	Water moves around in an endless cycle.
Why do authors have their characters change during a story?	Character changes show readers how to be better people and teach us lessons in life.

ACTIVITY 2.2
Start With an Argument

I have seen many successful units that are motivated by exploring and choosing one side of an important argument in the discipline. Examples include: Is utopia possible? Are genetically modified crops harmful? Should we decide elections with the popular vote? Is nature or nurture a stronger influence on who children become? You can see the learning potential in these arguments as students build up each side. They build up two or more opposing claims (kind of a two-for-one), which pushes them to think and read and talk even more—especially when you give them the agency to make the final decision.

There are also many "smaller" arguments such as these: Should students use cell phones in school? Should we have school uniforms? Should video games be banned? Are dogs or cats better pets? Or they could be used to help you build up an idea about how to communicate an argument and its decision effectively in writing, orally, or visually. Remind students with any argument in their lives, to think, "We need to build up both sides and then objectively evaluate their strength to decide which one is stronger."

I often work with teachers who say that the topic they are teaching isn't engaging enough for students. After they say that they can't change topics (often my first suggestion), I suggest finding some controversy or argument that students might buy into. Are there any two-sided decisions or issues with pros and cons? About half the time, we land on a question juicy enough to try out with students. Try this out in the following table. Put a seemingly noncontroversial topic you are teaching in the left-hand column and then come up with an argument question that might engage students.

Figure 2.5 Generating Argument Questions From Topics

Topic	Argument Question
Water cycle	Should we use desalination plants to make fresh water?
Honesty	Should we always tell the truth?
American Revolution	Were the revolutionaries patriots or rebels?
Division of fractions	Should we know why we should multiply by the inverse of one of the fractions?
Figurative devices	Should we use figurative devices in our writing or not?
Animal adaptation	Which is the most interesting animal adaptation of all?

ACTIVITY 2.3
Start With a Major Standard

In some cases, a standard might be big and interesting enough to be a big idea, which makes it a bit easier. For example, the common social science standard, "The culture of a group is influenced by its geography," is a big idea that can be clarified and supported by many examples. You can put the standard and put it at the top of the Big Idea column in Figure 2.6. Then under it you put the smaller standards, knowledge, and skills needed to build up that idea. And you can try to make the idea a bit more interesting by rewording it and/or letting students come up with an interesting product or performance. Sometimes you can turn it into an argument (refer to the previous section).

You can start with several standards. You might have a list of connected standards such as these:

- Cite textual evidence **to support analysis of what the text says** explicitly as well as inferences drawn from the text.
- **Determine the theme of a text** and how it is conveyed through particular details.
- Describe **how characters change** as the plot moves toward a resolution.
- Analyze how a **particular sentence or scene contributes to the development of the theme.**

In these abridged standards, I bolded the parts that worked for crafting a big idea such as "Authors of literature often communicate important themes though character changes." Try either one of the methods above in the chart in Figure 2.6.

When working with standards, we must always keep the big ideas in mind. It is highly tempting to teach each standard one by one, check off their boxes, and move on. Many curriculums do this. Most standards are not major enough to be the main goal of learning. Rather, they should be seen as the skills and building blocks for constructing and communicating larger ideas, concepts, and claims.

Figure 2.6 Generating Big Idea Statements From Standards

Standard(s)	Big Idea
Major standard:	*(If needed, reword the standard to be more student-friendly)*
Small standard: Small standard: Small standard:	

ACTIVITY 2.4
Start With Texts

Your curriculum unit might have a set of texts within it (or a longer text like a novel), but it doesn't include an idea to build from them. Read through the text(s) and highlight or note the key parts of the texts that you want students to remember and think about. These parts are potential building blocks for the idea. Then think about what idea, concept, or claim those building blocks can and should support in the minds of students. What meaty idea do you want them to learn from reading the text(s)? For example, in a unit on insect colonies, a second-grade teacher and I skimmed through the texts (two articles, a story, and a poem) to identify blocks focused on playing roles and working together. The first idea that came up was "Insects in colonies work together." We didn't think it was engaging enough, so we changed it to "We should be more like bees and ants."

ACTIVITY 2.5
Start With Student Ideas

As you navigate the waters of teaching over the years, you hear lots of things, including great ideas that you or the curriculum didn't come up with. Keep a list of student ideas for use in the current and future years. And if possible, even early on in a unit you can invite students to brainstorm ideas that they think are worth building. You can collectively choose one or more ideas that are worthy of lesson time, student energy, your energy, and so on. I worked with a math teacher who told me one of her students came up with the idea, "The equal sign is like a fulcrum." A science teacher's student wrote an article that communicated her idea, "Nature is more magical than any wizard."

Even though teachers will give, guide, and shape big ideas for students, we want to develop their abilities to come up with their own ideas. This means encouraging and helping students to come up with ideas that are not laid out neatly for them. For example, one fifth-grade teacher had students read accounts from different perspectives of the Boston Massacre to start building up their own ideas about how bias and language play roles in history and our interpretations of it.

One of the biggest challenges is that students often don't realize that lasting learning comes from building up ideas. They might hear you tell them to build an idea, or they might see a graphic organizer, or you might ask them to share their ideas with peers. But if they think that they need to do these things for points, less learning happens. Students need to develop the mindset that keeps them thinking, "We can come up with big ideas. Then we build them up to be as strong and clear as possible. And we help others do this too. This is how we learn best." Often, you will cull ideas from student writing, but be listening to their conversations and comments too. You can use a simple table like the one here.

Figure 2.7 Using Ideas From Students

Unit, Topic, Student Name	Student-Generated Big Ideas

ACTIVITY 2.6

Start With a Product or Performance

An engaging and meaty culminating product or performance provides a lot of information that is useful for crafting big ideas (see Chapter 3). Since the main purpose of the product or performance should be *to communicate* a big idea to others (i.e., not for assessment), you can think about the idea that students will communicate. For example, one teacher had given her students a history task of creating posters focused on the causes of different events and presenting them to the class. She then thought about the common concept that the products would communicate and drafted the idea, "Historical changes have different types of causes."

In Figure 2.8, fill in the rest of the cells in the left-hand column, even if you don't normally use any of the products or performances. Then think about the big idea that the product or performance might communicate to an interested audience.

Figure 2.8 Generating Big-Idea Statements From Products and Performances

Product or Performance	Big Idea
Podcast on	
Business proposal for	
Ted Talk on	
Short story about	
News article on	
Public-service message on	

Content Knowledge

Another vital *what* of learning is content knowledge. Ideas (concepts, claims, and solutions) need to be built up with building blocks. These building blocks include content knowledge, facts, evidence, examples, details, definitions, clarifications, quotations, illustrations, and events. For example, in the sample idea visual in Figure 2.9, notice the different types of information in the building blocks.

Most lists of teaching practices have "Connect to background knowledge" up near the top or at the beginning of lesson plan templates. And in many lessons, teachers ask students to "connect" to what they have already learned and experienced. Teachers often ask, "Have you ever …?" or tell students, "Make connections between what you are learning and what we learned last month about …" This particular element reframes this practice a little. Instead of just making a quick and fleeting connection to one's background knowledge or previous learning, it has students turn that connection into a useful and lasting building block. For example, a teacher might ask students to think of a time when they were sick and took medicine. As students share out, the teacher asks them to take notes on sticky notes for later use in building up the idea of how medicine works.

Some learning does include what I call "constructive memorizing." Students need to learn and remember information to keep their ideas strong over time. Examples include multiplication tables, important

Figure 2.9 Sample Idea for Building Blocks Information

Supply and demand affect prices of goods.			
If they make more bikes, demand for them goes down.		If they make more bikes, demand for them goes down.	Supply / Demand graph
Lots of people want that type of phone, so the price goes up.	Monopoly means no competition.		
A company stores diamonds to keep supply low.	I raised the price of lemonade and demand went down.		Monopoly means no competition.

dates in history, key definitions, lab procedures, scientific laws, mathematical principles, names and functions of organelles in biology, and so on. These are like the materials that construction workers bring and use at a construction site. In our case, students use these things to build up strong ideas. This is very different from memorizing *disconnected* pieces of information just for points on tests, which would be like piling up bricks randomly on a lot, getting some money for the pile, and forgetting about it. This analogy also shows that building ideas is harder work and takes more time, language, and skill than just memorizing facts and practicing skills for points.

Skills for Building Ideas and Making Decisions

Students need to become increasingly capable of building new ideas, choosing the strongest claims in an argument, and communicating them to others. They need to develop their "idea owner and contractor" skills, which means knowing how to effectively gather and use knowledge and skills to construct and communicate ideas. They need to be ready to build ideas at every turn and believe that, as María Nichols puts it, "each tentative thought has the potential to launch conversations as rich and varied as the range of voices involved" (2019, p. 37).

Students should exit each grade level having further developed their expertise in idea-building skills such as analyzing a problem or challenge; posing buildable and relevant ideas, solutions, and theories; supporting ideas with content, examples, and evidence; clarifying key terms; and objectively evaluating the weight and credibility of the evidence. In addition, students must develop their expertise in collaborating with others to accomplish tasks, co-construct ideas, and co-make decisions (National Academies of Sciences, Engineering and Medicine, 2018). Much of this expertise will come from—and will only come from—lots of practice in building and sharing ideas over the years in each discipline in school. There aren't any shortcuts.

Standards often include key academic skills such as analyzing, evaluating, comparing, and synthesizing. We want students to learn these skills. But why? Just because they are in the standards? To do well on tests? To get points? No, students should work on these skills to ultimately build up ideas and make decisions in academic and real-world settings. If you teach students how to make inferences, for example, the inferences can and should be used as building blocks for an idea—not just to answer inference questions on a quiz.

Builders on a construction site don't just know where to stack things. They have a range of skills that help them put materials (e.g., blocks) together in lasting ways. There are plenty of lists of cognitive strategies, thinking skills, literacy skills, disciplinary practices, and so on (e.g., Bloom, Marzano, DOK, etc.). Some lists even have some sort of hierarchy or continuum that assigns complexity or value to some skills over others. I often see such lists within curriculums and on classroom walls. They might be skills that students will develop on that day or during that week. Just make sure to teach them in the context of building up lasting ideas—not in isolation and not for points.

Students will develop their skills more deeply when they serve a purpose (like building a house) rather than just practicing (like hammering two pieces of scrap wood together). Even in units and lessons where skills (such as interpreting themes or argumentation) are prioritized, building up big ideas with those skills is more effective.

When you look at curriculums and long lists or jam-packed diagrams of thinking skills, zoom in on the skills that most effectively help students construct and communicate ideas. If you teach students to empathize with historical people, interpret the dialogue of a novel's main character, or solve a math problem, each skill used should help the student build up a claim or concept as strongly and clearly as possible. It should be strong and clear in the student's mind and in any mind of others to whom the student is communicating.

It is *very* tempting to teach skills out of context—because they are usually tested out of context and because they are often visible on well-known lists. A skill is not an idea, concept, or claim. Rather, students *use* skills to build up ideas and make decisions—just like skills carpenters use to construct a house; for example, do you want your contractor to say, "I have never built a house, but I'm really good at hammering, sawing, and measuring"? In school, a history student might be asked to compare two different accounts of an event. Comparing should not be the goal. The goal should be to use the information resulting from comparing to help the student build up an idea of what most likely happened—as a historian might do. I don't know many historians whose eyes light up when asked just to compare two events.

Activity 2.7 helps you look at a handful of popular thinking skills and reflect on how they can be used to build up ideas.

ACTIVITY 2.7
Using Skills to Build Ideas

Start by covering up all rows except the ANALYZE row in Figure 2.10. Then read the description of the thinking skill in the first column. Ask, "Why is this an important skill for life, work, or relationships?" Often, the answer will relate to idea-building (e.g., coming up with solutions to problems and making decisions in arguments). Then look at the classroom examples in the third column and put one or more of your own examples of how the skill can be used in your setting in the fourth column. Then proceed to the next row.

Keep in mind that many skills tend to be "carried over" from previous units of instruction. This is a good thing. It helps students to reinforce, revisit, and reconstruct while it also helps them gain needed practice in the skills they used in the previous unit(s).

Figure 2.10 Chart for Using Thinking Skills to Build Up Ideas

Thinking Skill and How it is Used for Idea-Building	Why it's Important in Life	Classroom Examples	Examples of How the Skill is Used to Build Ideas in Your Setting
ANALYZE means breaking down a complex story, process, or concept to understand it better and use the parts or pieces in some way—such as building blocks to build up an idea, conclusion, or solution.		Students analyze an article for loaded language, to build up an idea of how words influence emotions. Students analyze a financial report for a business to predict future earnings.	
SYNTHESIZE, SUMMARIZE, and DISCERN RELEVANCE means looking at a large or complex text, issue, or experience and identifying and prioritizing the parts that are most relevant for inclusion in the building of an idea or argument. The most important will be the largest support and clarifying blocks.		Students summarize the documentary to come up with an idea about how to address drought problems in a region.	

(Continued)

Figure 2.10 Chart for Using Thinking Skills to Build Up Ideas (Continued)

Thinking Skill and How it is Used for Idea-Building	Why it's Important in Life	Classroom Examples	Examples of How the Skill is Used to Build Ideas in Your Setting
SEE and COMPARE PATTERNS means seeing similarities and differences between two complex things in order to make a decision or come to a conclusion.		Students look for patterns in math problems to come up with a conclusion on how fraction multiplication works. Students compare two different geographic areas to decide where an animal needs to be relocated.	
SEE OTHER PERSPECTIVES and EMPATHIZE means to understand how others view an issue or event and use varying perspectives as support and clarifying building blocks in single idea-building or argumentation.		Students read journal entries from a historical person to see how she viewed an event.	
INTERPRET and MAKE INFERENCES means to make educated guesses and hypotheses about existing information, which can become ideas or building blocks for ideas.		Students consider what characters said in a story to infer their motives and interpret the author's message.	
EVALUATE means to assign value to an information source or to the information itself, such as giving weight to credibility, reasons, evidence, or examples that support claims in an argument.		Students evaluate the credibility of a web-based article and the information to support the claim that we should bring back extinct species.	

Figure 2.10 Chart for Using Thinking Skills to Build Up Ideas (Continued)

Thinking Skill and How it is Used for Idea-Building	Why it's Important in Life	Classroom Examples	Examples of How the Skill is Used to Build Ideas in Your Setting
SOLVE PROBLEMS means to analyze a problem or challenge, identify its causes, brainstorm possible solutions, and prioritize and build up the most feasible idea for solving it.		Students look at a complex math problem and plan out solution steps for solving and explaining it.	
APPLY means to modify a current idea to make it useful in a similar but slightly different situation.		Students apply solution methods from previous math problems to solve a more complex problem.	
USE CREATIVITY means to think about novel and effective ways to address challenges and communicate important ideas (e.g., art, language, music, movement, drama, coding, cooking, writing, etc.).		Students come up with an illustrated poem that represents key changes in a character from a novel.	

Language and Communication Skills

Language is the lifeblood of learning and growth. We use language to think, express, understand, and connect. Students have the right to learn as much language and as many different ways as possible to use language in learning and life.

Language was invented to cultivate relationships, get things done, build up ideas, and communicate them to others. We need to provide students with opportunities to do these things in school, often and with a wide range of texts and peers. When students are given a chance to interact with other students, they get to "try out" out their language to see if it is clear to others. If not, they clarify it. They also get to hear lots of language from various peers, absorbing how others use words and sentences and nonverbal cues to communicate.

All of the rich language use described in the previous paragraph is rare when students are preparing for multiple-choice tests. They don't need to talk to others, and if they do, it often consists of short exchanges focused on right answers or things like, "You chose answer C? So did I" exchanges. Students should not be subjected to language that is taught just for testing purposes (e.g., "You need to learn this academic vocabulary because it will be on the state tests," or "When you see this term in a question, it means you should choose …"). This is miseducation.

It helps to clarify what we mean by language. Unfortunately, in the United States there are standards and other societal expectations that have created limited pictures of the language that students are supposed to develop. While this paragraph is not the place to bring up the variety of intense debates on this topic, I will say that our responsibility is to help students continue to develop the language and skills that best prepare them to authentically communicate in a variety of academic, relational, and professional situations that they will encounter in the future. Some situations will require the use of more formal English, while other situations will require Spanish, African American Vernacular English (AAVE,) Arabic, sign language, drama, translanguaging, images and graphs (Baker, 2003), or a mix of any of these. Language for life is all about communicating as clearly and strongly as possible—using whatever works best.

ACTIVITY 2.8

Language and Communication Skills That Build Up Ideas

Just as language (e.g., vocabulary, syntax, and organization) is the lifeblood of learning and growth, communication skills are the muscles that do the heavy lifting of communicating messages. Like thinking skills, communication skills need to be thought of as skills for building up and communicating ideas to self and others.

This activity helps you think about how each skill can be used to build up and communicate ideas. Look at the samples in the second column and come up with at least one example of how students can or should use the skill in your setting to build up and communicate ideas. Feel free to add your own rows.

In Figure 2.11, I intentionally left out the commonly listed language dimensions of vocabulary, grammar, and organization because they actually develop better as students use communication skills. This makes the three dimensions of language harder to see, but they develop much better when we don't overdevote lesson time to working on each one and then testing students ad nauseam on them.

Use your knowledge of your students' language and communication skills, which will develop during the year, to identify the aspects that need to be modeled and practiced. One teacher, for example, noticed that her fifth-grade students' listening and note-taking needed extra work, especially listening for major transitions and discourse markers. She added extra modeling and practice into the next two units. Another teacher noticed strengths in his fourth-grade students' storytelling, so he had them craft and tell short stories to a class of first graders. Several students even created illustrated children's books.

Figure 2.11 Chart for Using Communication Skills to Build Up Ideas

Communication Skills	Examples of Using the Skill for Idea-Building	Your Examples
Reading	Students read articles to find evidence for and against bringing back extinct animals.	
Writing	Students write an explanation for why their museum artifact was valuable in learning about ancient Egyptian culture.	
Listening	Students listen to excerpts of famous speeches about democracy to build up ideas for their own podcast on how to improve it.	

(Continued)

Figure 2.11 Chart for Using Communication Skills to Build Up Ideas (Continued)

Communication Skills	Examples of Using the Skill for Idea-Building	Your Examples
Speaking	Students build up an idea about what equations are and why we use them to give a presentation to younger students.	
Conversing	Students record a paired conversation in which both share from different articles to build up the idea, "Energy is neither created nor destroyed."	
Interpreting (art, drama, music, etc.)	Students analyze various works of art from Harlem and Chicano Renaissances to generate and build ideas for their own renaissance.	
Representing (art, drama, music, etc.)	Students create paintings and compose songs that represent themes of respecting and learning from all cultures.	
Storytelling	Students read and listen to stories, pick a problem in the world, and work together to compose an oral story that addresses the problem.	
Organizing/prioritizing	Students work together to revise the organization of their presentation posters on artificial intelligence, come up with a catchy intro, and put the subtopics in a logical order.	
Using metaphors	Students write metaphor-filled poems from the perspectives of characters in *Esperanza Rising*, present them to small groups, and explain why they chose the metaphors.	

Ideas for Personal Growth

After you have a rough idea of the unit's big idea(s), consider which areas of personal growth you would like students to develop as they build up the unit's big idea and work toward their product or performance. True, growth areas should be and are fostered by people and experiences outside of school, but for many students, school is a powerful place for cultivating these—without sacrificing academic learning. Actually, in many cases, working on personal growth (e.g., social-emotional learning [SEL]) improves academic learning. Schools can offer unique and rich experiences that can become fertile soil for students to develop their sense of self, relationships, emotional maturity, and nonacademic traits that are vital in life (Weissberg & Gullota, 2015).

And yet, agreeing on the areas of growth that schools should emphasize or even lean toward isn't easy. In too many settings, schools don't do much about personal and social growth beyond a few inspirational posters in hallways. Some districts and schools do have various "profile" lists for grade levels or graduates. These profiles and lists can be useful in creating your own prioritized short list of focal areas that students can work on while they learn other things.

This section only covers a handful of key areas in which students should grow. I chose the areas that (a) tend to need extra emphasis, according to teachers, and (b) develop well alongside instruction that builds and communicates big ideas (see Chapter 4). I think that you will agree that the areas in Figure 2.12 are too important just to post on a classroom wall or cover in an add-on curriculum program. We need to work on them in tandem with and in service of other learning activities all year (see Chapters 4 and 5). If we don't value them and intentionally foster them, they are often easily set aside in pursuit of other (e.g., academic) goals.

Notice in Activity 2.9 that in the third column of Figure 2.12 it says Growth-Focused Idea Statements to Build Up. This means that students don't just see the statement (i.e., on a poster in the hall) and memorize it or say, "That's nice. What's for lunch?" Rather, they work to build up the ideas during the school year.

ACTIVITY 2.9
Ideas, Activities, and Practices for Fostering Growth

Read each category description in Figure 2.12 along with the examples of idea statements, which some teachers like to call mantras, in Column 3. Then read through the activities and practices that foster it in Column 4 and feel free to add any. Take notes on what you have noticed that your students need and don't need. Put examples of indicators and evidence that you would like to see in the last column. Then circle any activities that you already use and would like to use to further develop the dimensions of growth in your students. Add activities and practices that you use in your setting to foster these. Also, if you see the need, add a new category, description, and activities or practices that foster it.

Notice that the growth ideas in Column 3 are very hard to measure. So should we drop them? Does it matter if we don't have crisp numbers or spreadsheets for these? No. Because we are committed to the *complete* growth of all students, we must work on these areas and ideas and look for evidence of their growth *over time*. We can notice various aspects of their growth (what students say and how they act), and we can do all that we can to ensure that they are in the best environment for growth as possible. We can talk to students and ask them about the various areas what they are working on, how they want to grow, and so on.

For example, a fourth-grade teacher is having her students build up the science unit's idea, "Energy can be converted from one form to another." She encourages them to use their own examples and creativity to build up the idea and to create their poster presentations. The posters are meant to communicate the idea to family members. She has students engage in paired activities to build their oral language and social skills. She pushes them to persevere, learn from mistakes, and keep working hard on their products and on their presentations of them. All along she provides positive feedback related to the strength and clarity of their work and keeps an eye on the growth ideas they are building.

I realize that building up ideas for growth is another layer or dimension added to the already mountainous plate that is instruction. But growth can't be cultivated well enough in a special six-week SEL program or in homeroom-advisory time. It needs to happen in all lessons in all content areas.

Figure 2.12 Growth-Area Categories, Ideas, Evidence, and Ways to Foster Them in School

Growth Category	Description	Sample Growth-Focused Idea Statements to Build Up	Activities and Practices That Can Foster it	Indicators and Evidence
Positive self-perception	Students view themselves as learners and idea-builders; they have agency, feel that they can make a difference, that they have control over how they grow and think, can communicate, and have self-efficacy, confidence, and academic identity.	• I am a scholar. • I am a uniquely multilingual and multicultural human. • I can learn anything. • I can choose who I become. • I can make a difference.	Reflective journals Paired interviews Personal narratives Surveys Positive feedback	
Perseverance	Perseverance is the drive to keep working hard when things get difficult, including being resilient, learning from mistakes, responding to constructive feedback, and having self-discipline and patience.	• Rome wasn't built in a day. • Perseverance prevails over talent. • Success comes from trying again and again and again. • Little failures are stepping stones to success. • I can learn anything.	Allowing for revisions Positive peer feedback Stories of famous people who persevered	
Social skills	Those with social skills have the skills to connect with and relate to others, including empathy, perspective-taking, cultural competence, collaboration,	• It helps to walk in another person's shoes. • Forgiveness helps to heal the world. • We are stronger together.	Lots of paired interactions Learning social skills Highlighting positive comments and behaviors	

(Continued)

Figure 2.12 Growth-Area Categories, Ideas, Evidence, and Ways to Foster Them in School (Continued)

Growth Category	Description	Sample Growth-Focused Idea Statements to Build Up	Activities and Practices That Can Foster it	Indicators and Evidence
Social skills, cont.	respect, friendliness, kindness, fairness, and loyalty.	• Friends are loyal until the end. • People have different values.		
Character	Those who have character have traits that include being honest, generous, patient, optimistic, unselfish, open-minded, trustworthy, and fun; it assumes good intentions.	• Honesty is the best policy. • Patience is a virtue. • We must assume good intentions in others. • Sharing is caring. • Actions speak louder than words.	Talking about story characters Writing stories about characters with desirable traits Working on projects that promote good character traits in school	
Multicultural and multilingual identities	Students see themselves as uniquely and wonderfully multilingual and multicultural, with assets that grow and help them navigate multiple worlds and contexts.	• Speaking multiple languages improves the brain. • Having multiple cultures multiplies life's meanings. • Language influences culture and vice versa.	Prompting for ways in which different languages communicate something Using examples from cultural backgrounds as building blocks in idea-based conversations and projects Using multicultural and multilingual texts Tapping into home-based funds of knowledge	

ACTIVITY 2.10
Fortify Your Instruction With Growth Areas

With the fourth-grade science example that you just read in mind (also see Appendix C), use this activity to help you fortify one of your upcoming lessons or units with one or more areas of growth. In the second row of Figure 2.13, for each of the columns, put a growth-focused idea after the colon for that category. Then put activities and assessments underneath and consider how they might be used to strengthen the growth-focused ideas in the other columns.

Figure 2.13 Growth-Area Chart

Content-Based Idea to Be Built:					
	Positive Self-Perception Idea	Perseverance Idea	Social Skills Idea	Character Idea	Multilingual-Multicultural Idea
Activities to cultivate it					
Assessments to see progress					

Foundations of Pedagogical Justice

I have visited schools that are not pressured to raise state test scores. Teachers are free to choose texts and tasks and topics that engage students. Discussions about ethics, morality, historical mysteries, and controversial social issues are not cut short because of the pressure to cover a wide range of things for upcoming tests. When all classrooms have this freedom, engagement and learning increase.

What multilingual students learn and how they grow are foundational in achieving pedagogical justice. If we inundate students with a vast array of disconnected things to learn that have little connection to their lives, they lose interest. They might do some activities for points or to please the teacher, but not enough of the learning lasts and they don't feel much agency. In most curriculums, the emphasis is on reading and writing, both of which are sets of skills. If the content is disjointed or boring—and also linguistically challenging—multilingual students can become frustrated. And with very broad and shallow coverage, there is little reinforcement, recycling, and clarification. When any of these occur, it is unjust. And it is particularly unjust when (a) we know that it is happening and (b) we know that we can do something to fix it, starting with the suggestions in this and the next four chapters.

ACTIVITY 2.11
Fostering Pedagogical Justice

In Figure 2.14, reflect on how the learning and growth areas in this chapter (second column) can contribute to achieving one or more of the dimensions of pedagogical justice along the top (second row). For example, in the *Ideas* row, you might put, "When multilingual students build and share unique ideas, their sense of agency increases." Or in the *Communication skills* row, you might put, "Conversations develop content ideas and relationships at the same time."

Figure 2.14 Chart for Using What Students Learn and How They Grow to Influence Dimensions of Pedagogical Justice

	Agency and Voice	Engaging Challenges	Meaningful Interactions	Idea-Building	Assessment for Learning	Critical and Creative Thinking
Ideas (clear and strong concepts and claims)						
Content knowledge (that builds up ideas)						
Thinking skills (for and while building ideas)						
Communication skills (for building and communicating ideas)						
Language (for building and communicating ideas)						
Areas of personal growth						

A Vision for the Future

What students learn and how they grow can enhance or harm their education, their futures, and the future of the world. When we limit their learning and growth to the scope of what fits into what we can count, we limit who students become as individuals and as members of society. Do we want a society full of people who are slightly better each year at choosing answers but can't solve complex problems or relate well to one another? Do we want to send students off to higher education and out into the world with ill-formed ideas and inadequate preparation because our schools focused on visible points and percentages?

We must continue to envision and define the society that we want to have in the future and then work toward it. It won't be a utopia, but it will be more just and unbiased than what we have now. Pedagogical injustices (Chapter 1) are thriving within the current accumulation-focused approach to teaching and assessing. These injustices are limiting learning, growth, and opportunities for millions of students. Our students and society are suffering as a result. It's high time we overhaul what students learn and put more thought into how they grow.

CHAPTER IDEA

Here is a big idea that you can build up from this chapter. If another idea was sparked for you, feel free to build it up instead of this one. Remember to add personal examples, definitions, questions, and insights as building blocks along with new blocks gathered from this chapter. Some sample blocks are provided, which you can keep or not.

IDEA STATEMENT: Building up ideas (concepts and claims) is a powerful way to learn content, develop language, and foster engagement.		
		Building up ideas requires skills of supporting and clarifying.
Language is a tool for communicating, not for getting points on language tests.	Which ideas should students build up in each discipline?	
	Students should use building blocks from school and from their personal experiences.	

References

Ausubel, D. (2000). *The acquisition and retention of knowledge: A cognitive view.* Kluwer.

Baker. C. (2003). Biliteracy and transliteracy in Wales: Language planning and the Welsh National Curriculum. In N. Hornberger (Ed.), *Continua of biliteracy: An ecological framework of educational policy, research, and practice in multilingual settings* (pp. 71–90). Multilingual Matters. https://doi.org/10.21832/9781853596568-007

Mitchell, I., Keast, S., Panizzon, D., & Mitchell, J. (2017). Using "big ideas" to enhance teaching and student learning. *Teachers and Teaching: Theory and Practice*, 23(5), 596–610. https://doi.org/10.1080/13540602.2016.1218328

Meier, D. (2002). *The power of their ideas: Lessons for America from a small school in Harlem.* Beacon Press.

National Academies of Sciences, Engineering, and Medicine. (2018). *How people learn II: Learners, contexts, and cultures.* The National Academies Press. https://doi.org/10.17226/24783

National Research Council. (2000). *How people learn: Brain, mind, experience, and school—Expanded edition.* National Academies Press.

Nichols, M. (2019). *Building bigger ideas: A process for teaching purposeful talk.* Heinemann.

Nokes, T. J., Schunn, C. D., & Chi, M. T.(2010). Problem solving and human expertise. In *International encyclopedia of education* (Vol. 5, pp. 265–272). Elsevier.

Wiggins, G. (2010). What is a "big idea"? *Authentic Education.* https://authenticeducation.org/whatisabigidea/

Weissberg, R. P., & Gullotta, T. P. (Eds.). (2015). *Handbook of social and emotional learning: Research and practice.* Guilford Press.

Zwiers, J. (2019a). *Next steps with academic conversations: New ideas for improving learning with classroom talk.* Stenhouse.

Zwiers, J. (2019b). *The communication effect: How to enhance learning by building ideas and bridging information gaps.* Corwin.

Assessment 3

The main purpose of assessment should be learning.

Take a moment to reflect on the word "assessment." What emotions emerge? What word associations come to mind? If you want to take this activity to the next level, ask your students to engage in the same reflection. In all likelihood, the emotion that floats to the top will be something not far off from *dread*. If you ask them to elaborate, they will likely tell you that assessments are time-consuming, stressful, boring, or (D), "all of the above." If you ask your educator colleagues to elaborate, a common lament is that many of the "most important" assessments don't even provide information that is useful enough to be worth the time or the dread.

And yet, assessment doesn't have to be dreadful, nor does it have to be ineffective at showing students' learning. In fact, most educators agree that assessment is a vital dimension of teaching and learning (Wiggins, 2019). Yet somehow, its meaning and "spirit" have been corrupted in recent decades. Reductionist, accumulation-based views of learning, bolstered by our obsession with holding educators and kids accountable to a few data points (e.g., standardized test scores) have given tremendous power to what some call the "testing industrial complex" (Del Carmen Unda & Lizárraga-Dueñas, 2021).

For many multilingual students, yearly (and even monthly) multiple-choice-based assessments tell them over and over that they are "behind" in learning or that they don't have what it takes to be students (Chavez, 2018). Multilingual students work extra hard and they learn a lot, but the scores on the bubble-in tests don't always show it. They are often simply labeled, "Below Grade Level." Because the negatives caused by such assessment heavily outweigh the value of the information that the tests provide (see Chapter 1), we must overhaul how we assess the learning and growth that we described in Chapter 2.

Useful, engaging, meaningful, empowering, and motivating assessments are possible. But this is just one chapter. You will get some useful suggestions to get assessment overhaul started, but most of your actual assessments and assessment practices will come as you apply the suggestions to your setting and adjust them over time. Your students and their ideas are all unique (see Chapter 2), and they need customized assessments.

Let's start with this quote from Darling-Hammond et al. (1995):

> *The process of evaluating and revising and re-evaluating makes the assessment process fundamentally a learning process, one that promotes both self-evaluation capabilities and habits of work—the internalization of standards—for the students as well as staff. (p. 54)*

I underlined four key terms in the statement: *revising, learning process, self-evaluation,* and *internalization*. These four terms are vital in assessment, yet they are mostly missing in many assessments, especially the multiple-choice ones. In this chapter, we will look at ways to assess and design assessments with these features. Look for them and consider their importance as we seek to envision and design assessment that effectively motivates and shows student learning.

First, we must stop diluting our content and its assessment to satisfy the needs of what is visible and countable on computer-scored tests. We have done this limiting and counting for decades—and it has failed millions of students, many of whom are multilingual and multicultural. In the obsession to quantify students' learning, hold everyone "accountable," and achieve test-score parity, we have severely hampered learning and motivation to learn for many multilingual students. We have, in a sense, been gluing plastic apples to the tree in an orchard where all the farmer does is drive around and count how many apples are on each tree. If we overhaul our assessments, we can show others and ourselves that it is possible to assess rich learning without multiple-choice tests.

Second, we must remember our roles in the process. Consider this insight from Robert Tierney (1998):

> *I prefer to think of a teacher as a coach rather than a judge—a supporter and counselor versus a judge and award- or grade-giver. I would like to see teachers view their role as providing guidance, handholding, and comments rather than As, Bs, and Cs or some score. In my view of a more ideal world, I see teachers, students, and caregivers operating in a kind of public sphere where they are part of the team negotiating for a better self. (p. 387)*

We need to keep thinking about a more ideal world of education and how we educators, through supportive assessment, can help our multilingual students work toward better and better selves in their time with us.

Third, we must be ever mindful of the biases inherent in what we value as we are assessing. We tend to see through lenses shaped by our own cultural and linguistic practices. For example, monolingual English-speaking teachers might judge the quality of a multilingual student's final presentation differently than multilingual teachers. So for whatever we are assessing (ideas, skills, personal growth, etc.), we need to continue to reflect on how our own views skew our responses. We should collaborate with as many others (teachers, parents, and students) to "land" ever closer on the most effective indicators of quality possible for a given assessment for a group of students. So as you read through the sections that follow, expand your views of assessment even more to include a range of creative and linguistically diverse assessments that provide powerful windows into the minds and hearts of multilingual, multicultural, and neurodiverse students.

The rest of this chapter pushes the boundaries of what has traditionally been considered assessment in school. Traditional assessment has mostly been a collection of quizzes, classroom-based tests, rubric-based writing samples, and state tests used to see if students have accumulated knowledge and skills. These are assessments in which students tend to "pay for" points with the right answers and written responses (see Chapter 1)—that is, if they think the effort expended is worth the points in the end.

This chapter argues for creating and using a broader suite of more authentic and more engaging forms of assessment. The spectrum ranges from the smaller "on the fly, split-second" formative assessment practices to the larger and more summative products and performances that students work toward during a unit or beyond.

But given that we are assessing learning, let's first clarify two key terms related to assessment: "achievement" and "learning."

Achievement and Learning

Achievement is a highly misleading term. When people say that we need to raise student achievement, they usually mean raising test scores. Related terms include "low-performing," "high-performing," "successful," and "unsuccessful," which are also often tightly knitted to test scores.

Achievement is supposed to mean reaching and exceeding goals and expectations. Goals and expectations can be academic, social, emotional, artistic, physical, civic, environmental, and more (see Chapter 2). Achievement means *way* more than getting answers right on math and English language arts multiple-choice tests. It means doing meaningful things that are of value to the student and/or others. If we mean these things, then we can use the word "achievement." If we don't mean these things, then we should just use the term "test scores."

There are millions of smart and successful students and highly effective schools with lower-than-average test scores. To say that these students are not achieving is harmful and flat-out wrong. Millions of students and former students with low state test scores are learning, growing, thriving, building up ideas, achieving, and improving the world. Many very smart students are not doing well out in the world—not because they scored low on tests, but rather because schools miseducated them, devoting too much energy to shallow and boring test-score-raising lessons.

Consider the great swimmer who moves to another country and is told, "We only learn to be divers here. Start climbing up the ladder." Or the painter who moves to a new town and is told, "We only do music here. Now learn all these music standards. We will test you for an entire week on them in six months. You can choose one of three instruments: French horn, trumpet, or flute." You can think of your own analogy, but the point is how silly it is to squelch the diverse languages, interests, talents, identities, and dreams of our students.

If we must use the term "achievement," let's redefine it as successfully narrowing the gaps between where students are and where they can be—on things that matter—over a given period of time (see Chapter 2). And when we assess the things that matter, let's *not* compare students. Please! Much more harm than good comes from it.

The term "learning" has been watered down for decades. *Learning* in the accumulation approach is mainly defined by, not surprisingly, *accumulating* things like facts and skills, which usually are turned into scores on tests and writing assessments. Higher scores are interpreted as achievement, which some people think equals more learning.

The problem with memorizing facts and skills for choosing answers on tests is that students tend to forget many of them because (a) they weren't ever interested in them, (b) they didn't have any emotional connection to them, or (c) they didn't build up any ideas of value with them. Do you remember the Smoot-Hawley Tariff Act? Can you still factor a trinomial in math? What is *anaphora* in ELA? These were standards that I learned in school—and then forgot. Wait, did I really learn them if I forgot them? I got points for them, so I must have learned them for a little while . . . but . . . well, I think you get the "point."

You have likely seen your own students answer a question incorrectly that they correctly answered the day before. They got the points yesterday, which shows learning. But today it's gone. Should you take the points away? And if they answer it correctly tomorrow, do you give the points back? In accumulation-based teaching, students learn a lot of things that they will forget, mostly because they have not *used* and *will not use* the information, facts, and skills with any frequency in meaningful ways.

ACTIVITY 3.1
Defining Learning

What is the learning that we are seeking to assess? This activity helps you build up what you want learning to mean in your context. The last row in Figure 3.1 is open for you to add another descriptor if you want. Read the descriptors on the left and add examples of these in the right-hand column. Examples can come from student learning in your setting and from your own learning.

Figure 3.1 Chart for Defining Learning

Learning Means...	Examples of This in Your Setting
... *that new stuff sticks.* Learning might include facts, skills, concepts, arguments, language, stories, themes, ideas, procedures, explanations, and so on. If they don't stick, a person hasn't learned them. Does this mean we test students twice a week on the same things over and over? No. Instead, we have students build up disciplinary ideas over time (see Chapter 4). As they build, they reuse and reinforce the most important information and skills. Some things from October might show up (gasp!) in student presentations in the spring. The brain tends to hold on to information that has been used, used often, used in collaboration with others, and used to build up concepts and claims.	
... *being able to use and adapt it in novel contexts.* This is the opposite of memorization. If I tell you that the meaning of *brummagem* is the same as the meaning of *meretricious* and gave you a matching quiz with these two items, you would match them and get the	

Figure 3.1 Chart for Defining Learning (Continued)

Learning Means...	Examples of This in Your Setting
points—but without ever being able to use the words (assuming you didn't already know them or look them up). Yet if you learn what they mean and use them to communicate in some way, and ideally use them multiple times, you will learn them.	
... *it is useful in life*. It has a purpose other than being tested on it. Think about all the different types of jobs for which people continue to learn every day. Teachers learn about students and new ways to teach. Doctors learn about new ways to diagnose and treat illnesses. Computer programmers learn new ways of coding to design applications. We need to strive to make learning in school more useful in students' lives and in the world.	
(Other?)	

What Should We Assess?

When I ask this question to teachers and administrators, I often hear the short answer, "The standards." Sounds logical, right? We just tell students to learn the standards and then take a test that we trust in order to assess all of the most important standards for the year. We don't look at the test (it's against the rules), but we trust that the knowledgeable item writers have done their job to create valid items for every single student in the state and that the numbers that show up months later will show the world exactly how well our students learned the standards this year and how good our school is.

Unfortunately, as you well know, *effective* assessment of in-depth human learning is a lot more complex ... and more engaging ... and more valid. This type of assessment starts with a picture of the areas of learning and growth on which we should be spending our assessment energies. You can refer to Chapter 2 for more elaborated descriptions of these areas if needed.

The Quality of Big Ideas

We should effectively assess the clarity and strength of student ideas and decisions (Mitchell, 2016). This means assessing how well students use evidence, examples, steps, and/or details to support an idea. *Quality* means the extent to which an idea (concept or claim) is strongly supported by evidence, examples, and reasoning, as well as how it is clearly communicated to others.

First, work on assessing one idea—let's say a concept such as "The water cycle keeps rivers running," or "Conflicts in history bring about change—and vice versa," or "Stories give us insights into how others think and feel," or "Multiplying fractions means taking a part of a part." Decide how you want to assess the different aspects of quality. Here are some features you can borrow and tweak, depending on the ideas you are assessing.

The student(s)...

- Uses enough different examples and evidence to make the idea strong and clear
- Uses solid and strong examples and evidence from reputable sources
- Uses clear explanations and key details to communicate with others
- Enhances communication of the idea with nonverbal, kinesthetic, and visual aids
- Uses the most effective language(s) (e.g., speaking, prosody, writing, movement, visuals, sounds, vocabulary, syntax, and message organization) to communicate the idea to a given audience

As an example, two fourth graders are communicating the idea "Multiplying fractions means taking a part of a part" by creating a cooking video. Just one example of multiplying in a recipe is not enough, and the examples need to be clear and correct for the video. They don't just write answers; they divide up ingredients to show the "part of a part" concept. They ask viewers to act out multiplying with their hands and add a little chant, "When you multiply fractions, you need to start, by knowing that you get, a part of a part." They do a practice run for the teacher and two different student groups for feedback on clarity and strength before recording the video.

We must also assess the quality of argumentation, which means considering how well students do these things:

- Build up *both* sides as strongly and clearly as possible, without bias
- Critique and evaluate the value of each evidence block
- Decide which side is stronger or "weighs" more
- Clearly explain why the chosen side weighs more
- Clearly explain any implications or next steps, if applicable

While we can design rubrics with levels and points in the interest of assessing both strength and clarity, we must be careful not to sully student motivations with point-seeking. Rather, it is more important for students to see models and get helpful feedback and then reflect on what they can improve in building up the idea and better communicating it (Newmann et al., 2007).

As you set up each idea-building process, you can tell students the types of artifacts and even the idea-building blocks they will need to use. One example is the visual organizer used for the dancing bees idea in Chapter 2 (Figure 2.1). In the blocks are the information and skills that you will eventually assess. Or let's say you are teaching the idea "Gravity increases as the distance between two objects decreases." You want students to build up this idea and then show their understanding of it in the product-performance at the end of the unit. You might tell students, "By Friday, I would like to see at least five blocks from articles, two from watching videos, two from reading, and one from your own life or research. I want to see these on the idea-building visual that you create, along with questions that you have. Prepare to share them to help your partner and be ready to clarify if your partner asks you questions."

Skills

It is very tempting to assess skills out of context. Standards are full of skills, which fit nicely into single lessons. I sometimes ask teachers what they taught yesterday and often hear skills such as making inferences, summarizing, synthesizing, comparing and contrasting, cause and effect, and the like. I ask *why* and often hear, "It's in the curriculum," or "It's a standard." Less often, I hear something like, "Because it's a key skill for helping them build up the idea of…," which is music to my ears.

So when we choose skills to assess, we shouldn't go through the lists of standards and see which skills come up the most. Instead, we should choose the most useful skills for communicating and building up ideas that we want students to build up in the unit or longer. In this book, *in context* means doing something in the process of building up and communicating ideas. If we think that making inferences is important for idea-building, then we figure out how to assess it *in the context* of building up and communicating ideas. We make sure students know what the skill is, we model it in various idea-building ways (e.g., using it to build an idea from movie clips or songs), and we tell them that it is an important skill for life (e.g., relationships). We tell them that we and they will assess its development over time, a bit like we would assess the use of the carpentry skill of an apprentice at a construction site.

Other important idea-building skills include summarizing texts, empathizing, comparing, inferring causes and effects, interpreting, analyzing, problem-solving, and evaluating. Before reading on, take a moment to think about how one or more of these skills is used to build up an idea in a discipline that you teach.

Language

Do not leave language assessment solely up to yearly language tests, which often only test certain aspects of English. These tests, like most standardized tests, tend to be generic, unengaging, decontextualized, and inauthentic. Multilingual students can and must use their languages in more nuanced and authentic ways—and for greater purposes—than getting lots of answers correct on language tests. I sometimes hear, "Oh, this will help them on the ___ test." I respond with, "Maybe, but it will for sure help them build up the key disciplinary idea, help others build ideas, communicate with others, foster their agency and identity, and build relationships."

Language is a grand set of tools plus the ability to use them. It was invented to be used, not to be dissected and tested. So we should assess how well students *use it* to build up ideas, make decisions and argue, collaborate, foster relationships, and get things done in life. We can assess word knowledge, syntax, and organization—not because linguists said that these are important aspects of language to test—but *because these things can help or hinder communication*. I tell students, "We assess language to let you and us know what to keep doing with language as well as what to work on to improve your learning and your communication with others. Some words are clearer than others. Some sentences are less confusing than others. Language development is a lifelong process."

We should assess language in use, and we should assess useful language. This includes the use of students' entire language repertoires, including the use of more than one language, which is sometimes called translanguaging. We should observe students as they talk to one another. We should listen to them read texts and ask them what certain key words mean. We should analyze their writings and recordings of their talking. All along we evaluate the clarity of their communication while figuring out what feedback we can provide to help them make it clearer (Darling-Hammond & Adamson, 2010).

We need to be their language coaches and advocates rather than their language testers.

In the first part of the year, you can gather lots of observational data on language use and work with it to identify the strengths and the dimensions of language to work on. These dimensions include content vocabulary, grammar, organization (of sentences), pronunciation, decoding, reading comprehension, fluency, prosody, gestures, body language, eye contact, consistent verb tenses, verb conjugation, punctuation, use of pronouns, complete sentences, cohesion (between sentences and between paragraphs), use of text features, and figurative language. That's plenty to look for—always in context and always for communication.

WHAT COUNTS AS ASSESSMENT

If we really feel the need to count things, let's count these things:

- The number of times a student pauses, midmessage, to look up to find the right way to say something
- The number of head nods while listening
- The number of minutes students talk to one another in class
- The number of high-quality building blocks (content knowledge, supports, and clarifications) students have in their idea-building visuals
- The number of times students ask partners to clarify and support questions
- The number of sentences that students use to communicate higher-order thoughts, complex ideas, and arguments
- The number of times a student says more than one sentence without being prompted
- The number of times we hear languages beyond English used in classroom communication
- The number of times a student smiles during class

Assessment for Learning: Tools and Methods

Assessment for learning and growth means using tools and practices to gather useful information that (a) we (teachers) use to provide feedback and adjust instruction and (b) students use in response to teacher, peer, and self-feedback (Gottlieb & Honigsfeld, 2019). Assessment for learning and growth means looking through *valid* and varied windows at what students are understanding and doing with their understandings. It means looking at a range of artifacts and evidence of learning. And it means getting to know students and their ideas as well as we can. All of this assessment, which ranges from summative to formative, is done to improve learning and growth.

While many of the following suggestions are effective for all students, they are especially effective for multilingual students. They are strategies for allowing students to leverage their languages and unique funds of knowledge to show their learning and growth. But this means that we must encourage their creative uses of language, knowledge, and experiences for and during the assessment. We must encourage them to push themselves to communicate as clearly as they can, including the use of either or both languages, visuals, movement, and stories.

This chapter can help you choose and design the assessments and assessment practices that are most likely to motivate students to engage in the idea-building, interactions, and actions that lead to lasting learning of the high-priority areas of learning and growth outlined in Chapter 2. Along the way, reflect on how these types of assessments and their features can foster pedagogical justice for multilingual students.

Products-Performances

Let's not start by designing assessments. Rather, let's come up with engaging products and/or performances that inspire students to learn and communicate their learnings. In this way, students will see the task as a way to push them to construct an idea and then communicate it to others in some manner that's not just for getting points. Picture a seventh grader presenting a solution to ocean pollution to a small group of other students. Or a third grader creating a podcast about how we all can be more caring to members of the community. Then we think about how to use the task for assessment.

Products-performances are powerful ways to both motivate and show learning. I use a hyphen because there might be one or the other or a combination of a performance that includes a product. For example, students will often create a product and then present it in some way. It should be motivating and purposeful.

At first, students will think that the product-performance is just an assessment for a grade. Remind yourself and your students that the main purpose of the product-performance is *not* assessment—it is to learn and to communicate one's idea to others. Assessment is secondary. You will see a powerful difference when students understand this—though it may take a while. As much as possible, provide choice and room for creativity. How often are we allowed to say to students, "Surprise me"? And how often do students hear this invitation and feel the creative and engagement juices start to flow in their minds?

Think about what products-performances might clearly and strongly communicate the big idea to others, allow students to be creative, and foster their sense of agency. The product-performance should be in the learning limelight—it should be the engaging thing that students are working and learning toward. The product-performance should inspire students to build up a unique idea and then communicate it as clearly and strongly as possible. Even after any presentation of the product-performance, emphasize to students that this is their idea right now and that they will continue to build it this year and beyond.

For products-performances, you will want to show models and co-analyze them with students to identify various features that make them effective. You can put these features into teacher and student "help and evaluation" tools. These are primarily meant to help students create stronger and clearer products-performances and secondarily for evaluation purposes.

Products-performances can be real-world-based, and they can stem from what is called problem-based or project-based learning (PBL). PBL has been around for while in various forms, yielding a range of outcomes. They usually include solving robust problems and addressing challenges in the community, school, and beyond. A project tends to include research, discussion, the creation of a product, and an explanation of its usefulness. The best learning comes from projects in which each of its pieces is enhanced with a focus on idea-building and communication. Every unit, including those with projects, should have at least one engaging product and performance that motivates students to learn (i.e., gather building blocks for ideas), organize, and communicate what they learn.

Students can also work on self-growth projects in which they set personal goals for growing personally throughout the year (Gay, 2010). They can build up growth-based ideas and even create products or performances that communicate their growth to others. For example, a student can work on being more empathetic during the year and share a final poster on empathy with parents (as a parent, I would rather read a poster like that than a test score).

ACTIVITY 3.2
Products-Performances in Your Setting

In the following chart (Figure 3.2), read across each row, and in the third column jot some ideas for how you might use it in your setting to inspire students to engage in building up key ideas in the disciplines you are teaching. For the second column, think about how you can prepare students to come up with strong and clear products-performances. Do some further research (including chatting with colleagues) on how teachers have been using these in their schools.

Figure 3.2 Products and Performances Chart

Product-Performance	Key Features and Preparation You can Discuss and Model	How You Might Use These in Your Setting
Podcast	Prosodic strategies, pauses, organization of content, and repetition	
Video/screencast	What to show on video and how to display it; scripting for engagement and clarity	
Billboard public service announcement	Ways to capture the attention of drivers; effective phrases that match the visuals	
Plan and give a lesson on your idea for younger students	How teaching is a powerful way to learn; give students insights into lesson plan elements: hook, purpose, essential question, kinesthetic and visual strategies, and reading strategies	
Story (oral or written)	What you want them to learn by creating stories; what they want listeners-readers to learn (themes, etc.); features such as figurative language, dialogue, plot, and character changes	
Journal entry of the historical person	How they will do their research to get into the mind of the historical person; how biased we are in the present; what to put in the entries that show their empathy and learning of the content	

(Continued)

Figure 3.2 Products and Performances Chart (Continued)

Product-Performance	Key Features and Preparation You can Discuss and Model	How You Might Use These in Your Setting
Bill that will become a law	Types of problems that bills (laws) are intended to solve; the language used in them; how bills become laws	
Business plan for nonprofit group	The problems that nonprofit organizations address; different types of running costs; how to raise funds over time	
Design a science experiment	Making a hypothesis, dependent variable, independent variables, controls, data recording, and interpreting	
Murals about local history events, and so on	Types of messages that a given community needs to see as they walk by the mural, possible components, painting styles, and symbols	
Article for newspaper or magazine	What types of information do readers need and why; predicting their questions to answer them (e.g., who, what, where, why, and how)	
Design an educational video game or app	The possible areas of learning that the app or game will foster; how the game or app will work; what makes it engaging; why it is needed	

Formative Assessment

All assessments should be formative.

Formative assessment is the ongoing **observation** of evidence of learning. It includes reflecting on the **value of the evidence** and how to use it to respond with helpful **feedback and** adjust instruction (Glossary of Education Reform, 2014). **It is the** minute-by-minute assessment that we engage in during learning and during other forms of assessment mentioned in this chapter.

Formative observation plays a major role in learning and is the topic of thick teacher resources. My main suggestion here is to focus formative observation efforts on idea-building and communication. Trying to formatively assess the many standards equally for each content area for each year will be your undoing. Instead, focus on how students improve the quality of "building blocks" (examples, evidence, and clarifications); the reading, watching, and listening skills used to gather "building blocks"; the conversation and social skills used to help each other; and the writing and representation skills used to communicate the idea to others. Most key standards fall within and support these areas.

For example, sixth graders were building the idea that improved farming methods helped to form civilizations. They had to write a story, journal, or drama from the perspective of an alien (from a planet that wanted to form a civilization) who goes back in time and observes the beginnings of Earth's civilizations for several hundred years. Students built up the idea by reading texts and watching videos. They worked with partners on their projects. The teacher took notes, mental and written, on what students were doing well, individually and collectively. She gave immediate and useful feedback as quickly as possible and adjusted her instruction when she saw that enough students needed some extra help (e.g., interpreting a primary source). In one conversation, she noticed that students weren't asking each other clarifying or supporting questions, so she modeled these for them and nudged them to practice the questions in their next conversation.

A common form of formative assessment is *asking questions*. These might be questions in a discussion, on a quiz, on homework, for a writing prompt, and so on. Teachers ask a lot of questions, and we need to be careful not to overdo it. If we are not strategic with questions, we run the risk of overwhelming students and pushing them into thinking that learning is all about answering questions. Focus your questions on ideas and the skills for building and communicating them. Ask questions with answers that help students to build up ideas. This gives us a sense of what students know and can do, while it also provides useful information. Ask for building blocks such as, "What does *specialization* mean? How would it stem from irrigation? Tell a partner. What makes a civilization a civilization? What job would you choose back then? Why? What would you do with extra grain that you grew?"

In all of the assessment tools and practices in this chapter (and in all that we do in class), we should also be formatively observing language. This means looking at the many strengths and strategies that multilingual students use to communicate their ideas. This includes using different languages, dialects, gestures, facial expressions, and prosodic cues. The more students have chances to use language (receptive and productive) in authentic ways, the more we can see their linguistic strengths and needs.

WRITE-TALK-WRITE (DRAW-TALK-DRAW)

This assessment-activity helps you to see what students have learned through two lenses: writing (or drawing) and talking. It also helps you see the difference that talking makes between students' pre- and postwriting. And many teachers notice the difference that prewriting makes in the quality of the talking that follows. Here is the procedure:

1. Prompt students to write the answer to a meaty prompt or question, such as an essential or controversial question. This writing can also be a drawing or notes or filling in a visual organizer.

2. Instruct students to turn their writing over or put it inside a folder to avoid looking at it.

3. Instruct students to pair up and tell each other about what they wrote. Remind them to share building blocks to help the other person. When listening, students ask clarifying and supporting questions (students can switch partners and talk a second time). If possible, record one or more pairs while they talk.

4. Students take notes after the talk time.

5. Students write (without looking at their prewrite) a stronger and clearer postwrite answer using the new language and content they discussed in their pairs.

6. Students turn in pre- and postwrites, and you compare them, assessing for content and language use. You also analyze the video for strengths and needs related to oral interaction skills.

Learning Interviews

Years ago, I asked teachers what they thought was the best way to assess student learning. They said, "Interview them." But they also said they didn't have the time because of all the content they had to cover that week, that they were behind in the pacing guide, and that grading their work took up so much time. Interviews can get to the essence of what a student has learned about a topic and what idea(s) they have built up. Many teachers with whom I have worked did make the time and told me that it was well worth it with respect to the information they gained about what their students had learned and still needed to work on. One teacher even called them "mini-doctoral defenses."

When you ask a student to answer the unit's essential question (e.g., What is energy and how does it change forms?), the student's answer and ways of answering can tell you a lot. If she says one sentence ("Energy makes things happen") and stops, this tells you that she has a strong idea statement in her mind, but she needs to work on clarifying and supporting her thoughts without expecting to be prompted. When you ask follow-up questions (e.g., What things does energy make happen? What is energy? How does it make those things happen?), her answers can tell you more about her content understanding and how much she has built up her idea about energy.

You can also work with your students to come up with interview questions. Students can play the role of experts in the field. They can think about what they would ask potential co-workers or collaborators to make sure they have developed ideas. Ask students to help you come up with a description of what great answers would consist of (e.g., more than one sentence, multiple and strong examples from school and life, clarification of big and important terms, and responding with confidence and excitement). Students can even interview each other and make a video recording that you can later watch and assess.

Conversations

Conversations don't usually make it near the top of "how to assess" lists, but you can get a lot of information by listening to two students talk about a topic (Zwiers, 2019a). Some teachers have students practice for this type of assessment by having conversations with various partners throughout the year. In addition to improving conversations, such practice sessions are helpful on multiple levels such as developing language, content, social skills, agency, and relationships.

I recommend having students prepare for the conversation with an organizer such as a semantic map, an idea-building visual, or an argument balance scale (Figure 3.3), which you can collect afterward as part of the assessment.

Putting notes on these organizers beforehand helps students to share more in their conversations. I have students silently and separately fill in building blocks that they think their partner won't have. This helps to create information gaps (see Chapter 4) to fill. Sometimes I will give students different texts to use. You can also co-craft a "content and conversation skills checklist" that helps students self-assess to improve the effectiveness of their language, body language, eye contact, warmth, interest, content, equity of voice, agency, clarification of terms, and support of ideas.

Tests and Quizzes for Learning

Classroom-based tests and quizzes can be beneficial to students, albeit with some authenticity strings attached. Tests and quizzes *for learning* are ways that help students and teachers to see the "building blocks" that students have and need at a given point in time. I might give a quick quiz with several questions on the events preceding World War I. The quiz provides formative information while it also zooms in and informs students of what's important for building up the larger idea of the unit. Tests should not be a long string of disconnected questions (like you tend to see on long tests),

Figure 3.3   Sample Idea-Building Visuals

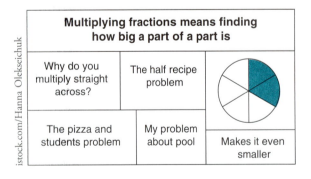
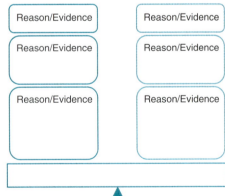

but rather a short set of cohesive prompts that let students communicate their evolving ideas.

Tests and quizzes should be thought of as "backup tools" to assess any important information or skills that weren't assessed with the tools already discussed—for example, if you don't feel that a performance or product in science (e.g., podcast) provides a clear enough look at students' knowledge of photosynthesis or of the skill of controlling variables. Short-answer questions are best, as they allow students to describe, in connected sentences, their thoughts.

A few helpful questions that can guide assessing with tests and quizzes include these: Can students learn from tests? Can they retake them? Do they get immediate feedback on specific questions? Do they get to explain their answers? Can they collaborate?

DISCUSSING LEARNING AND ASSESSMENT

We can have honest discussions about learning and assessment with students. We can say something like, "In some ways, education is still learning how to assess learning. Some think that counting up your correct choices on multiple-choice questions and giving points for using isolated skills represents your learning. But you and I know that it doesn't. You will still need to take the tests this year, and you should try to do well on them. But in class, we will not spend every day preparing for the tests. We will not focus on piling up answers but rather on building up complex, big, and wonderful ideas in your minds. We will try to make the building of ideas as fun and motivating as possible so that down your many different roads in life, you can use them if you need them."

Most assessments are limited in what they can tell us. We should improve them as much as possible and squeeze what we can out of them, but we can't water down rich teaching and learning for the sake of assessment. We must always remember that lots of learning can happen as a result of instruction that does not show up in the observations and assessments that we give to students. For this reason, we must stay committed to the goal of high-quality learning in every lesson.

Student Self-Assessment

We need to apprentice students into being good self-assessors. Most do not assess their own work with the same critical eye and focus on excellence that teachers use. So as often as possible, we co-construct criteria (e.g., checklist or rubric) for high-quality work and co-analyze work samples so that they see how to apply criteria. It can be a painstaking process, often starting off with "That looks good enough for me" statements. Then, over time, we improve their assessing of their own work. Self-assessment can be one of the most helpful life skills of all. Just think of all the people who have succeeded in various areas because they kept on assessing and improving what they were doing.

I recommend focusing self-assessment on the building and communicating of ideas. This means to apprentice students in applying criteria that are useful for idea-building, such as coming up with strong support and clarifications, unbiased evaluation of evidence, and creative and powerful ways to communicate the idea to others (see Chapter 2). Over the years and with enough practice, students can save a lot of your time used providing feedback after formatively assessing their work. Why? Because students are doing a lot of the assessment and giving themselves feedback before you have to.

Using Assessment Information

In addition to crafting effective ways to assess learning and growth, a significant challenge in teaching is organizing the evidence. A lot happens in students' brains every day, some of which has to do with our teaching. We need to do as much as we can to use the *helpful* information about students' learning of concepts, claims, language, facts, communication skills, confidence, and social skills to push our instruction to be as impactful as possible. Here are two suggestions.

Portfolios

A portfolio is a strategic collection of artifacts and evidence of student learning, such as the performances and products described in the previous section. Portfolios can be digital, in a binder, or in some other folder or container. It is one of the best ways to get an overall picture of learning because it offers multiple views of what students know and can do about a topic. But the term "strategic" is important here. Just dropping a lot of random student work into a folder won't help much. The portfolio should focus on showing the building up and communicating of ideas, as described in Chapter 2. This means that the portfolio contains various artifacts (products, performances, projects, tasks, and even tests and quizzes) that offer views of the strength and clarity of a student's idea(s). In short, the portfolio should focus on showing different viewpoints and depths of the student's idea-building and communication of it.

For example, a fifth grader builds up the idea in science that plants use air to grow. She and her partners designed an experiment. She reads about different experiments with controlled variables. She creates a poster with her partner. They each write part of the explanation. They ask adults if they know where all the matter of a huge tree comes from. They create a podcast on their conclusions and the possible uses of the knowledge. These go into her portfolio, which the teacher uses to evaluate the student's use of scientific language, interpersonal communication skills, and understanding of the scientific method and molecules. Some of the items have been scored for grading purposes, but most of the comments and feedback are focused on highlighting the quality of the work and any changes to improve strength or clarity.

There are various ways to use portfolios beyond just looking at them for assessment purposes. Because they are unique collections of students' ideas and building blocks, there are opportunities for students to share with peers, parents, the community, and the world. They are also a great fosterer of student confidence and agency. You can say or write something like, "Look at the great idea you built up and all the work you did for it! Wow! Keep it up!" Students take a lot more pride in what they have built than in what scores they get on tests.

Learning Evidence Charts

Learning evidence charts help you to keep track of the many areas of learning that sometimes get forgotten in the bustle of teaching many vibrant minds all at once for five hours a day.

First, decide what to assess. We would like to assess everything, of course, but it is more feasible to come up with a "top 10 or so" to avoid being spread too thin. Figure 3.4 provides a quick list of the areas of learning and growth described in Chapter 2. Your school, district, or grade level will likely have others. Look at the list and think about which areas are the highest priorities for your students for a unit. Ask students what *their* priorities are. Add to this list, if needed, and come up with specifics for the ones that you want to emphasize the most.

Figure 3.4 Possible Areas to Assess in a Unit

Content ideas	Critical thinking
Creativity	Relationships
Agency	Honesty, integrity, and responsibility
Strength of ideas	Emotional wellness and well-being
Clarity of ideas	Hard work, resilience, and perseverance
Speaking	Respect, perspectives, and empathy
Listening	Lifelong learning, personal growth, and curiosity
Reading	Healthy lifestyle (quality of life)
Writing	
Conversing	

Once you have a rough idea of 10 (or so) areas to work on and assess in a unit, put them into a chart like the one in Figure 3.5. Discuss these with students to get their input and to explain the value of the areas on the left-hand side.

Figure 3.5 is a sample Student Evidence Chart. Students are different, so different students might end up with some different areas in the left-hand column. You can, for example, tell them that there is room for three substitutions (yet some are fixed, like idea-building). This keeps it somewhat manageable while giving students voice and choice in their learning and growth.

Figure 3.5 Sample Student Evidence Chart for a Unit

Subject/Unit: Fourth-Grade History/Gold Rush			
Area to Assess	**Assessment Type**	**Quality of Evidence (Student)**	**Quality of Evidence (Teacher)**
Content idea(s): *(People got rich in the Gold Rush, but not from finding gold.)*	Product: Museum exhibit Performance: Story and drama on a person during the Gold Rush		(Teacher comments)
Clarifying terms	Observations of student interactions; analyses of story and museum placards		

Figure 3.5 Sample Student Evidence Chart for a Unit (Continued)

Subject/Unit: Fourth-Grade History/Gold Rush			
Area to Assess	**Assessment Type**	**Quality of Evidence (Student)**	**Quality of Evidence (Teacher)**
Supporting ideas	Observations of student interactions. Examples in final story and museum exhibit placards		
Conversing	Observations and recordings of conversations		
Reading comprehension	Written summaries and graphic organizers stemming from reading texts focused on idea-building		
Student agency	Surveys of students and interviews with randomly selected students		
Critical thinking	Discussions and written analyses of the credibility of sources used		
Creativity	Analyses of the story and the drama presentation		
Relationships	Observations of interactions and interviews with students		
Hard work, resilience, and perseverance	Observations of interactions and work time; analysis of student work; interviews and surveys		

In the student column, your student can put any kind of representation of quality (shading in a bar) that you all think would help. Students can write comments too. In the teacher column, use any comment system that will provide helpful feedback at key points in the unit. Students can keep these handy and pull them out for periodic progress checks and comments from the teacher. The teacher can collect these at the end of the unit and end of the year.

All the areas on the chart should reinforce students' building of content and/or growth ideas. Some assessment types can assess multiple areas (e.g., observations of interactions), so it's important to keep your notes organized according to which area you are emphasizing at a given time. Some might get less assessment emphasis in a current unit, so you can carry them over to the next unit. Some areas might be on your evidence charts for the entire year. It also helps to look at the charts before and during instruction as a reminder of areas to highlight on certain days.

ACTIVITY 3.3
Unit Progress Chart

Choose five top areas of learning and growth for your students that you think are important enough to assess. Try to include one or two areas of personal growth. When you do this for real, involve students in the choosing process as much as possible. You will be impressed by how insightful and engaged they become when given a chance to be a part of their own learning. This is an initial chart that can evolve over time.

Figure 3.6 Student Progress Chart Template

Subject/Unit			
Area to Assess	Assessment Type	Quality of Evidence (Student)	Quality of Evidence (Teacher)

Features of Assessment for Learning

Assessments need to do much more than assign numbers to how much students have memorized, how well they read a text, or how much they have matched up their writing to rows in a rubric. Assessments must help students think about how to enhance and deepen their learning (i.e., self-assessment) while they help teachers provide feedback and adjust instruction. Assessment in this book's approach focuses on how well students are building up ideas, making decisions (arguments), and growing personally. It is unfair to students to make them think (and stress them out) that an assessment is about a grade; we must overhaul this focus to instead be on improving learning and growth.

The points don't (or shouldn't) matter to many students. When a student scores high on a quiz or test, does she think, "I learned a lot about ... I did well, so this is interesting, and I hope it sticks," or "Each of these right answers will help me in the future"? If she scores low, does she think, "I scored low, which shows me that I haven't been studying hard enough, so I will study harder and better next time?" Likely not. Often, the scores, if they do matter, do not inform students of better ways to build up ideas, learn, and grow. They tend to be, for many students, unimportant or indicators of failure.

Pedagogical justice requires that students and educators enter into a different paradigm of assessment. Assessment is meant to serve, not to rule. This means that learning is the priority and that assessments should push for working toward rich learning, foster learning, show ongoing strengths and areas to work on, and show culminating learning (though the learning never really ends). Points and grades can be used within these priorities, but we should do all that we can to keep points from being the main reason to learn.

ACTIVITY 3.4
Improving Our Assessment and Assessments

Read through the key features of assessment for learning in the middle column of Figure 3.7. Circle the ones that you agree with and that need the most work in your setting. The left-hand column is the initial, basic version. I chose to improve a science poster presentation, so I put it on the left side and then thought about how to apply each feature in the middle column to it. Look at the improvements in the right-hand column. Now gather a small stack of sticky notes and cover up the left and right columns (or just write in the margins). Pick a different assessment used in your setting and engage the same process.

Figure 3.7 Features of Assessment for Learning and Examples

Basic Version	Key Features of Assessment for Learning	Improvements
Science poster presentation	Requires and inspires students to show their building of an idea (or their choice of side in an argument) to an authentic audience to help them further build up the idea (i.e., not just the teacher for points).	Explain that they are building up a solution to a problem and communicating it to others who should act on it.
	Offers students some choice in the products or performances that they will use.	Provide more than one choice of presentation format.
	Provides clear directions and modeled responses, if needed. They should understand how their work will be evaluated, along with the criteria being used for feedback.	Gather models from previous students and critique them with current students.
	Offers appropriate levels of entry and challenge for a range of students.	Encourage visual and movement messages.

(Continued)

Figure 3.7 Features of Assessment for Learning and Examples (Continued)

Basic Version	Key Features of Assessment for Learning	Improvements
	Values students' use of background knowledge and languages	Encourage students to incorporate home language and examples from home into presentations.
	Fosters learning and/or growth. The assessment itself should be a positive educational experience during which students improve, learn, or grow. For example, they should walk away with a more solidified or clarified idea, along with a stronger sense of agency and academic identity.	Have audiences take notes and ask questions to build up ideas. Encourage audiences to say or write at least one positive comment to the presenter (for an agency).
	Encourages students to self-evaluate, especially with respect to the clarity and strength of their ideas and how well their products and performances are communicating their ideas to others.	Include a short strength and clarity self-rating tool for students. Have them practice in front of small groups for feedback.
	Allows, encourages, and supports revision, multiple chances to submit, and learning from mistakes.	Allow multiple chances to submit (if there isn't time to present to live peers, present on video).
	Positively influences areas of growth over time (e.g., agency, creativity, social-emotional learning, perseverance, etc.).	Include a short questionnaire on agency and creativity.
	Is valid. The assessment process assesses what it's supposed to assess.	Look for commonalities and overlaps in the various parts of the final product-performance.
	Is feasible, practical, and doable with respect to the time and resources that you have.	Strategize ways to have students present to one another in small groups and provide feedback.

Many existing assessments don't have enough of these features to truly be effective at assessing all students in powerful and fair ways. But we can start improving these now so that in several years we will have a robust suite of assessments and assessment practices that students actually like and that show teachers and students vital information about learning and growth.

Linguistically and Culturally Enhanced Assessment

Many students come from cultural backgrounds in which learning is grounded in context-based experiences, challenges, stories, informal apprenticeships, and collaboration (Herrera et al., 2020). Many do not have lots of school-like quizzing during meals at home. "Assessment" at home varies, of course, but many assessments focus on practical and real-world here-and-now tasks and knowledge. Adults in the home are "experts," and children are apprenticing into more mature roles within the family and community over time. Then they enter school, and assessment is very disconnected from anything remotely practical for life. Plus, the assessments are in a non-home language.

Therefore, we must try to overhaul our assessments with as many culturally appropriate dimensions as we can. For example, rather than having students answer a string of comprehension questions, have students show their comprehension of a text and character development by creating an oral sequel or a short graphic novel and explaining it. Or have students solve a real problem going on in their school or community and create a local renaissance fair using art and poetry to address the problem and propose solutions. Have students become like apprentices who are studying to be historians, mathematicians, artists, scientists, and the like. They come up with articles, drafts of poems, and initial interpretations of historical events, which they bring to you (or another expert) for feedback and revision.

If English proficiency is not the main thing being assessed, students should be allowed to use their first language(s), movement, drawing, music, and other forms of expression to communicate the idea that they have built up. Throughout the unit, as students gather "building blocks" (see Chapters 2, 4, and 5) they should be encouraged to work with others in their first language(s). The "negatives" of less usage of

English are far outweighed by the engagement, relationship building, sense of belonging, sense of agency, and content learned.

Collaborative Assessments

In every assessment type described in this chapter, you can also assess collaborative versions of them. Yes, I know we have all experienced the "I did all the work in this group project, and they all got the same grade as me!" problem (wait, was I one of the members who didn't work? Anyway…). But with a few tweaks here and there, and even some slightly uneven contributions, collaborative projects can be very educational, relational, and informative. Many multilingual students are still adjusting to the hyperindividualistic nature of U.S. schooling. Being a part of a team that works toward an engaging goal or end-product-performance can foster learning, language, and relationships while also allowing you to assess these things. Remember, one of the top priorities for most employers (and significant others) is being able to work with others and communicate. So, let's pay them more attention by assessing them. Experiment a little with these. You might even try collaborative tests!

Engaging Students in Designing and Analyzing Assessments

Not many large-scale testing companies ask the students whom they will test what should be on their assessments. But you can. Brainstorm with students what they think would be good ways to show their learning. Make a list of things that you want them to learn (and areas in which to grow), add the things that they want to learn and grow in, and then co-pose some ideas for projects, products, and performances. You can have them work in pairs for several minutes and then share with you and the rest of the class. Jot the possibilities down and then reflect on how you might use them in the current unit or in the future.

Assessing the Overall Ideas in the Classroom

Every few months, it helps to get an overall sense of the ideas being built in your classroom. Gather student ideas from your classroom. It is best to have a graphic organizer like an idea-building visual or semantic map that you can quickly analyze and compare across students and across time. You can group the ideas into subject areas. Some teachers have students keep a visual for each idea in the back of their binders or in a special folder. Compile a list of questions or features like these in order to guide the creation of this archive as well as use it throughout the year.

- Are the ideas important in the content area? In life?
- Are the ideas as strong and clear as possible?
- Is this student's idea-building improving during the year?
- Do the ideas have some "building blocks" that come from student backgrounds, lives, home language, or community (not just from school learning or texts)?
- Are there any key building blocks that are unclear or missing?
- Are any of the ideas from last year?

Assessment for Personal Growth

Assessment for personal growth means that we and our students are keeping track of how much they are growing in the five areas outlined in Chapter 2.

Activity

Chapter 2 introduced the five areas in the left-hand column of Figure 3.8. In the middle column are possible questions to put into student questionnaires, rating tools, and self-reflections, which you and

Figure 3.8 Questions and Observation Strategies for Assessing Personal Growth

To See Growth in How Students...	We Can Ask Questions Such As...	And Observe Students When They...
Think about themselves (agency, self-efficacy, integrity, self-discipline, confidence, and honesty)	Do you feel that learning is easy? Do you feel that you can learn most things? Are you good at building up ideas? Are you good at communicating? Are you honest? Do you like challenges?	• Write or talk about themselves, their abilities, their talents, dreams, etc. • Interact with others • Share their thoughts and ideas

(Continued)

Figure 3.8 Questions and Observation Strategies for Assessing Personal Growth (Continued)

To See Growth in How Students…	We Can Ask Questions Such As…	And Observe Students When They…
Persevere (being resilient, learning from mistakes, and listening to constructive feedback)	Do you keep trying to do well at things, even when they get difficult? Do you like it when others, like teachers, give you feedback? Do you make changes based on it? Do you learn from mistakes?	• Engage in challenging academic work • Make mistakes • Make changes in response to feedback • Engage in challenging, active, physical activities and skills
Relate to others (social skills, empathy, and perspective-taking)	How are your friendships going? What do you do when your friends are sad? Can you relate to how others, even way back in history, might feel? Can you see events in ways that others see them?	• Talk with each other • Disagree with each other • Write from the perspective of others • Interpret character dialogues in stories
Show character traits (honest, generous, patient, optimistic, assumes good intentions, unselfish, open-minded, trustworthy, and fun)	Are you honest? How are you like (character in story)? How are you patient? Do others trust you? Are you open-minded? What are the traits of heroes?	• Write and talk about themselves and others • Converse with others • Solve life problems • Express feelings
Develop multicultural and multilingual identities	Do you see yourself as uniquely and wonderfully multilingual and multicultural? Do you value your unique backgrounds and knowledges as strengths for learning and life? Do you use and share examples from your life to build up ideas in class and beyond? Do you value the power and beauty of being able to construct meaning across cultures?	• Compare perspectives, cultures, and communication styles • Talk about, write about, and represent themselves in class • Share their multilingual and multicultural goals • Express feelings about their multicultural and multilingual identities inside and outside of school

students can use to monitor growth over time. Feel free to add your own questions and questions generated by students. In the right-hand column are ideas for observations that you think are valuable for seeing evidence of growth. Add your own, if needed.

You can put areas that you and your students prioritize into the Student Evidence Chart (Figure 3.5) in the previous section, or you can create a separate chart. You might also want some specific tools and strategies for assessing. Try to use whatever tools you are using every two months or so to let students know how they are doing in these areas. Make it a habit to observe growth as much as possible.

One fifth-grade teacher, for example, has students meet in growth groups every month to go over a rating tool that they developed together. Students share their progress and challenges, along with examples that they feel safe sharing in the groups. The teacher has noticed that friendships often grow out of this collaborative sharing and sharpening.

The more that students develop a "practical meta-awareness" of these areas and think about signs of growth in them, the more they are likely to value these areas and work on them in school and beyond.

How Assessments for Learning Help Us Achieve Pedagogical Justice

This chapter briefly touches on ways to overhaul assessment. In the accumulation-based approach, anything that isn't countable tends to not be valuable. Most of the assessment ideas here center on idea-building and growth, which value students' uniquenesses, voices, and contributions. But these things are hard to quantify. And yet, if we can land on the moon and split the atom, we can figure out how to effectively assess all students.

This chapter's ideas for overhauling assessment—imperfect as they may be—provide rich and useful information. A multidimensional assessment that students don't consider to be painful or boring is helpful on several levels: It is more valid, we see authentic uses of language it is creative, and students learn content and skills in context.

Pedagogical justice is achieved by emphasizing idea-based, non-test assessments because they allow students to share what they have learned rather than what they have not memorized. Idea-based assessments value multilingual students' voices, creativity, personal and cultural building blocks, and ways of using language.

Students focus on communicating their unique ideas, and we assess the quality of their ideas and their communication in order to revise and improve them. This offers second and third chances to show their learning, which accelerates their language abilities and solidifies the content.

CHAPTER IDEA

Here is one idea that you can build up from this chapter. If another idea was sparked for you, feel free to replace this one. Remember to add personal examples, definitions, questions, and insights as building blocks along with new blocks gathered from this chapter. Some sample blocks are provided.

IDEA STATEMENT: Assessment for learning focuses on seeing students' strengths and next steps in the development of knowledge, language, and skills needed for building and communicating big ideas.		
Learning interviews can be powerful ways to assess.		Assessment is more accurate when the task is engaging.
Products and performances should prioritize communicating ideas to others.		
		We must be supporters rather than judges.

References

Chavez, S. (2018). Effects of standardized tests on English language learners at the elementary school level. *Capstone Projects and Master's Theses*, 363. https://digitalcommons.csumb.edu/caps_thes_all/363

Darling-Hammond, L. & Adamson, F. (2010). *Beyond basic skills: The role of performance assessment in achieving 21st century standards of learning.* Stanford University.

Darling-Hammond, L., Ancess, J., & Falk, B. (1995). *Authentic assessment in action.* Columbia University Press.

Del Carmen Unda, M., & Lizárraga-Dueñas, L. (2021). The testing industrial complex: Texas and beyond. *Texas Education Review*, 9(2), 31–42. http://dx.doi.org/10.26153/tsw/13911

Gay, G. (2010). *Culturally responsive teaching: Theory, research, and practice* (2nd ed.). Teachers College Press.

Glossary of Education Reform. (2014). Formative assessment. https://www.edglossary.org/formative-assessment/.

Gottlieb, M., & Honigsfeld, A. (2019). From assessment of learning to learning for and as learning. In *Breaking down the wall: Essential shifts for English learners' success*. Corwin.

Herrera, S., Murry, G., & Cabral, R. (2020). *Assessment of culturally and linguistically diverse students* (3rd ed.). Pearson.

Mitchell, C. (2016). Study: Current, former ELLs take fewer advanced, college-prep classes. *EducationWeek*. https://www.edweek.org/teaching-learning/study-current-former-ells-take-fewer-advanced-college-prep-classes/2016/11

Newmann, F., King, B., & Carmichael, D. (2007). Common Standards for Rigor and Relevance in Teaching Academic Subjects. Iowa Department of Education.

Tierney, R. (1998). Literacy assessment reform: Shifting beliefs, principled possibilities, and emerging practices. *The Reading Teacher*, 51(5), 374–390.

Wiggins, G. (2019). The case for authentic assessment. *Practical Assessment, Research and Evaluation*, 2, Article 2.

Pedagogy 4

Very few hands go up when I ask teachers if their students enter the classroom each day hoping to continue building up an idea that they started earlier in the week or hoping to start building up a new idea that day. When I ask them about common student mindsets about learning, I hear things such as, "Just get by. Do what the teacher says. Get ready for the upcoming test; then forget the stuff. Do as little as possible but still pass. Get your points and move on." And much more. I believe that there are too many classroom settings where thoughts like these are prevalent. Multilingual students with such thoughts tend to face extra challenges in school (see Chapter 1).

Minor changes to accumulation-based teaching won't work. An overhaul takes time, energy, trial, error, and working through some cognitive dissonance about learning. But changing pedagogy is the most important and foundational transformation for serving our multilingual students. What a student does and thinks about for many hours a day is highly influential in their development. Many students are immersed in five to six hours a day of accumulation-based instruction that overwhelms and disengages them while simultaneously molds their minds into short-answer choosers rather than big-idea builders and problem-solvers. These are, as you remember from Chapter 1, pedagogical injustices that are especially detrimental to multilingual students.

This chapter attempts to address these injustices by describing a significantly different approach to teaching and learning, called the

Idea-Building Approach. It is focused on rich academic learning, cultural and linguistic cultivation, and personal growth.

The Idea-Building Approach

Figure 4.1 is a visual representation of the Idea-Building Approach. It is grounded in the ideas of the many educators and thinkers in this book's acknowledgments and references. It is the result of two decades of research, collaboration with educators, and classroom observation and reflection.

As you can see in Figure 4.1, this approach is very different from that of accumulation-based learning depicted in Chapter 1 (Figure 1.3). For example, you can see that the results in Figure 4.1 focus on the learning and growth of each student, not on grades or test scores. It also values student differences throughout the learning process. Each idea that each student builds is unique. It is not a temporarily memorized set of facts or ideas borrowed from someone else to be tested on. The idea is meant to stick and continue to develop over time. Rather than just providing students "access" to content, idea-building provides ownership of it.

The icons on the far left and far right represent the changes in a student's mind before and after the learning and growth process. Everything that happens in between (e.g., lessons in the unit) inspires and fosters the differences in learning and growth over time. The central element is the big idea(s) that students build up during their learning experiences. The supporting 10 elements enrich and amplify the building of the idea—and vice versa—throughout the learning process. The time this process takes varies, though the bulk of it in school will span multiple weeks during a unit of instruction.

Growth, as you remember from Chapter 2, consists of five categories: self-perception (agency, self-efficacy, and identity), perseverance, social skills, character, and multilingual-multicultural identities. Teachers use these categories not only to help students learn but also to help them become the confident, hard-working, relational, creative, and multifaceted individuals that they were meant to be. Teachers should try to weave a range of growth-fostering activities and practices into lesson activities to build up a growth-based idea (see Chapter 2). These include student–student interactions, goal setting, positive peer feedback, choice, creative products and performances, and reflection journals.

Ideas play an important role in personal growth because they help students remember important concepts and building blocks for being human—for example, honesty is the best policy; might is not usually right; we learn from our mistakes; I am unique and important, and other concepts such as these. Growth-focused ideas should be woven into learning as much as possible. This can happen during class discussions, group work, practice activities, quizzes, reading, and writing. Refer to Appendix C for more growth-centered ideas.

What follow are short descriptions of each element in the Idea-Building Approach. As you read them, consider how well your current curriculum and instruction align with them. You can see examples of planning with these elements in Chapter 5 and Appendix B.

Figure 4.1   The Idea-Building Approach to Learning and Growth

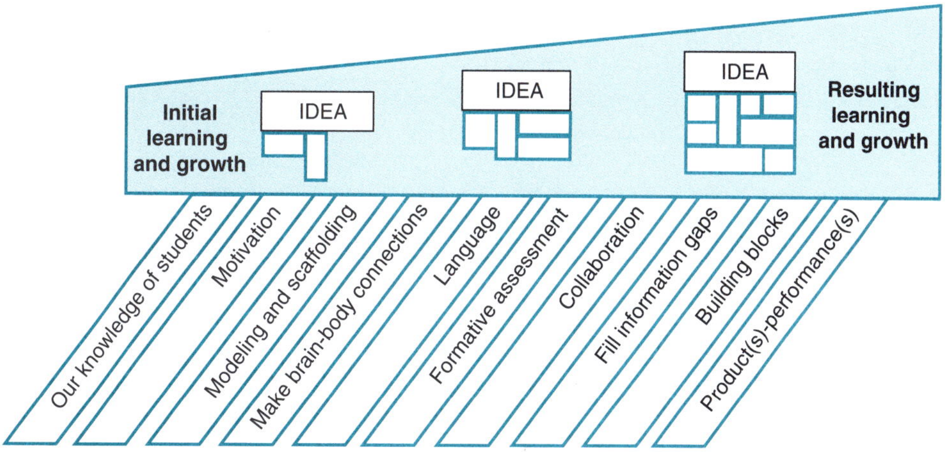

Outline the Results

It's necessary to outline what you want students to learn and how you want to see them grow, both of which are represented by the two icons on the right side of the model (refer to Chapter 2 for more on these). School learning is represented by the icon of the building. It symbolizes the more academic focuses of the learning, such as the learning of core content ideas, skills, and language that will help students in subsequent schooling and life. Personal growth, which is symbolized by the tree icon, represents self-perception, perseverance, SEL (social-emotional learning), character traits, and multicultural-multilingual identities.

> Think of the negatives that can emerge without the element of Outlining the Results.

I use the term "outline" because we can never perfectly predict what students will learn by the end of a unit or school year. We can outline our top priorities, which are a synthesis of what we noticed in recent units that students still need to work on (for both learning and growth), content standards for our grade level and course, and any curriculum we might be using. Then we can make a list (ranked, if possible) of what students should learn, ideas they should build, and how they should grow. These are often found in the front matter of curriculum guides and at the beginning of units and lessons. Think about what kinds of knowledge and skills are needed by experts in your discipline and adjust them according to your students' grade levels. Then take another pass at the list to prioritize the most important things to focus on. This will help you craft a possible idea or argument, described in the next section (also see Chapter 2).

These results should not have anything to do with test scores. Rather, they need to be about the lasting things that we want to see improve in the minds and lives of students as a result of being in school.

In Monica's fourth-grade classroom, two-thirds of her students were multilingual, most of whom spoke Spanish and English. Two spoke Somali and English, and one spoke Farsi and English. Monica was teaching an ELA (English language arts) unit that focused on understanding how authors of stories and poetry use character traits and changes to convey life messages and themes about life. She looked at a list of standards in the curriculum guide and chose the ones most related to this focus, based on her students' interests and needs.

Draft the Big-Idea Statement(s)

Come up with one or more big-idea statements that will last in students' minds and motivate them to learn. A concept, claim, or standard is more likely to be an effective big idea if it (a) is valuable for students to use and cultivate in their minds and (b) is conducive to clarification of key terms and support through examples, evidence, details, relationships, or steps. For example, if a student says, "Some ancient civilizations fell because they got too big," there are many terms that are ripe for clarification (*civilization, fell,* and *big*) and an obvious need for examples, of which there are many. And it is an important and interesting (it's counterintuitive) idea in history and social studies.

Think about thesis statements or topic sentences that you would like to see students build toward and then communicate at the end of a unit. Think about which ideas, concepts, and claims are worthy of ongoing construction inside your students' minds over the course of their lives. Which ideas will be useful to students if they pursue this discipline?

You can draft the big-idea statements knowing that ideas might change during the year or even during the unit. Students might come up with even better and more engaging ideas as they work together in the discipline.

The idea might also change depending on your knowledge of students. For example, after some interviewing and pre-assessment, you might find that they already have some solid ideas that you or your curriculum had planned on teaching. Or you might find that some expected foundational ideas (e.g., from last year) are not strong enough and you need to develop them before moving on.

THE CENTRALITY OF BIG IDEAS

The big idea at the heart of learning is central for four reasons. First, all the other elements either contribute to or result from the idea-building process and the idea-building needed for it. If you take the big idea (concept or claim) away, you might learn some new content, you might collaborate, you might develop language, and so on. But without a purpose (something newly constructed), the learning fades. The process of communicating toward the focused goal of building up an idea—or building up two competing ideas in an argument—gives cohesion to the "materials" and skills used in the process.

Second, we want to build up students' expertise in a wide range of disciplines. Experts do not memorize lists of information for tests; they think in "chunks" in order to keep all of their knowledge organized, prioritized, and purposeful. These chunks tend to be concepts, claims, and ideas in the Idea-Building Approach. They use these chunks to get things done.

Third, big ideas tend to last. When students do the cognitive work of searching, interpreting, finding, gathering, processing, and using information to construct something in their minds (and in a product or performance), that thing tends to be better remembered than just static, memorized information traded to the teacher for points.

(Continued)

(Continued)

Fourth, idea-building fosters ownership and agency. Students get to choose what goes into building up their ideas. When they build it, it's theirs. They use unique knowledge and skills from their lives, as well as knowledge and skills from classroom texts and experiences. When they share their ideas and building blocks with others, it is authentic sharing—others don't have the information, but they are interested in using it, and they show their interest. It is not about "right" answers but rather about co-constructing the strongest and clearest idea possible.

Monica used the essential question in the curriculum to draft the big idea "We can mine important life lessons by looking at how characters act and change in stories and poems." She shares this with students who already know that they will be building up this idea (or something similar) during the unit and into the future.

Design Products and Performances

When you have a rough picture of the idea(s), content, and skills that you want students to learn, come up with possible products and/or performances that will inspire students to use lots of language and engage in lots of thinking in order to build up the idea(s) (see Chapter 3 for more on these).

An engaging product-performance provides a concrete and tangible goal to work toward (Darling-Hammond & Adamson, 2010). A great many students are much more excited about creating products and performances, especially when they get to collaborate with others. In many ways, products-performances approximate real-world learning and work. How many jobs out there require you to work the whole year to pass a test? Rather, they want ideas, results, solutions, products, performances, growth, and so on.

As students work on their product-performance, they should receive plenty of helpful feedback from peers, teachers, and others with respect to content and clarity. It should be feedback that they can use to revise and improve their work. For example, a student might practice a short oral presentation with a small group of peers to get their comments on how to improve it.

Monica gave her students several choices for performances and products that they could work toward and that would communicate their big idea:

1. Create a mural of several authors and their messages with a written description (in their home language and/or English) of the perspectives and messages of the authors and artists.

2. Write a short story or poem (in home language and/or English) with messages related to character traits, actions, and changes.

3. Create a painting, photograph, or collage that illustrates it (or picture book).

4. Create a screencast that explains the works and how they compare to several other stories or poems that they read and brought with them from home.

Know Your Students

When you have a rough idea of the idea(s) that students will build up and the likely products-performances for the unit, strategically gather as much information as possible on your students. Figure out ways to learn about their strengths, needs, potentials, goals, and interests. Some of the data come from last year (e.g., from previous year's teachers, tests, and student work), but most of this knowledge gathering will happen in the first months of the school year and from previous units leading up to the current one. Of course, "knowing students" doesn't really end because they change so much during the year.

Ask them about their families, friends, hobbies, sports, favorite foods, languages, activities, movies, and so on. Get to know their interests. Ask them about these as often as you can. Students like to be known by teachers. Not only does the knowledge help you as you design and teach lessons, but it also helps you to strengthen relationships with them. Strong relationships with students are one of the most important factors for learning for many diverse students (Delahooke, 2019).

Get to know their growth in the areas of personal development. Growth area categories, as described in Chapter 2, are self-perception, social skills, perseverance, character, and multilingual-multicultural identity. In order to gather information on these, you can use growth-area interviews, surveys (strengths, needs, interests, hobbies, goals, etc.), and open responses (oral, written, visual, artistic, etc.).

Get to know students' learning preferences. Do they like to learn visually, kinesthetically, dramatically, creatively, cooperatively, or in other ways? How do they like to be assessed? Which topics interest them? What gives them energy? What drains the energy from them? How do their backgrounds, languages, and cultures align with learning activities and assessments? What motivates their learning? What are their language strengths and needs?

Get to know their content knowledge, ideas, and skills that are *related to upcoming learning*. This includes thinking about the results: ideas, content, skills, and changes that you hope to see by the end of the unit. So in a sense, you start by considering both ends of the learning. You try to strengthen your notion of what students will build up and how they will grow (right side of the model), while at the same time bulking up your knowledge of students that will relate to what they need to learn (left side of the model). This allows you to understand students' preexisting understandings in order to build them up or challenge them if they are incorrect (Bransford et al., 1999). For example, a student might say, "The moon is not always round."

Here are some suggestions for getting to know current ideas, understandings and skills:

- Hold idea interviews with students (e.g., What is your idea? What are examples that support it? What do you mean by___?).
- Have them write you an idea letter.
- Have them make an idea visual (e.g., semantic map, idea organizer) that shows an idea or other knowledge related to the upcoming learning.
- Have them create an oral recording (podcast) describing their idea to listeners not familiar with it.

Knowing students helps you to adapt instruction and assessment with a culturally and linguistically sustaining lens (Alim & Paris, 2017). Students' home and community languages and cultures must be known, valued, and leveraged to help students build up ideas, communicate, and grow. Students have a wide range of knowledge, perspectives, interests, and backgrounds. We need to value all assets and consider how they can strengthen students' learning and growth.

It means getting excited about all the things that students can bring to the learning table—and shaping instruction in response.

Consider which topics and texts interest the majority of your students and provide the most opportunities for connections to their backgrounds, as well as among students. These connections become building blocks for collaborative and language-rich idea-building, as well as avenues for the five areas of personal growth. (Accumulation-based learning, by contrast, tends not to value getting to know students and their differing backgrounds. Students are simply expected to learn the same way because they will take the same tests—which also value student differences very little.)

> Think of the negatives that can emerge without the element of Knowing your Students.

Knowing students helps us (a) see their academic and personal strengths, (b) see the many ways in which students can and want to learn, (c) expand how we see different access points for different students, and (d) see their humanity.

Monica had frequent "check-ins" with students to ask how they felt about school, relationships, and life. She asked groups of her multilingual students how they felt about the language demands of the lessons and if there was anything she could do to improve learning and communication in the classroom. She gave out short surveys at the beginning of each unit to get a sense of their engagement and existing knowledge and skills related to the unit. During the unit, she used an app on her phone to take observation notes on each student's academic progress, personal growth, and engagement.

Use Building Blocks

When you have a clear enough sense of the unit's focal idea(s), the products-performances that students will work toward, and sufficient knowledge of your students, it's time to think about the content and skills that students will need in order to build up the idea(s) and do well on their products-performances.

One way to organize these blocks is to use an idea-building visual like the ones in Figure 4.2. You also saw examples of these in Chapter 2. Put the idea on top and then start filling in the blocks. First, write down the useful knowledge and skills that your students might *already* have (i.e., connections to background knowledge). Throughout the unit, you will be able to encourage students to use these for building.

Figure 4.2   Idea-Building Visual and Argument Balance Scale

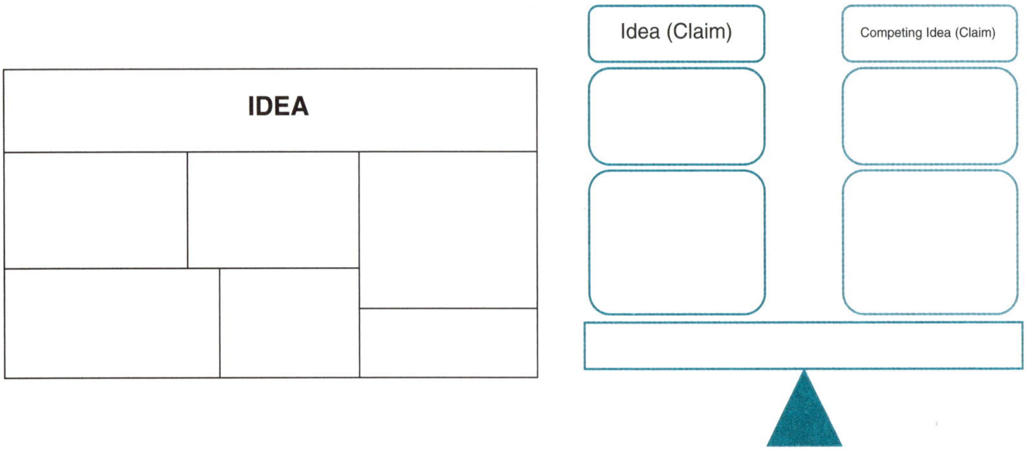

Then write down any new content that students will likely need to learn and use to build up their ideas even more. These include facts, examples, evidence, definitions, stories, anecdotes, insights, information, texts (written, visual, etc.), and any other useful information for supporting the unit's idea. Include any content that students will need in order to do well on their performances or products. Circle the blocks that you think your students need the most. These blocks will give you an idea of what to emphasize in your instruction.

Second, think about the "clarify blocks." These are the blocks that clarify key terms needed to understand the blocks and communicate the idea. If one student says she thinks that the idea is *Geography shapes peoples' cultures*, then her partner can ask, "What does geography mean? What does shape mean? What does culture mean?" A lot of building comes from answering such questions.

Third, think about which skills, in addition to supporting and clarifying, students will need to (a) build up an idea or effectively argue and (b) create and deliver a successful product and/or performance. These include disciplinary, literacy, communication, and idea-building skills such as analyzing, comparing, synthesizing, evaluating, problem-solving, interpreting, applying, evaluating, and seeing others' perspectives. These skills also serve as building blocks. Flip back to the Idea-Building Skills section in Chapter 2 for a refresher on how such skills help students to build up ideas and choose sides in an argument.

Keep in mind that when students see a graphic organizer with boxes on it, it will be *highly* tempting to robotically "fill in the boxes" as quickly as possible. We need to remind students that it's not about filling in boxes or even piling up blocks, nor is it just about the final product or performance and its grade. It's about building up ideas—as strongly and clearly as possible—so that they will last in their minds and keep building over the years. And it's about improving their abilities to work together and to communicate their ideas to a wide range of other people.

The accumulation-based approach tends to devalue knowledge and skills that come from students' backgrounds, cultures, and personal lives. These are students' "personal building blocks," and they are absolutely vital in the Idea-Building Approach. Using them in idea-building shows students that their lives contribute to knowledge-building and problem-solving in life. The valuing of personal blocks by teachers, peers, and school shows that *differences* are rich and valuable—that variety within and across ideas is a precious spice for learning. An added bonus is that when students share their personal blocks with other students, there are plenty of interesting information gaps to fill with loads of rich language in the mix.

Monica looked through the curriculum materials and texts and took notes on the various "school" building blocks (clarification and support) that she wanted students to use for the idea. She also asked for personal building blocks from stories from their home cultures and stories that they had read outside of school. During the unit, she told students to use building blocks from both school and from home to make their ideas stronger and more interesting. She also had them color-code their personal blocks on visual organizers.

Fill Information Gaps

Filling information gaps is why language was invented (Zwiers, 2019b). It means that a person (student, speaker, author, actor, or artist) provides information to another person who doesn't have it and wants or needs it (Billings & Mueller, 2017). If this book, for example, has information that is new and useful to you, you will read more closely than if you already knew the information or if you were just reading it to answer questions for points. Without an information gap, language tends to be just for show, it's less used, it's of lower quality, and it sticks less.

Teachers need to be aware of how much information gap potential there is for each activity. If not much (e.g., if all students have read the same text), then the teacher needs to engineer a useful gap (e.g., by giving students different texts to read) or think about how students might share different information (e.g., opinions or connections to their lives, varying emotional responses, life experiences, and answers to different questions).

When students are reading, the author cannot audibly answer, of course, but students need to develop the habit of pushing for the text to be clear and trying to interpret all messages as clearly as possible. The more we can model (using read-alouds) and scaffold (e.g., taking notes) this habit, the better. Clarifying is another way to fill information gaps. Encourage students to ask each other clarification questions, even if they think everything is perfectly clear. It usually isn't.

Here are some questions that might help as you prepare a lesson with lots of clarifying:

> Think of the negatives that can emerge without the filling of information gaps during lessons.

- What types of language will students need to clarify their idea(s) to others?
- If there is writing, what aspects of writing will help them to get their stellar ideas across to others?
- If there are oral messages, what types of oral-language conventions (pausing, prosody, and grammar) will best convey their intended meaning?
- And if there are visuals or video, what features will be most effective?

Monica noticed that the curriculum materials lacked opportunities for students to fill information gaps. So she made it one of her priorities. She looked at every activity and asked, "Are students using language to get or provide information that they or others need to build up ideas?" She modified her turn-and-talks to make sure that partners and group members had different information about the authors and works of literature and art they were using. She made sure students read texts that they didn't already know and that they needed for idea-building. She emphasized that their writing would serve to fill information gaps for their readers and help them build up their own ideas.

Motivate

One of the main causes of high-quality learning is motivation (Stipek, 2002). And one of the main causes of low-quality learning is a lack of motivation. When students are not motivated, they don't tend to push their brains to understand, build, or communicate. A handful of points might get them to do a little more, but it often doesn't reach what we would call high-quality learning.

There are different types and strengths of motivation, as shown in Figure 4.3. We want the strongest types of motivation to dominate in our instruction and assessment as much as possible. We can't always teach topics that are interesting to every student, but we can strive to motivate student learning in as many ways as possible before defaulting to threatening students with lower grades.

A key aspect of motivation is *intrigue*. Intrigue is the term I use for setting up learning experiences in which students desire some sort of closure or resolution of "helpful tension" or an unknown ending. It is somewhat similar to that feeling you get when you want to answer a major question and you don't have internet access. For students, intrigue might take the following forms:

- Learning the ending of a good story
- Solving a mystery
- Solving a problem
- Finding out what "really" happened during a historical event or period
- Answering a meaty question
- Learning why a lab demonstration didn't go the way they thought it would

- Finding out which side of an argument they (or other students) will end up choosing
- Figuring out if a hypothesis is true or not

As you can see in these examples, resolving intrigue tends to come from getting and using new information to create or discover. Intrigue gives students energy and perseverance to maintain attention because they are anticipating and working toward getting the desired information or relieving cognitive tension. They are not sure what it will look like or how it will show up, which makes it intriguing.

We can't just post the unit's essential question on the wall and expect students to be magically intrigued by it. Even I'm not interested in half (maybe three-quarters) of the essential questions I see in curriculums, and I am fairly curious overall. Students tend not to be very interested in curriculum writers' questions. So the more we can create experiences in which students are asking big questions, wondering big wonderings, posing big hypotheses, wanting to find out the endings, and being "bugged" by not knowing something, the better the intrigue and the ideas that follow.

An important type of intrigue is narrativity. This means that your instruction has story elements, such as characters who solve a problem (i.e., plot). Narrativity is obvious in language arts classes, especially when reading an engaging story. It is also quite strong when looking at characters and events in history, especially when students don't know the outcome. You can also find narrative-based intrigue in science. For example, students might observe an unexpected phenomenon (e.g., a chemical reaction) and then hypothesize and figure out how the characters (chemicals) worked together to cause it. Even conversations have narrativity: the participants and their knowledge are the "characters" who work together to come up with a new decision or new idea (see "Story-fy" section in Chapter 5).

ACTIVITY 4.1
Motivation Chart

This activity shows different types of motivation and how each one fosters intrigue and engagement. In the left-hand column, the amount and intensity of motivation correspond to the size of the font—roughly speaking. And yes, these will vary on different days with different students and different topics. For each row, add examples from your setting in the right-hand column.

Figure 4.3 Types of Motivation Chart

Type of Motivation	How It Fosters Intrigue	Examples
Learning about a topic of interest	The student anticipates being satisfied with new knowledge about the topic.	
Arguing and making decisions	Students don't know which side of an argument they or others will eventually choose, which is a bit like not knowing the outcome of a story or sporting event.	
Solving real problems and challenges	Students are intrigued by learning new ways to solve real problems and how they can contribute to solving them.	
Collaborating with peers	Students want to see how their contributions to a team effort are used and validated by others; they also want to see what kinds of friendships and shared experiences might result from working together.	

(Continued)

Figure 4.3 Types of Motivation Chart (Continued)

Type of Motivation	How It Fosters Intrigue	Examples
Creating meaningful products and performances	Students are interested in seeing what they can produce and how they might perform in order to communicate their ideas to others and see how others change as a result.	
Building up a unique idea (using building blocks from their own lives)	Students wonder what the final idea will look and sound like, especially how the examples from their lives will be used to support it and communicate it to others.	
Finding out how something ends (intrigue)	Students get hooked on the characters and plot of a story, often making several predictions, and want to see how it ends.	
Answering meaningful questions (inquiry)	Students are intrigued by many topics and questions and want to know the answers.	
Using creativity, art, hands-on materials, movement, drama	Students look at materials and wonder what the final product will look like once they apply their creativity to it.	
Earning grades and points	Students wonder what their grade will be on graded assignments and in the course.	
Doing well on yearly state multiple-choice and standardized tests	Some students wonder what their scores will be and what teachers will do when they receive the scores.	

When we can't fill the entire curriculum with interesting topics—which is often—we can rely on other forms of motivation on the list. Sometimes three or more can be woven into instruction. For example, a teacher might turn an essential question such as "How does erosion change the shape of the land?" into an argument such as, "Which has changed the land more, rivers or glaciers?" Now with two competing sides, students are asked to build up both ideas as much as possible using evidence from their lives and research. They then collaborate to create a multimedia poster to show their final decision to the principal. Notice the different types of motivation from Figure 4.3.

Monica took the endings away from several stories so that students could wonder, predict, and discuss how they thought characters would change and how the stories would end (before seeing the original endings). They then discussed why the author wrote the story or poem. She also reminded students that one reason for reading stories and poems with different perspectives is to spark ideas for writing their own stories or poems. She also encouraged students to write based on their unique journeys, perspectives, and cultural practices. One of her Somali students, for example, wrote about her first year of school in the United States.

Model and Scaffold

Modeling offers a chance for students to observe how a more proficient person does something that they will eventually do. Apprentices, for example, often watch a lot of modeling and look at (or listen to) lots of models of products. In accumulation-based pedagogy, modeling tends to focus on memorizing reading skills, choosing the right answers, writing for levels on a rubric, reading to answer questions, and doing things for points. In the Idea-Building Approach, modeling focuses on reading to build up ideas, writing to communicate ideas as strongly and clearly as possible to real readers, conversing with others to collaboratively build up ideas and choose sides of arguments, critically thinking about sources of information, and building up growth-enhancing ideas in life.

Scaffolding is the use of supports (e.g., visuals, movements, stories, and interactions) that are reduced as students build independence in learning and showing their learning. The focus of scaffolding is important. We should not scaffold so students can do better on tests. This tends to be a bunch of little supports aimed at short-term learning of correct answers. In contrast, in this approach we are scaffolding a building—the students' building of an idea (you never see workers using scaffolding to create lots of short piles of bricks). The scaffolding in the Idea-Building Approach is bigger and stronger and focused on helping students connect knowledge and skills needed for lasting concepts in their minds. We still remove the support over time, and when we do, students are left with a strong and clear concept or decision.

Monica frequently modeled how to fix reading comprehension problems as she read aloud. She emphasized that mistakes in reading happen and that the goal is to learn from them, move on, and always seek to understand the text. She modeled how to turn key information about characters into building blocks in her sample idea up on the front screen. She used frequent scaffolding practices (student interactions and peer editing) and scaffolds (movement and visual organizers) to support students' building and communicating of their ideas. Monica was impressed with how well and how long students conversed without her help after she gradually removed conversation scaffolds during the unit.

Collaborate

Collaboration means interacting, conversing, and working together to construct shared meanings (Palincsar & Herrenkohl, 2010). Lessons that are grounded in accumulation-based learning tend to lack sufficient collaboration and conversation between students. It is an individualistic approach that doesn't prioritize students sharing or helping each other build up ideas. There may be some teacher-centered class discussions and some quick pair-shares, but such interactions tend to foster minimal language and thinking. Students need lots of practice in putting complex thoughts into words when collaborating with others in real time.

Dialogue plays a crucial role in collaboration. "Dialogue" means productive back-and-forth interaction. Wells (2015, p. 68) argued that for millennia, "when situations arose that posed challenges that went beyond current members' knowledgeable skills, individuals pooled their resources, attempting through collaborative action and dialog to construct solutions." We are wired to collaborate orally with others, yet schools have neglected such "pooling" in favor of isolated and individual memorizing and practice.

Dialogue is stronger when there is some intrigue, or uncertainty, in the mix. Peter Johnston explains, "It is the perception of uncertainty that enables dialog. Dialogue, in turn, sustains uncertainty. If there is certainty, or only one view, there is nothing to discuss and nothing to learn. Uncertainty is the foundation of inquiry and research" (Johnston, 2012, p. 59). This uncertainty not only applies to the topic being discussed but also to the dialogue itself. Like a story, we seldom know beforehand what will happen in a conversation or how we will change as a result.

Dialogue is a vital tool for construction, discovery, and transformation. Therefore, we must design lessons with plenty of dialogue-rich collaboration. There are many collaboration- and conversation-based activities that you can use (see Zwiers, 2019a). But make sure that students know that they are sharing, listening, and collaborating *in order to* construct novel and stronger ideas (concepts, understandings, decisions, etc.). Also, be careful not to overdo talk protocols. While talk protocols (e.g., cold calling with names on sticks, group roles, timed responses, rigid steps for sharing, sentence frames) can scaffold the development of conversation skills and content, they can also sidestep a lot of the messy and powerful aspects of building ideas with others found in "unbounded" conversation (Nichols, 2019). Students need to cultivate their individual and collective senses of agency, which is not possible if protocols take up most or all of the lesson time.

Collaboration also includes developing peer relationships, which are one of the most powerful yet most neglected nurturers of learning. When lessons simply treat students as recipients (as can often be the case in classrooms with multilingual students), the default is to have them quietly soak in the learning from the teacher or texts. Yet students of all ages crave warm and positive relationships with peers and teachers. Not only can such relationships increase learning directly (learning from one another), they can strengthen students' sense of belonging, self-worth, motivation, and perseverance. For many students, sharing academic challenges is much more tolerable (and even more fun) than facing challenges alone.

Students in idea-building classrooms also work on their social skills during each collaboration. This includes improving at listening to others' contributions and valuing them. It includes appropriate turn-taking and using nonverbal cues such as smiling, nodding, back-channeling, and body language.

Think of the negatives that can emerge without the element of Collaboration.

Monica designed pair and small-group activities so that students needed each other to accomplish the task (e.g., enhanced jigsaw, peer editing). She modeled social skills such as nodding, smiling, and asking questions. She encouraged her multilingual students to share in either or both languages while making sure others understood their contributions. She encouraged them to teach words and phrases of their home languages to group members, and she encouraged the group to use them in their projects.

Develop Language

Language is the cog of cogs in the complex workings of learning and growth. Imagine students in your classroom not using language. How much learning would happen? How much growth would happen?

Unfortunately, in most lessons around the United States, teachers, tests, and curriculums assume that students use a certain type and level of English. They aren't very flexible or open-minded regarding the various ways in which students communicate (e.g., using other languages, images, colloquial terms, nonverbal strategies, etc.). They often focus on narrow notions of "academic speaking and writing," which are usually five-paragraph-esque, generic, and expository.

Language is needed to give and share information in the construction of ideas, so we need to do all that we can to help students use it well. This does not mean that we overwhelm students with lots of sentence frames full of "academic language" or ding them for not using complete sentences. It does mean that we highlight, model, and scaffold language *that is useful* to students for building and communicating their ideas.

It also means that we get to know—as well as we can—how students currently use language to build up and communicate their ideas. Instead of using language listed in a curriculum or borrowed from generic vocabulary lists, we need to monitor how *clearly* students are using language (listening, speaking, reading, writing, and conversing) and consider how to help them improve it, if needed—for the purposes of clarity, not correctness—each step of the way.

Clarity is key, which means that students max out their communication resources. They might use their home language, both languages (translanguaging), slang, a drawing, or certain facial expressions to communicate to others as clearly as possible. Over time, we help students to communicate in a wide variety of settings, some of which include using more formal language (e.g., writing letters, giving speeches, writing articles, and recording podcasts) and some of which encourage students to communicate their ideas less formally and more creatively.

Language support varies a lot from year to year and student to student. It is messy, and we must remain patient and confident that students, when motivated to communicate, will push themselves to use clearer and clearer language to get things done—even if they are talking in groups out of earshot from us. As students communicate to build up ideas, and as they interact with a variety of texts and peers for a purpose, language develops. This is actually how language has been developing for thousands of years, in and out of school.

> Think of the negatives that can emerge without the element of Developing language.

Monica's teacher's guide suggested a long list of new words, from which she selected a handful that she thought would be useful for idea-building. In the first two weeks of the unit, Monica focused more on helping students interpret challenging language in the texts they were reading. She analyzed texts for language demands and chose some passages to read aloud and engage students in "language zoom-ins" in which they discuss how the language of the passages works to convey meanings. She often asked for translations in students' home languages, and they discussed interesting ways in which languages differ. In the last week, Monica focused on helping students push themselves to use language for productive (writing and speaking) communication of their ideas to others. This included strategies for speaking (intonation, pauses, stress, message organization) and for writing (punctuation, organization).

Make Brain–Body Connections

Connecting brain and body means having students engage in movement, sensory, drama, readers theater, music, labs, simulations, and play experiences. These experiences are more than just fun. They are often the most powerful and lasting types of learning (Hostetter, 2011), and they are vital for the learning approach in this book. Also, they are egregiously missing from most lessons around the country, especially in grades 4–12.

When they are used, though, educational magic happens. For example, I was recently in a class where students made up actions and acted out new content vocabulary that was helpful for building up an idea about plate tectonics. Other teachers had students act out a historical event, turn a short story into a song, act out different life cycles, and sit on each side of a long board over a fulcrum (like a seesaw) to show how to balance equations in math. The magic comes from learning being active and fun at the same time.

> Think of the negatives that can emerge without the element, Make brain–body connections.

More specifically, the power of brain–body learning experiences stems from the intertwined engagement of the body and the mind at the same time. When the body is involved, it helps students better remember content and language (Cook et al., 2008). For multilingual students, in particular, brain–body connections help them to remember lots of new language that surrounds them each day.

You can see more examples of these in Chapter 5 and Appendix B.

> *Monica's curriculum had very few brain–body (active learning) strategies in it. So in the character-theme unit, Monica started by having students choose important scenes in stories and act them out. After modeling a story-based chant that she had written with a focus on character traits and changes, Monica had groups pick a story to turn into a short chant or song. She had groups do a "talking tableau" for a poem or story in which they posed and froze together, and each actor told the audience who they were and what their pose represented. And she had students brainstorm movements to remember certain elements such as* trait, theme, dialogue, conflict, figurative language, *and* plot *to help her teach the items the following year.*

Formatively Assess

All along the learning process (idea-building and communicating), we must observe, reflect, provide feedback, and adjust instruction—sometimes all in the span of a few seconds! But we can't waste our formative assessment time and energies on trivial and forgettable things. We must engage in formative assessment *to help students build up meaty ideas, communicate them, and to grow.* Our feedback, for example, should focus on helping students as they gather building blocks, use language(s), and employ other strategies to be as clear and as strong as possible with respect to content, evidence, examples, and details. The focus should lean more toward constructing and communicating deeper understandings than toward correctness and surface understandings.

Throughout the unit, students are building their ideas and working on their products and performances. A vital component of the idea-building approach is allowing and helping students to revise their ideas, products, and performances (Darling-Hammond et al., 1995). As students receive feedback on strength and clarity, they make adjustments—or even major revisions—in order to maximize the strength and clarity of the idea.

For example, a student is reading to get building blocks for an idea about healthy food choices. The teacher notices that the student isn't rereading any parts of the text and isn't taking notes. The teacher says, "Don't forget that it helps a lot to reread any parts that seem important or that you don't quite understand. I do that all the time. And it really helps to write down a quick note to remember important information that you can turn into building blocks for your idea(s)."

Peers can also provide feedback. Students can partner with a wide range of others in the classroom to get feedback on clarity and strength, especially when they communicate their ideas with their products and performances. Peers offer varied perspectives on how clear and how strong an idea is, which gives the student who is sharing more ways to improve the idea. The teacher's perspective is important, of course, but it is not the only one to be valued in the classroom; if students just practice communicating with teachers, they miss out on many chances to expand their abilities to communicate with a wide range of others in life.

> *Monica listened closely to the content and language used in students' paired and small-group interactions. She often prompted students to ask to clarify and support questions. She analyzed their writings and visual organizers to make sure they included school and personal building blocks. She provided feedback on clarity, strength of evidence, interpersonal skills, and agency. She also held weekly check-in interviews with students to assess their confidence and feelings about their learning and school experience.*

ACTIVITY 4.2

How the Idea-Building Approach Elements Work Together to Achieve Pedagogical Justice

Cover up the second and third columns. Before moving your paper down to uncover what I wrote in the second column for each row, come up with your own answer for how the element fosters pedagogical justice for multilingual students. Then compare your response to the description in the middle column for each element. Add any notes that you can think of in the middle column. Then add examples from your setting in the right-hand column. Do this for each row.

Element	How It Fosters Pedagogical Justice	Your Examples
Outline the results	When we outline the results of students growing personally and effectively building and communicating their ideas, multilingual students are more prepared to do this in school, postsecondary education, and the world—as opposed to simply "envisioning" higher test scores, grades, or one-size-fits-all essays.	
Draft the big-idea statement(s)	Trusting multilingual students to build their own big and lasting ideas in a discipline gives them more purpose to learn, think, and communicate. This trust builds student confidence and agency.	
Design products and/or performances	Student creation of products and performances that communicate an idea to others inspires multilingual students to be subjects (makers and deciders) rather than objects (passive receptacles and test-takers).	
Know your students	Knowing your students' initial ideas, building blocks, interests, and goals helps you to design instruction and assessment that	

(Continued)

Element	How It Fosters Pedagogical Justice	Your Examples
	empowers rather than bores or overwhelms. In knowing students, we send the message that their uniqueness is a strength rather than an unwanted deviation from what is considered the norm (i.e., middle-class monolingual).	
Use building blocks (school and personal)	Multilingual students learn knowledge, facts, and skills to build or decide something, not just to get answers right on tests. When they use building blocks (cultural, linguistic, and content) from their own lives, this values their backgrounds, adds to the ideas of others in the class, fosters agency, and makes learning last.	
Motivate	All students have the right to engage in motivating learning experiences that value their perspectives and contributions. The building and communicating of original ideas tend to be more motivating than increasing test score percentages.	
Fill information gaps	Rather than just rehashing facts that they all know ("sharing for the show"), students speak, listen, read, and write to help one another build up their unique ideas. Students share definitions, opinions, and examples to strengthen and expand, rather than just slice up and accumulate.	
Collaborate	Daily collaboration with a wide range of peers develops vital language and social skills that are often neglected in accumulation learning. Collaboration also helps	

(Continued)

(Continued)

Element	How It Fosters Pedagogical Justice	Your Examples
	multilingual students to practice their language in safe settings and build relationships.	
Develop language	When we develop students' uses of language to communicate (not just to develop their language for testing purposes), we empower them with language that lasts because it is used purposefully and reinforced rather than just memorized. This is why content area classes are so important for language development.	
Make brain–body connections	Because mind–body instruction provides extra-verbal and active cues, the more that students can engage in movement, music, art, and drama to build up ideas, the better *all* students (and multilingual students, in particular) comprehend the content and language being learned.	
Model and scaffold	Modeling how to build up ideas directly shows multilingual students what the gathering, processing, and communicating processes look like. Scaffolding these processes keeps students engaged and pushing themselves to strengthen and clarify their thoughts and language uses along the way.	
Formatively assess	Students benefit from ongoing monitoring by teachers who provide feedback that is helpful for building and communicating ideas. This allows multilingual students to "try out" their thoughts and language on others and to iteratively revise their products and performances.	

Cultivating Students' Cultures and Languages

The elements of the Idea-Building Approach strengthen and are strengthened by the cultivation of students' varying cultures, experiences, and languages. For a deeper look at this topic, refer to work focused on culturally and linguistically responsive and sustaining pedagogies by Geneva Gay, H. Samy Alim, Sharroky Hollie, Gloria Ladson-Billings, Django Paris, and Zaretta Hammond. The elements build on their work and seek to revolutionize instruction so that it not only responds to and sustains students' cultural and linguistic strengths, but it cultivates them as a result of all that we do in school.

Cultivation means going beyond teachers' comments on how much they value students' assets. It means that in every lesson, every assessment, and everywhere students look and listen, they see how their cultures and languages are valuable and powerful. "Lip service" valuing isn't enough. We cannot say that we value student assets and then never use them to add value to learning or assessment. Assets need to be *useful*, and students need to see how they are useful in school and life. We need to create tasks and purposes in which students know that the assets they bring are useful to meaningful learning. When they co-build up an idea, for example, they can share cultural and linguistic building blocks and directly see their usefulness ("asset-ness") in the responses of their peers, on paper, and in their own minds. This feels much more valued than just hearing positive comments from the teacher.

Idea-building gives purpose to the use and development of language. Successful and meaningful uses of language motivate students to push themselves to use more and clearer language. Students at different levels of English proficiency can participate and learn at high levels. Students at beginning levels build up ideas, which is very different from how accumulation-based instruction treats students, often implying, "If you don't use correct language or do well on tests, you aren't smart or you haven't tried hard enough." It is pedagogical injustice to make students feel this way. Idea-building, on the other hand, fosters pedagogical justice because it meets students where they are, supports and nudges them forward as they build up ideas, and grows their sense of agency as they construct and communicate concepts and claims.

A commonly asked question is, "How do I make all of my units in all of my subject areas culturally and linguistically responsive, relevant, and sustaining?" One way in which the Idea-Building Approach addresses this need is by authentically valuing the content, skills, and communication styles that students bring to the building of each idea in each content area. It also values the diversity of ideas across students. It's OK and exciting when students share unique ideas with unique building blocks from their unique backgrounds. In the accumulation approach, by contrast, tapping into students' assets just to answer questions and choose the right answers is less effective.

A major challenge in culturally and linguistically sustaining education is changing the system and what it values as learning and evidence of it (see Chapters 2, 3, and 6). Ultimately, most accumulation settings rely on tests to tell them how well students are faring in the system. And the tests, as we saw in Chapter 3, are strongly biased toward the cultural norms, funds of knowledge, and language practices of middle-class monolingual English speakers. If this challenge is not addressed—if we can't get the system to value students' diverse assets, language uses, and outcomes—then the many efforts to be culturally and linguistically responsive will fall short.

Yet we also must be discerning, even within the content of this book, to consider the who, how, and what that goes into the strength and clarity of ideas. There is no rigid "universal" set of standards for an idea. An idea and its building blocks can and need to change, depending on the situation and people involved. Different kinds of evidence and clarifications are valued differently. For example, I am white, middle-class, multilingual (Spanish, Italian, and English), and grew up speaking English in the Pacific Northwest. I have had a range of experiences working in schools, living in other countries, reading many books and articles, and conversing with many different people. What I value and convey in this book about ideas, growth, and communication is influenced by these experiences, all of which differ from those of others.

We must therefore be mindful to overhaul learning with multiple lenses—not just the lens presented by me in this book. The approaches and suggestions in these chapters can be a start, but the scope is limited. Seek out other perspectives and wisdoms from others, many of whom are mentioned in this book. And collaborate with other educators who have a passion for the success and well-being of your students. Ultimately, the power and potential of idea-building and idea-communicating comes from helping your students see how their multicultural and multilingual assets contribute to ideas that make *their* worlds and *the* world a better place.

Authentic Communication

In order for students to build ideas and grow, the Idea-Building Approach both depends on and fosters authentic communication. Communication is authentic when it is used for real purposes (not just for show), which means it gets something done (e.g., builds up a valuable idea) and fills information gaps (Zwiers, 2019b). For example, when students share their personal building blocks with one another, they use language to share and receive *useful* information, which fills information gaps.

Sfard even argued that "communication, rather than playing a secondary role as the means for learning, is in fact the centerpiece of the story—the very object of learning" (2015, p. 250). This is a very different focus from testing content and skills. Think about how the 12 elements in this chapter depend on and foster communication abilities and why these abilities are so important in life. And you can think about how, if students are deprived of opportunities to develop communication skills and learn through communicating, this fosters pedagogical injustices described in Chapter 1.

In the Idea-Building Approach, students do all of these things:

- Listen, watch, and read to gain new content and skills as **building blocks** that help them build up ideas; and speak, represent, and write to communicate **new content** to others

- Are intrigued, interested, and **motivated** to communicate to build up the idea that resolves the intrigue and then communicate the idea to others

- Develop and practice increasingly clear **language** to understand and share building blocks, communicate their ideas to others, and negotiate meaning through extended dialogic idea-building

- Communicate to **collaborate**, helping selves and each other to build ideas, which tends to include lots of clarifying and supporting and stronger relationships

- Share insights, aspects, and building blocks from their respective backgrounds and **cultures**

- **Grow** in their sense of agency, emotional well-being, creativity, identity, and confidence as they communicate their novel ideas to others who validate their contributions

- Receptively communicate in order to develop successful **products and performances**; and they productively communicate to (a) help others with their development and (b) to share their ideas with others by way of the **product-performance**

- Receive and respond to helpful feedback from ongoing **formative assessment** by teachers, who also assess to adapt instruction

Communication is one of the most important skill sets of all for academic, social, and professional purposes. Idea-building and communication have a symbiotic relationship. The stronger the idea, the more and better the communication, and vice versa. But as we all know from experience, just "teaching" communication to teach communication (i.e., teaching reading for a reading test) isn't nearly as effective as scaffolding communication to create or accomplish something (e.g., learning about an environmental problem to create a public service announcement focused on ways to solve it).

CHAPTER IDEA

Here is one idea that you can build up from this chapter. If another idea was sparked for you, feel free to replace this one. Remember to add personal examples, definitions, questions, and insights as building blocks along with new blocks gathered from this chapter. Some sample blocks are provided.

IDEA STATEMENT: Idea-building, like a healthy tree, will produce deeper roots and more fruit—and it will take time.		
		Roots include social skills, language, and content concepts, agency.
Fruit includes abilities to foster relationships, be creative, improve the world.	Relationships are really important to students.	
	Students like to build and create—not memorize someone else's ideas.	

References

Alim, H. S., & Paris, D. (2017). What is culturally sustaining pedagogy and why is it important? In D. Paris, & H. S. Alim (Eds.), *Culturally sustaining pedagogies: Teaching and learning for justice in a changing world* (pp. 1–17). Teacher's College Press.

Bransford, J. D., Brown, A. L., & Cocking, R. R. (Eds.). (1999). *How people learn: Brain, mind, experience, and school.* National Academy Press.

Billings, E., & Mueller, P. (2017). *Quality student interactions: Why are they crucial to language learning and how can we support them?* NYSED. http://www.nysed.gov/bilingual-ed

Cook, S. W., Mitchell, Z., & Goldin-Meadow, S. (2008). Gesturing makes learning last. *Cognition*, 106(2), 1047–1058.

Darling-Hammond, L., & Adamson, F. (2010). *Beyond basic skills: The role of performance assessment in achieving 21st century standards of learning.* Stanford University.

Darling-Hammond, L., Ancess, J., & Falk, B. (1995). *Authentic assessment in action: Studies of schools and students at work.* Teachers College Press.

Delahooke, M. (2019). *Beyond behaviors: Using brain science and compassion to understand and solve children's behavioral challenges* (1st ed.). PESI.

Hostetter, A. B. (2011). When do gestures communicate? A meta-analysis. *Psychological Bulletin*, 137(2), 297–315.

Johnston, P. H. (2012). *Opening minds: Using language to change lives.* Stenhouse.

Nichols, M. (2019). *Building bigger ideas: A process for teaching purposeful talk.* Heinemann.

Palincsar, A. & Herrenkohl, L. (2010). Designing collaborative learning contexts. *Theory Into Practice*, 41(1): 26–32.

Sfard, A. (2015). Why all this talk about talking classrooms? Theorizing the relations between talking and learning. In L. B. Resnick, C. S. C. Asterhan, & S. N. Clarke (Eds.), *Socializing intelligence through academic talk and dialogue* (pp. 245–254). American Educational Research Association. https://doi.org/10.3102/978-0-935302-43-1_19

Stipek, D. (2002). *Motivation to learn: Integrating theory and practice.* Allyn and Bacon.

Wells, G. (2015). Dialogic learning: Talking our way into understanding. In T. Dragonas, K. J. Gergen, S. McNamee, & E. Tseliou (Eds.), *Education as social construction contributions to theory, research and practice* (pp. 62–90). The Taos Institute.

Zwiers, J. (2019a). *Next steps with academic conversations: New ideas for improving learning with classroom talk.* Stenhouse.

Zwiers, J. (2019b). *The communication effect: How to enhance learning by building ideas and bridging information gaps.* Corwin.

Instruction 5

> Only the educated are free.
>
> —Epictetus

To meet the needs of multilingual students and achieve pedagogical justice, we can't just push for a handful of "sheltered instruction" activities, tell teachers to use lots of visuals, tell students to use lots of sentence frames, or adopt new computer-based "solutions." Many professional development and reform efforts have done these things already, with minimal success in the things that matter. We need to overhaul *all* levels of instruction.

But how? We start with the elements of the Idea-Building Approach described in the previous chapter. We apply the elements to the structure and organization of learning in the classroom, starting with curriculums, and then we zoom in on units, lessons, and activities. If you find yourself asking for more examples, refer to Appendix B.

Overhauling Curriculums

Many of the large, all-in-one curriculums do not align well with the suggestions in this book. These curriculums tend to focus on covering state standards, transmitting information (without really *using* it), accumulating answers and points, giving back the right answers, and preparing for tests. Large curriculums (especially for English language arts [ELA]) are jam-packed with suggestions and activities, trying to "cram it all in" in less than a school year. Moreover, in many of these "silver-bullet" offerings, multilingual learners are literally sidelined to the margins in the form of generic scaffolding strategies and tips that were never intended to promote idea-building or higher-order thinking to begin with. Lessons tend to prepare students for quizzes, benchmark assessments, and standardized tests. You can spot these types of lessons when you can't see logical connections between activities within a lesson or between lessons.

Overhauling a curriculum for idea-building at the curriculum level is challenging for several reasons. First, a curriculum has many moving parts and resources. It can get overwhelming to modify a semester- or yearlong curriculum to be cohesively focused on idea-building and growth, especially given the limited amount of time that teachers have for this kind of work. It's easier to just to keep using them, as is.

Second, course content is often hard to change. You usually have curriculum materials that were designed to work together a certain way. Moving units around, or adding or subtracting them, can end up taking more effort and time than you have available. And not having a curriculum at all—that is, coming up with your own—is even more daunting.

Third, course curriculums tend toward focusing on accumulation and standardization rather than idea-building and valuing student differences. The deeper these foundational differences are, the harder it is to replace the "flawed parts" with the 12 elements outlined in Chapter 4.

Despite the challenges, course-level overhauling is worth doing if we want to improve school-based learning for all students—and for serving our multilingual students in particular.

ACTIVITY 5.1
Curriculum Overhaul Tool

The first column in this tool contains core features that each curriculum should have. If you are searching for and deciding on a curriculum (i.e., piloting), try using a tool like this one. To be blunt, you won't likely find any curriculum for sale (no matter the price) or online that has these in abundance. Most curriculums still have accumulation features. So this tool will be more useful for those of you who have a curriculum with potential or are designing your own curriculums. I work with many districts that do both.

The second column contains questions for analyzing your curriculum, and the third column is for adding your answers. Choose a course syllabus or outline and start jotting down answers to help you see if an overhaul is needed. Feel free to add features or questions based on the information in Chapters 1 through 4.

Figure 5.1 Curriculum Overhaul Tool

Feature	Questions	Your Answers
Big Picture	Why is this curriculum (course) necessary?	
	Does this curriculum help students to learn the most important big ideas of its topic?	
	Do the lessons provide students with high-quality building blocks, and do they prompt for and value personal building blocks from varied cultural backgrounds?	
	What areas of personal growth (see Chapter 2) are woven into the units of this curriculum?	
	Do the ideas encourage multicultural perspectives and voices (not just focused on dominant themes and ways of knowing)?	
Assessment	Do the assessments and products and performances engage students in building up ideas and motivate them to communicate their ideas through them?	
	Do the assessments allow and encourage students to express their learning using languages beyond just English? Can students use other forms of communication?	

(Continued)

Figure 5.1   Curriculum Overhaul Tool (Continued)

Feature	Questions	Your Answers
	How is the course graded? Is it traditional (points for right answers) or focused on assessing the quality of ideas and communication? Or a mix of both? Does it provide suggestions for feedback to students as they build up their ideas and for ways to score and grade students' larger performances and products? Do the unit topics and their essential questions build on one another, preparing students for the next unit? Does the order make sense?	
Organization	Are there big ideas that the units help students to build over the entire course? Are they in a logical order? (Think above the unit level of ideas to consider if there are ideas that span across all units and that are highly useful in the discipline and in life.) Which unit is least necessary or least interesting, in case you run out of school year? (Consider the least necessary idea(s) to put near the end of the course, in the likely event of running out of time because you prioritized depth over breadth.) Is there anything missing? (Think about what information or skill work students might need to build up ideas.)	

I realize that most teachers and schools won't be able to overhaul curriculums in major ways. For this reason, I recommend an incremental approach, beginning with a run-through of the overhaul process to see what changes might be manageable this year. Teach the curriculum with the changes and gather some evidence from students (other than test scores) and from other teachers (if multiple teachers teach the course) in order to reflect on how the changes made a difference. And more importantly, *don't forget the students.* Ask them what they liked and didn't like about the learning in the course. Ask them which strategies, assessments, resources, and so on they thought were effective. Ask them about the ideas they built and the relationships with peers they developed. Ask them if they prefer building ideas over memorizing information and practicing skills for tests.

Overhauling Units

Overhauling at the unit level is more tangible and flexible than overhauling at the course level. Teachers have more control over what happens in a unit, especially in schools and districts that encourage their teachers to design and redesign units of instruction. The downside, of this overhauling (and of great teaching), is that it's a fair amount of work.

In a nutshell, we overhaul a unit by strengthening the dozen elements of the Idea-Based Approach described in Chapter 4. So grab a unit plan that you will teach in the upcoming months and use the suggestions in this section to overhaul it. You can also look at Appendix B for overhauled unit examples across grade levels and content areas. As you overhaul your unit with these suggestions, reflect on how much more encouraging and engaging it is becoming for achieving pedagogical justice for your multilingual students.

Objectives

First, look at what the unit is meant to teach. It helps to look at any objectives or standards often listed at the beginning of the unit. See if a concept or claim (big idea) is stated or implied. If there is an essential question, it can help in identifying the idea. If not, try to find the most important objective or standard, or try to see some commonalities between the standards listed in the list. See if standards converge on a larger idea in the discipline. You might even have to comb through the lessons or look at the unit assessment(s) to identify or come up with the unit's big idea or argument. See Chapter 2 for additional ideas on generating big ideas for a unit.

If your unit has an essential question, make sure it is engaging. I have seen many essential questions that bore me even before I get to the question mark (e.g., How can we use punctuation to make our writing more effective?). Effective essential questions tend to have a core idea to build or a decision to make in order to answer it.

In one sixth-grade ELA unit, for example, the essential question was "What is a community?" I saw a lot of focus on rights and responsibilities in the unit, so I changed the question to "What rights and responsibilities to others should we have, and why?" in order to make it more engaging and to have more potential for idea-building. Then I came up with this big-idea statement: *We all have rights and responsibilities to others*. This is like a thesis statement for starting to answer the essential question. This idea statement might change or vary as the unit develops, but it helps to have something solid to start with. Remember, the "tests" for a good idea statement are as follows:

- Are we happy when a student says it? (Is it something that we want students to learn?)
- Do we want to know a lot more (e.g., clarifications and examples)?
- Is it buildable?

Assessment

Then ask the following questions about the assessments in the unit:

- Do the assessments during and at the end of the unit show meaningful learning and growth?
- Is there an end product-performance that engages students in building up an idea *and* motivates them to communicate their idea to others?
- Are students given some choice and creativity in how they learn, build, and communicate?
- Do assessments encourage and value the use of students' diverse interests, stories, and cultural practices?
- Do students understand the high expectations for the products-performances and know how they will be evaluated?

Make changes to ensure that all of the answers to these assessment questions are yes. For example, I changed the final assessment of the sixth-grade unit, which was writing an essay, to creating public service announcements about rights and responsibilities. The announcement could be a poster or a drama presentation or even a digital creation. There would be a written component to describe the interpretations and justifications supporting the products and performances.

If you think that any of your unit's assessments might lean toward being boring or ineffective, improve them or lose them. I have seen teachers make some small changes to assessments and vastly improve the engagement and learning of a unit. For example, one teacher I know always tries to turn the less interesting essential questions into controversial questions that students answer in a poster presentation. Another teacher turns final essays into articles that students submit to different publications.

Building Blocks (New Content and Skills)

Once you have a solid enough sense of the big idea or decision for a unit, along with the products-performances, then it's time to figure out what building blocks (new content and skills) are needed for students to be successful at building and communicating the idea.

You can make a list of the informational building blocks (facts and skills) that are vital for building up the idea and for coming up with high-quality products-performances. You can also use an idea visual (which students might also use) in Figure 5.2 to lay out your initial set

Figure 5.2   Sample Idea-Building Visual for Unit Planning

We all have rights and responsibilities to others.					
Mr. R. learned to share his water in the story.		What is a responsibility?	We need to take care of parks.		People should vote.
What is a right?	Which rights are not given to us?	We have a right to a good education.		We need to follow the rules.	
			Being nice helps make the world nicer.		Everyone needs respect.

of building blocks. These will then inform what you do in your lessons. Here is my sample from the sixth-grade unit.

Look at your list (or visual) and circle the blocks that are new to most of your students. If you are not sure about which building blocks to emphasize, you can have a casual chat session with students using images and questions to get a better idea of their strengths and needs.

Keep in mind that some of the most important building blocks come from reading texts and seeing the world with a justice-focused perspective. This means that as students read and build up ideas, they use a lens that considers who created the text and why. Every student needs to be a "critical consumer" of content (i.e., of the ideas they build and of the building blocks that they use) in any text, and they should read to understand the varying ways in which texts (all kinds of texts and messages) influence readers and the world—positively and negatively.

For building up the idea in Figure 5.2, for example, I might put definitions and examples (building blocks) from texts or from school or life in which students' rights (social, political, and pedagogical) are not supported. Then I use these blocks to sketch out lessons that will help students "gather and process them" in the first two-thirds of the unit. For example, one lesson might include reading an article that defines civic responsibilities.

Organization

When you have a solid enough list of building blocks that the unit's lessons will emphasize, it's time to organize the lessons within the unit. You can start with your existing curriculum's organization, of course. If you don't like the order or if you have added other topics, texts, case studies, activities, and projects, then you will need to reorganize.

The first lessons should engage students in the overall unit focus and idea-building or decision-making. There is often an experience, simulation, presentation, experiment, or juicy question that gets students thinking by moving, viewing, and/or creating. These lessons are opportunities for clarifying what students will do, create, decide, and produce or perform at the unit's end.

The next lessons provide students with new building blocks. These are the "middle" weeks when students will emphasize gathering and processing new information using a variety of texts, experiences, fieldwork, and projects.

In the final week(s), students work more on their final project, product, and/or performance. They still might do some gathering and processing of new blocks, but the emphasis is on using and refining the building blocks from the previous mini-projects, lessons, and activities in the larger project. You can tell students to start thinking about and even working on their final product-performance in the first weeks, but you won't give them much time in class to work on it until their expertise, skills, and materials are gathered and their ideas are more developed.

Purposeful Questions and Answers

Questions tend to abound in school. The purpose of asking questions and giving the right answers should be to learn. Yet many teachers ask questions to assess whether or not students know things. Even if teachers do ask questions to move the discussion along and dig more deeply into a topic, students often think they are being tested. When teachers and students all see that questions and answers can serve the purpose of idea-building, then learning can become more engaging and effective. For many students, if they don't think an answer is helping them or is worth whatever reward (good feeling, helping the teacher, and points), they won't answer. And if they are called on (e.g., their names get pulled out of the cup), they will tend to answer with the bare minimum. But if they think their answer will contribute to their or others' idea-building—especially if they think others don't have the information already—then they are more likely to share beyond the bare minimum.

How Overhauled Units Foster Pedagogical Justice

Units overhauled for idea-building and growth focus classroom energy on students' development and ownership of unique ideas. The unit products and performances are opportunities to communicate these ideas to others. This unit structure—because it is less focused on "checking off the standards boxes" than accumulation-based units—gives multilingual students the needed depth and focus for learning. There is teacher direction, but with plenty of encouragement of creativity and flexibility. There are plenty of chances to constructively interact (students helping others learn), which strengthens relationships and social skills. These things contribute to student agency and a positive academic identity. And when multilingual students have a chance to bring in their backgrounds and ways of using language for idea-building, they and their learning thrive.

Overhauling Lessons

In idea-building instruction, the design of learning experiences tends to get "creatively messy." Following the pacing guide with pristine fidelity, as you know, doesn't work well for many multilingual students. Neither does inundating them with disconnected grade-level texts, comprehension questions, and practice quizzes. Students need to *build*, which takes time and focus. Educators need to be artists and scientists as we design engaging lessons, activities, case studies, and projects that help them build and grow.

Let's say you have a unit mostly outlined. You have a rough idea of the big idea(s) that students will build up (or will decide, if an argument), along with the essential question(s) and likely performance task(s). You have lesson topics and have put them in a logical order, more or less. Now you need to flesh out the lessons into opportunities for idea-building and communicating.

In all likelihood, you will need to change the focus and nature of your lessons. Many schools use a variety of "step-based" lesson plans (e.g., Danielson, 2009; Hunter, 1984). They might have five steps, seven steps, nine steps, or more. Most of them start with the teacher providing a "hook" or modeling a skill. Teachers then gradually release responsibility of the skill or thinking to students, having them do the learning tasks with less and less help over time (a.k.a., I do–We do–You do, etc.). This process is a form of scaffolding (see Chapter 4), in which supports are taken away over time so that students build independence and proficiency in whatever they are building and learning (Wood et al., 1976).

Another type of lesson is an inquiry-based lesson, in which students start with a juicy question or odd experience and come up with answers and explanations for what they saw, heard, hypothesized, and so on. One popular inquiry-based format in science, for example, is called a "Five-E" lesson, which starts the lesson with engagement and then moves into exploring, explaining, elaborating, and evaluating. Notice the potential for idea-building and language use in these various parts of the lesson.

In this chapter, we focus on two types of lessons: idea-building lessons and idea-communicating lessons. Both types have some overlap with the more specific lesson plan formats mentioned in the previous two paragraphs, but there are some differences. Idea-*building* lessons focus on learning the "building blocks," whereas idea-*communicating* lessons spend more time on putting the blocks together into a product or performance that communicates the idea to others. In idea-building lessons, there is more emphasis on receptive and interactive language use. In idea-communicating lessons, there is more emphasis on productive language use and development. Both types emphasize personal growth, communication, and student–student interaction.

Both types of lessons can be short, fitting within a 30- to 50-minute window, or long, lasting several days. The length will depend on the curriculum you are using, the type of texts used, personal preferences, and the needs of students. This year they might need a two-day lesson on a topic, and the next year they might need a 50-minute lesson.

Idea-Building Lessons: Prepping–Gathering–Processing

In an idea-building lesson, three "modes" form a foundation for lasting learning of informational and skills-based building blocks: prepping, gathering, and processing. These are related to into-through-beyond and pre-during-post lesson progressions, often used for teaching reading. Yet in the Idea-Building Approach, we broaden the scope of these three modes and apply them to any type of learning in a lesson that focuses on learning new knowledge and skills used to build up concepts and claims.

Prepping

Prepping means setting students up for success in the lesson and the unit. Prepping tends to take more time and energy in the initial lessons of a unit and in the first minutes of most lessons. It includes clarifying what is expected of students for the lesson (or unit) and the initial engagement strategies, reviews, and connections to previous learning. Also during prepping, teachers can model and provide students with background knowledge and language they will need in the lesson, as well as pre-assess to get to know students' knowledge, interests, and abilities.

> How does having high and clear expectations foster pedagogical justice?

Here are some helpful aspects of prepping for idea-building.

High and Clear Expectations. A huge pillar of this overhaul work is having high and clear expectations for what multilingual students can do and trusting them to take on more responsibility and complexity over time. These high expectations should not be assessment-based demands ("You must do all these things or else you will get a low grade!"), but rather they should be encouraging and guiding ("I know you can do these things and am excited to see the results."). We also need to clarify our expectations so that students know what we are looking for in terms of idea-building, products-performances, social interactions, character development, and personal growth. Such clarification is extra important for multilingual, nondominant, and neurodiverse students because curriculums and assessments typically make a host of assumptions about what students can and can't do. See Appendix B for examples.

Attention Focusers. Attention focusers are strategies to pique students' interest and focus their attention on the work of the unit. They are ways to foster motivation for doing the hard work of gathering and processing new information. They are often in the form of short videos, demonstrations, labs, images, and engaging read-alouds, often with meaty essential questions guiding them. These questions should be relevant to student lives and, when possible, two-sided (controversial). For example, a teacher might drop a penny and a feather in a vacuum-sealed tube. They fall at the same rate. She asks the class, "Why?" Another teacher reads a historical account that contradicts commonly held beliefs about an event. He asks, "What's true?" Or a math teacher shows a clip of the huge garbage island floating in the ocean, and asks, "Mathematically, what should we figure out, and what should we do?" All attention focusers should get students excited about building up answers and ideas.

Attached to the focuser can be an explanation of why students should work to build up the idea or make a decision, such as in the following examples:

- You will answer a question that has puzzled historians for years.
- You will create a product that helps scientists solve or explain ___.
- You will engage in lesson activities and read these stories to build up an idea for how we can be better people—and to write your own story that communicates a different life lesson.

- You will find out which of these ten animals is the culprit.

- You will create a work of art (or music) that has never existed on this planet before, and it will communicate a powerful truth to its audience.

Connections and Reviews. Connections and reviews ask students to bring up related information that they already have learned. Often, the teacher asks questions that start with "Have you ever . . . ? Do you remember when we learned about . . . ? Who has . . . ?" And for reviewing (e.g., if students don't seem to remember what they need for this lesson), you can start with, "In order to build up our ideas about ___, let's review and keep in mind what we learned last month about ___ and the ideas we built up about ___. Here are some key points and images to remind us. Let's revisit some building blocks from our previous unit that we might use in this unit."

Pre-assessing Knowledge, Interests, and Abilities. You can ask key questions to get a better pre-picture that will inform the instruction in the lesson. Some of your students' knowledge, skills, and interests will impress you, and you should try to use them in the lesson. You can have them raise their hands ("Who has . . . ?"), put up number or fingers ("How confident do you feel at ___? Put up between one and three fingers"), draw on mini-white boards ("Draw your idea of the water cycle"), fill in anticipation guides, do a Quick Write, put sticky notes with answers up on posters up front along a continuum, or the like. All of this information can help you with the current lesson (with some quick adjustments if you can), but you might need more time to adjust things in the next lesson.

> How does providing useful language foster pedagogical justice?

Providing Background Knowledge and Language. If, from the previous paragraphs, you find out that students need a little extra information, language, or skill development for the lesson, then try to provide it early on. Also think about which aspects of language are needed. It is common to provide vocabulary (i.e., pre-teaching it), but (a) don't spend too much time on words out-of-context, and better yet, (b) consider not pre-teaching words at all and instead teach the words as they arise in the lesson. Lesson time is precious, and *in-context* is always better than *out-of-context*. Consider the types of grammar-syntax and text organization features that will help students both comprehend and communicate during idea-building and after. For example, a teacher teaching argumentation had students work on the organization structure for a paragraph for each building block.

She emphasized starting with a topic sentence and following it with clarifying and supporting details. Why? Because it would be clearer for their readers. And if students need a little refresher on certain skills they will use in the lesson (analyzing, inferring, comparing, synthesizing, interpreting, etc.), it's likely worth the time.

Teacher Modeling of Skills. Students can often benefit from seeing a skill or process modeled before they try it out. But they should be motivated to watch the modeling beyond just being assessed on it. Motivation can stem from the attention focusers plus the overall topic and tasks they will engage in (see the Motivation section in Chapter 4). The modeling shouldn't be too long; it's not supposed to be a lecture, and you should think aloud at strategic times to share how you, an expert, are thinking about what you are doing (with an emphasis on gathering or processing new information). One teacher modeled how to fill in both sides of an argument balance scale visual organizer (see Appendix B) with the issue, "Should we go to Mars?" The students then did similar work in pairs with a different issue.

Gathering

In order to build up ideas in each lesson, students need to "gather" building blocks. This means taking in initial information in the form of facts, details, examples, evidence, definitions, and so on, which are useful for constructing concepts and claims. The teacher could (and too many do) spend the bulk of lessons lecturing (presenting), but we all know how ineffective long lectures are.

Instead, here are some methods for helping students gather the initial building blocks that they need during a lesson.

> How does gathering new learning through experiences foster pedagogical justice?

Experiences. Experiences (e.g., experiments, mysteries, crime scene simulations, history simulations, games, dramas, field trips) involve students. These are not as common as written texts, but they can be much more powerful for gathering and remembering information. For example, when I taught eighth graders about energy, I had different groups perform a lab in which they sent cars down ramps of different heights and gathered data on the distances the cars traveled. They then shared their varied findings with other groups and had to come up with a working hypothesis about energy, its origins, and its transformations. A science teacher used pictures of animal tracks to figure out which kind of animal stole food from a camp. An ELA teacher had student groups act out different scenes from a play. A math teacher presented two statistics that supported two sides of an argument and asked, "Which side is more right?"

Fieldwork and Service. Assign gathering experiences that engage students in the world, often with real-world people. For example, students might interview family members or people in the community who have various jobs or positions in government. Students usually gather data on an issue or problem, data that they will use to inform or support a solution to the problem. One teacher had students develop interview questions for family members on their views of technology use by young people. Students can also get involved in a service project, which has numerous benefits: working together with others to make a real difference, developing relationships with the community, learning about others, and authentically using and learning language to communicate.

Case Studies. Case studies zoom students into an engaging story or perspective within the larger unit topic (e.g., roles of women in the Civil War; a family that lives in a rainforest, the evolution of the peppered moth, a successful student business, life after the Trail of Tears). Case studies like these provide students with a deeper and often more human side of the concepts or claims they are building. One teacher, for example, used a case study of Martin Luther King Jr.'s decision to not cross the Edmund Pettus Bridge in Selma, Alabama, on March 9, 1965. She posed the question, "Should King and demonstrators have crossed the bridge that day?" Students needed to build up both sides by learning a lot more about the context, politics, and key figures in that time.

Other variations of case studies include realistic fiction stories and children's books. These narratives, written at varying levels and often including helpful visuals and illustrations, can intrigue students and stick with them. I worked with a fourth-grade teacher who used Jane Yolen's children's book *Encounter* (1996) to teach about the arrival of Columbus through the eyes of a young Taino boy. She used the case study not only to build an idea focused on empathy and perspective-taking but also to discuss colonization and the silencing of voices throughout history.

A variation of a case study is a family interview. Students craft questions for family members in order to learn more about a member and potentially use (with permission) some of the information as building blocks for ideas they are building. Questions can yield powerful stories as well as information on language practices, family culture, values, beliefs, histories, and much more. Students are encouraged to ask follow-up questions to clarify and support and to practice their conversation skills. An added bonus is the deepening of relationships between family members.

Collaboration. Collaboration helps students to orally share blocks that they and their peers can use. Examples of this collaboration include whole-class, group, and paired conversations, along with structured interactions such as pair-shares, Socratic Seminars, jigsaws, and peer editing. One popular activity, called Stronger and Clearer Pairs (Appendix B), prompts students to share their emerging ideas and current building blocks with three partners in a row. Each student gets a minute or so to talk. The partner asks clarifying questions as needed. Collaborative interactions can happen before, during, and after the other strategies in this section.

Nonwritten Texts. These texts communicate ideas and building blocks to "readers-watchers-listeners" in multimodal ways (e.g., videos, podcasts, images, songs, art, dance, oral stories, advertisements, websites, speeches, and presentations). Lectures would also fit into this category, as students usually need to listen and use visuals (e.g., slides with images). But be ever cognizant that most students can productively listen to a teacher's "lecture/presentation" for no more than a few minutes without a pause for taking notes, drawing, sharing with a partner, or organizing the information in some way. Any type of teacher lecture presentation should be focused on providing clear and strong building blocks.

Rather than just think "Here is a break from reading wordy texts," we want students to think that nonwritten texts are powerful providers of building blocks for ideas. And we also want students to be able to "read" a wide range of "texts" in the world. This means being able to read people, situations, problems, and injustices throughout life. They need to recognize when they are being persuaded, manipulated, deceived, silenced, and used—and when they are being valued, validated, respected, and lifted up.

Technology/AI. Technology (computer programs, internet, social media, apps, artificial intelligence [AI], etc.) offers a range of different uses and text types, often combined. Subscription-based computer programs tend to focus on reading and math support, usually focused on skills. Apps can provide a variety of information and ways to learn, including second language development, digital flashcards, book collections, lessons for playing a musical instrument, educational games, speech therapy, software coding, ways to create books, and literacy development.

The internet is also a huge collection of information sources, many of which are helpful and many of which are not. Social media can be used to connect, share information, and build relationships, but it can also be harmful and waste time. Artificial intelligence apps can answer a wide range of questions and even cull information from the internet to write essay-like responses to prompts. This can be a problem if students just turn these responses in, claiming to have written them on their own.

Whatever technology (app, site, program) you use, use it *as a tool* for helping students build and communicate ideas. This means to think of it is a provider of building blocks, a nurturer of idea-building skills, and a helper for organizing the blocks and communicating the idea to others.

Written Texts. In school, written materials tend to use lots of paragraphs, complex sentences, and challenging words. Common texts include articles, primary sources, textbook chapters, novels, poems, opinion pieces, biographies, and manuals. Reading comprehension is mostly about figuring out relationships in the text that help the reader construct the intended meaning in the reader's mind. These relationships can be between topics, paragraphs, text features, and words. Most of the relationships depend on one or more thinking skills, such as cause and effect, inference, interpretation, compare/contrast, supporting ideas, empathy, metaphorical thinking, and clarifying. Students need to see all texts as potential providers of useful building blocks and some texts as "idea inspirers."

Many multilingual students don't like written texts because their schools mostly used texts to test their comprehension. Overhauling this mindset is challenging but vital. It's time to say something like, "I'm not going to ask you questions to test your understanding. We might ask questions at times, but their focus will be on helping you choose and clarify and shape the text's information into building blocks that you will use to build up your own idea on this topic."

It is common to ask and answer a wide range of questions during the gathering phase of a lesson. Often, the questions are in a text, on worksheets, or from a teacher. And most students are tired of being asked questions that test their comprehension. Rather, sparingly ask questions that help students to clarify and strengthen the building blocks—ask questions that help them build. And even more importantly, have *students* authentic questions as they are reading, thinking, and talking with others. They can ask the author of the text ("What does that mean?") and ask their peers questions that help them gather needed information for building. In a pair-share, for example, one fifth-grade teacher tells her students, "When you are listening, ask at least one clarify question that you really want to know. You are listening to gather building blocks from your partner, and those blocks need to be as clear as possible."

Gathering building blocks also requires the following:

- A range of skills for understanding and interpreting texts, experiences, people, and the world. You can emphasize skills that are most needed for gathering building blocks (e.g., listening, watching, interpreting, inferring, identifying cause and effect, and empathizing).

- Receptive language abilities. These include knowing how to use text features, discern loaded language, use transitions, and understand complex sentences.

- Abilities to *evaluate* which information is valuable enough to remember. This is akin to taking a close look at a building block to decide if it is strong enough to use in the building.

Finally, the gathering mode in a lesson is prime time for *filling information gaps*, a key element of the Idea-Building Approach. One common form of gap-filling is reading new information that one needs and wants for building—which is, by the way, typically why adults (like you) read (books like this). It is also effective to have students read different texts, interact, and share with each other, such as what happens in jigsaw activities. When students share building blocks, they fill information gaps for one another.

Gathering one's own personal building blocks, along with the personal building blocks of others, creates powerful opportunities to learn about others, have one's own experiences and knowledge validated, fill information gaps, and build relationships with each other. See Chapters 2 and 4 for more on how building blocks are used to build up ideas.

Processing

Gathering information and doing nothing with it doesn't tend to last very long in the brain. After students gather the information and consider it to be useful for building up an idea, they then need to *process* it. Processing means using and working with the information in different and deeper ways than just memorizing it for tests and quizzes.

Here are some effective methods for processing building blocks during lessons.

Movement. Movement (e.g., hand motions, whole-body movement, games, drama, and standing up to talk) connects muscle movement and gestures to important information to be learned. These kinesthetic experiences help students to make brain–body connections that make learning last. This is one of the most powerful yet least used methods for teaching all students. It is even more powerful for multilingual students because it can help them see and remember new language that is often attached to the movement or experience.

For example, a teacher might encourage students to move their bodies to show a science idea such as the water cycle. As they move and verbalize key terms (evaporate, condense, precipitate, etc.), these terms and the processes stick in the brain much better than just looking at a picture of the cycle. In addition, having students come up with actions can solidify them even more. Some teachers have students act out new words in a text or scenes in a story. Other teachers have students stand up to talk in pairs and even have pairs come up with actions to remember new concepts. Math teachers have students act like variables and coefficients to physically balance equations; other teachers have students go outside to measure things to create their own problems.

We tend to see more movements in primary grades, but their use tapers off way too quickly in Grades 4 and up. They are *not* too juvenile for secondary students, even though some older students might act like they are not interested. For example, you can use hand motions to teach cell division, balancing of equations, foreshadowing, and types of historical causes. Students, regardless of age, tend to enjoy the experiences, and they better remember the concepts (see more movement ideas in Appendix B).

Students should also be tasked with coming up with movements that help them learn. In this way, they engage even more by creating an action that communicates a term or concept to be remembered. They should also be encouraged to use or adapt movements from their own cultural backgrounds and practices. They can work together, compare, decide on the most memorable movement, and explain their reasons for the movement.

Hands-On and Sensory Experiences. Students also need sensory experiences (e.g., experiments, music, rhythm, tactility, manipulatives, art, kinetic sand, objects, money, arts, crafts, being outside, etc.). They need experiences that engage senses other than the main two senses that we see throughout most lessons: visual (e.g., watching the teacher and reading) and auditory (e.g., listening to the teacher talk). There is a wide range of studies grounded in brain research that show that learning thrives when different strategies engage students' senses of touch, music, smell, and even taste (Willis & Willis, 2020). You can have students work with their hands (clay, painting, origami, fidget toys, etc.) while communicating. It can distract students at times, but for many students, it focuses their thinking and gives more solid reasons to use language.

Hands-on experiences do different sensory things for the brain than just reading or listening. For example, any time students can hold, touch, feel, and manipulate real items, materials, and objects, the likelihood of language comprehension and lasting learning increases. True, such things can be expensive and challenging to manage, but the learning power is always worth it, especially for multilingual students who need that extra connection to concrete things when lots of language surrounding them is abstract and overwhelming. For example, you can use kinetic sand to teach geometry; you can use modeling clay to teach animal adaptations; you can provide a variety of art materials (beads, feathers, yarn, toothpicks, leaves, etc.) to create a mixed-media representation of themes in a story.

Story-fy. "Story-fy" means to turn a process or concept into a narrative, or to give it narrative-like qualities. Students can get tired of memorizing facts, concepts, and processes, so it can help to jazz learning up a bit with characters and plots. For example, a teacher turned the process of generating and using electricity into a story, starting with the sun and having electrons as characters. Another teacher had students turn diary entries from the early colonies into short stories.

A variation of story-fying is to have students play the roles of certain parts of a process. For example, students learning about erosion meet in pairs to have conversations about their impressive feats of erosion—one partner as a glacier and one partner as a river. Another teacher has students turn math concepts (adding fractions with different denominators) into short skits. Other teachers turn historical events into mysteries, some with multiple endings that students can choose and argue for. Becoming or relating to characters, wondering how a character will change and act, and wondering how a story will end is intriguing (see the Motivation section in Chapter 4 for more on intrigue).

Visuals. Visuals include any visual aid that can help students "see," build up, decide on, or communicate an idea (chart, diagram, graph, graphic organizer, T-chart, table, cycle, work of art, etc.). Visuals show rather than tell, though there is often some telling and reading as the visual is created or used. Most visuals serve to scaffold a process or thinking skill, showing relationships visually. For example, Venn diagrams show similarities and differences, cause-and-effect diagrams show causes and effects, semantic maps show ordinate and subordinate levels of information, and an argument balance scale shows the support of each side of an issue and the evaluation of each side's strength.

Students can use typical visuals such as charts, semantic maps, timelines, and the like, but remind them that visuals are not ends in and of themselves—not just forms to be filled in and turned in for points. Rather, they are *tools* for organizing building blocks and skills toward the goal of building up larger concepts and claims. For example, a teacher might have students fill in a jigsaw matrix after reading different texts about the factors that helped the Mongol Empire expand. The teacher reminds them that the charts are for them to use for developing their ideas for their final projects.

Moreover, there is a lot of processing power in having students come up with their own visual representations of the ideas they are building. I have been in classrooms where students are busy creating and talking about visual organizers for crafting poems, coming up with metaphors, charting photosynthesis, showing strategies for preserving coral reefs or preventing acid rain, understanding probability, displaying lab results, showing family traditions, and others. This crafting also nurtures student choice and agency.

Projects. Projects can deepen the thinking for idea-building and communication. For example, students might engage in projects such as constructing a bridge out of cardboard, deciding if more dams should be built, writing an opinion article for the school paper, designing and giving a survey of healthy behaviors, writing a story about a family's migration experiences, crafting a poem, creating a business proposal, designing a park, or generating an experiment for measuring the speed of sound. These projects overlap a lot with the products and performances in Chapter 3. Often, the project will be the process of creating the product-performance for the unit. As students work on the projects, they further gather and process the building blocks. For example, students working on a mural project will talk about where to put certain characters in the mural and why. They have learned about famous people, and now they use and share that knowledge. And the teacher—rather than just saying "Go!" and "Good luck!"—uses lesson time to maximize the potential of the project for students' learning, conversing, reading, and thinking.

Collaborative Processing. Some of the most powerful learning time is messy and loud collaboration. In collaborative processing (e.g., conversations), students don't just exchange information. They strengthen and clarify it. They challenge and evaluate it. They converse about how to best use it in their ideas, products, and performances.

For example, in this collaborative activity, students look at John Smith's two very different accounts of the ceremony in which he was "saved" by Pocahontas. Each student reads an account and shares their views on why they are different. The teacher then asks students to talk about why the myth persists and how Pocahontas was (and is still being) used by colonists. You can have students orally process drafts of their articles and stories; you can have small groups decide whether or not people should read and write poetry; you can have pairs work together to come up with a complex math problem, and so on.

As Theodore Zeldin points out, "Conversation is a meeting of minds with different memories and habits. When minds meet, they don't just exchange facts: they transform them, reshape them, draw different implications from them, engage in new trains of thought. Conversation doesn't just reshuffle the cards; it creates new ones" (1998, p. 14). These "new trains of thought" and "reshuffling of cards" are what students want and need to do in order to prepare themselves for the future in which success requires much more than test-taking prowess.

Music, Songs, and Chants. Music offers another dimension of sensory experience that strengthens learning. The brain tends to enjoy and remember concepts, metaphors, and emotions presented and sparked by music. I even remember a clapping chant from ninth-grade biology (which was a long time ago): "The chromosome is the carrier of the gene." Chants and songs are often repeated, but it's repetition that students don't mind much, and the musical notes help the words stick better than if students just memorized sentences. Even if you don't think yourself to be musical, there are plenty of online songs covering just about any idea.

Downloadable songs are great, if you can find ones that align with the learning, but making up your own songs and chants can be even more fun and effective. And, of course, it's powerful to have students come up with songs and chants as well—not just for fun, but to help themselves and their peers build up key ideas. You can have students create the rhythm with items in the classroom, clapping, banging on desks, utensils, and so on. They focus on a core term or building block of the idea they are building. For example, history students might come up with something like this:

We dig dig dig,
We find an artifact.
Is it fairly recent?
No, it goes waaaaaay back!
I want to find its age,
So pass me the machine,
That figures out how old it is
With carbon 14!

Writing. Taking notes while reading, listening, or watching is a common form of processing. But just taking notes isn't usually enough if students don't do a little extra processing with them (e.g., look back at them, organize them, use them in a visual, etc.). Even better is putting new information into one's own words with connected sentences. This can also help students to process building blocks and provide more lasting "ownership" of the content. But remember that prompted writing (for a grade or because the teacher just wants students to write) is not usually authentic enough. Keep reminding students that writing helps them and others remember and refine building blocks for use in their final products and performances. Final pieces of writing should communicate big ideas to others.

ACTIVITY 5.2
Design an Idea-Building Lesson

Use this activity to overhaul a lesson of your choice—maybe even a lesson you are teaching tomorrow. Write in the big idea and key building blocks and then circle the methods you want to include from the central Gathering column. In the list of methods for gathering notice that Read written texts, the most commonly used method for gathering, is last. This is meant to challenge you to try to put one or more of the other methods in your lesson, before resorting to reading written texts. Then think about how students will process what they get and put these in the *Processing* box. Finally, think about how you want to prepare students for *Gathering* and *Processing* and put these in the *Prepping* box. Prepping elements will often happen at the beginning of the lesson. Then fill in the last two rows with language and growth areas to develop during the lesson.

Figure 5.3 Tool for Designing an Idea-Building Lesson

Big Idea:		
Building Blocks to Gather and Process in This Lesson:		
Methods for *Prepping* Students	**Methods for *Gathering* Building Blocks**	**Methods for *Processing* Building Blocks**
Clarify expectations Hooks (motivation) Reviews and connections Pre-assess knowledge, interests, and abilities Teacher modeling Provide background knowledge and language	Experiences Fieldwork and service Case studies Collaboration Nonwritten texts Technology/AI Read written texts	Movement Hands-on and sensory experiences Story-fy Visuals Projects Collaborative processing Music, songs, and chants Writing
Language		
Growth (self-perception, perseverance, social skills, character, multilingual-multicultural identities)		

At the end of every idea-building lesson, each student's idea(s) should be more built up than before the lesson. Usually, this means that students have used the lesson activities to better clarify or strengthen an idea. The teacher should develop a solid understanding, based on formative assessment, of the strengths along with the clarification or support that students need next. For example, you might see that several students' ideas had some effective personal examples of earthquake experiences and that many would benefit from the textbook chapter's explanation about how earthquakes are caused by the shift in plate tectonics.

Idea-Communicating Lessons: Modeling–Practicing–Workshopping

Idea-communicating lessons emphasize helping students put their building blocks together into a product-performance that communicates their big ideas to others. They tend to follow idea-building lessons in a unit. There might still be some gathering and processing in the lesson, but the bulk of the time is on putting together products and performances and improving how these communicate ideas.

Idea-communicating lessons are more effective when they have three modes: modeling, practicing, and workshopping. There can be plenty of overlap between these modes (e.g., you might quickly model a skill during workshop time), but they will tend to be in this order.

Modeling

Students benefit from teacher modeling and the showing of model products and performances. Many students have not seen, created, or performed similar products-performances in the past. Teachers can model a variety of processes and skills such as how to do these things:

- Clarify written explanations
- Add and use dialogue in a story
- Explore different options for writing a poem
- Compose a painting
- Compose a song

- Add animation to a slide presentation
- Give a speech
- Provide peer feedback
- Put building blocks in a logical order
- Evaluate the strength of evidence in an argument

Modeling should be short. You might start by saying something like, "I have noticed that you might benefit from extra modeling of creating metaphors for your poems. I am creating a poem and want to add some new metaphors. Here's how I think. I write down the basic or simple things I want to communicate in the poem. Then I think about something in nature that is like it. For example, . . ." Or you may notice that students' written explanations could use modeling on how to use paragraph construction and transitions to clarify thoughts. You also might model how to respectfully ask for clarification or support in a conversation.

It also helps to analyze the models. As a class, you ask students to work together with you to come up with features or traits of high-quality models. You might ask, "What makes this article so powerful? What helps it communicate its message to its readers?" You might hear features such as an engaging first sentence, interesting analogies, clear statistics, helpful graphics, and so on.

Practicing

"Practice" has been around in lessons for a long time, but most often it has been focused on doing well on points-based assessments. There is a big difference between practicing skills for a quiz or test and practicing performing or creating a product of value. When you practice for a quiz or test, there is not as much mental or physical investment—especially if you are not hyperfocused on points.

In the Idea-Building Approach, practicing focuses on skills and abilities that are used for doing well on products and performances that communicate their ideas to others. This learning tends to last longer because the stakes are a bit higher and more engaging; you will show a product and/or "perform" in some way to authentically help others understand (and build up) the idea that you are communicating. Many students even engage in extra practice (even at home!) when they know the practice leads to more than just a number in a gradebook.

Idea-building practice does *not* include typical "practice" activities that have been around for decades, such as worksheets, reading-to-answer questions, fill-in-the-blanks exercises, writing sentences that need to have certain words or grammar, memorizing vocabulary exercises (flashcards), doing things at "stations" that don't help students build up ideas, and so on.

Often, students will practice the skills that you have modeled, but you can also have students self-evaluate their need to practice certain skills. Some students might practice their poster-design skills, others their writing, and others their speaking in preparation for giving a presentation. You can tell them to try to self-identify something they want to practice or work on in today's lesson, or you can suggest what to practice.

Practicing can range from being highly supported by you to no support at all. In most practice sessions, you will circulate to observe and provide feedback when needed. Address misconceptions or confusion and provide authentic praise and encouragement as much as possible. After practicing, have students reflect on how they improved as a result of the practicing that day, as well as if they need more practice.

Here is a short list of skills that students typically don't get to practice enough:

- Having productive back-and-forth conversations with peers
- Using body language and intonation to communicate ideas
- Building up both sides of an argument and objectively evaluating which side weighs more
- Combining school information with personal information to construct complex ideas
- Sharing ideas, products, and performances with peers and getting useful feedback for revision
- Creating and revising visual images, symbols, and art that represent academic ideas
- Using transitions to connect sentences and paragraphs

Workshopping

Workshopping means synthesizing all of the building blocks learned and skills practiced into products and performances. Just like in a real workshop, where there are tools and materials all around, there is a lot going on. Workshop time in a lesson should be a bit messy and loud, with mental sawdust flying all around.

Students are often working on different things at different times. Some are drawing, some are acting, some are writing, some are getting feedback, some are doing last-minute research, some are rehearsing lines for a drama, some are painting—there are so many possibilities! Your mission, should you accept it, is to monitor and support students as they work. This includes providing guidance, language suggestions, acting tips, feedback, and much more.

Workshopping also provides nice opportunities for checking in with students one-on-one to get a sense of the strength and clarity of their ideas, along with how they plan on communicating it in their product-performance. You can use a rubric or a similar list of traits that you made when showing or analyzing models previously. You can ask them questions that encourage them to work on areas on the list, nudge them to clarify and support their idea, get them to think about using additional tools or materials, use you as an audience, and so on.

If the workshop time is not buzzing with engagement and activity (mental and otherwise), then you need to do something about it: clarify roles and tasks if there is confusion, strategically partner and "un-partner" students, and work alongside certain students to get them into higher gears of thinking and doing.

ACTIVITY 5.3
Design an Idea-Communicating Lesson

Use this tool to overhaul a lesson that focuses more on helping students create final products and/or performances. After putting the big idea in the top box, put the products, performances, and skills that students will be producing and working on in the lesson. These can be "likely" because sometimes you don't know what students need to work on until you see them working. Then in the *Modeling* box, put what you think you need to model to help with product and performance development. This is often at the beginning of the lesson, but it could be in the middle as well. In some cases, the modeling will be for a smaller group of students rather than the whole class. Then put what students need to practice (often what you have modeled) in the *Practicing* box. Then envision how workshop time will most effectively happen and put it in the *Workshopping* box. Finally, put language and growth areas to develop in the last two rows.

Figure 5.4 Visual Organizer for Designing an Idea-Communicating Lesson

Big Idea:		
Products, Performances, Skills:		
Modeling	**Practicing**	**Workshopping**
How to design or make How to speak or perform To use language Analyzing models	Whole class Small group (student names): Individuals (student):	Features and traits to highlight Strategic groups One-on-one work Tools and materials
Language		
Growth (self-perception, perseverance, social skills, character, multilingual-multicultural identies)		

Developing Language(s) in Every Lesson

Given that language is so important for learning, we must always be aware of language used in previous units, assessments, lessons, and activities, all of which inform us of students' language strengths to encourage and the needs to address (Language tests, by the way, are usually not very helpful here because they do not and cannot test for use of language in authentic contexts on a daily basis). Therefore, in a particular lesson, think about the language that you want to hear as students engage in the activities, whether they are in idea-building or idea-communicating lessons.

How do we teach language? My terse answer is that we don't teach it. Rather, we cultivate it. We set up situations in which students are motivated to communicate using the language. We model and supply language for them to process and try out on others. It's a bit like learning a first language. How many four-year-olds memorize words for points or study verb conjugations during dinner so that they do well on quizzes? Very few. Instead, they use the language to get things done, express their opinions, gather new "building blocks" for their ideas, and so on.

Similarly, in the classroom, the number-one way to develop language is to design learning experiences and interactions that motivate students to use language as they construct and negotiate meanings with real others. We model, scaffold, interact, and let *them* interact. In such settings, students will learn lots of language that we never know about.

The number-two way to develop language is to address it as needs arise (sorry if you like everything planned ahead of time!). For example, you might observe that a student, while reading, is having trouble understanding figurative language, using transitions, or comprehending new words in a text. You then model and highlight the language needed for understanding and processing the information. Or while observing a conversation, you notice a lull or detour, so you quickly model the type of respectful and productive language that keeps the conversation on track toward building up an idea.

The number-three way to develop language is to explicitly teach words and grammar—in-context! Sentence frames and vocabulary walls can be used, but use them sparingly, optionally, *and for the purpose of building up and communicating ideas.*

Fostering Growth in Every Lesson

All lessons should foster personal growth as much as possible. This means that you have an ever-present "growth lens" that influences your planning and in-the-moment instruction. Most activities can be used to strengthen one or more growth categories and growth ideas. For example, to foster...

- *Positive self-perception*, you can be highly encouraging with your feedback while students engage in lesson activities and with comments on their work. The more specific, the better. A teacher might observe a pair-share and say, "I love how you are leaning forward and asking great clarify questions. That really helps show your interest in what your partner is saying, and it helps you build up your idea. Well done!"

- *Perseverance*, you can talk about the importance of perseverance in life, showing examples of famous people who persevered; you can ask students how they or family members have persevered; as students work and share, you can share what they do as building blocks for a growth idea on the wall such as "Success is 90% perspiration"; and you can give students extra time on their tasks to persevere and then speak highly of the results with comments such as, "Look at how your perseverance paid off on this wonderful product! Wow!"

- *Social skills*, you can have students meet with a wide range of partners to talk about a wide range of topics and collaborate on a wide range of tasks. As they interact, you can notice trends to highlight (social-based ideas) and improve across the class. You might notice that students are not facing each other, not using effective eye contact, talking too much or too little, excluding members, not using respectful responses, and so on. You might highlight the idea that members of a community support each other through thick and thin.

- *Character*, you can remind students to work on certain traits during a lesson, a week, or a month. You might say, "OK, as we agreed, we are going to work on the trait of being unselfish this week. What does that mean? Why is it not easy to improve. Why is it so important? So when we are talking or collaborating, we need to listen and share as much as we can." Traits can also come up when reading about a character in a story or when other unforeseen situations arise (e.g., disagreements, copying from others, borrowing without asking, bullying). You can point to a character idea visual on the wall ("Choose kindness!") and ask, "How are we thinking and doing things that build up our character idea?"

- *Multilingual and multicultural identities*, you can encourage the use of all languages during classroom activities. You can have students engage in activities in which they talk about what it means to be multilingual and multicultural. You can remind them of the many wonderful aspects of being able to navigate multiple linguistic and cultural worlds, communicate with millions of people who don't speak English, and be more creative and linguistically empowered to succeed in school and life.

Overhauling Activities

Overhauling activities consists of applying some of the elements of the Idea-Building Approach to them. These elements include building up an idea (or building up two sides of an argument-decision), intentional clarifying and supporting, filling information gaps, modeling and scaffolding, and strengthening brain–body connections.

For example, for the common think-pair-share, you can overhaul it by saying to students, "You just read two different stories about the theme of ___. Before you share, think first about one or more building blocks from your story or your mind to share that will help your partner build up their idea. When you listen, ask at least one clarify question (What do you mean by . . . ? How?) or one support question (Can you give an example of . . . ? Why?). I will also model how to use criteria to discuss which supports are strong enough to keep and which are weak enough to leave out. And when you find an important word or concept, figure out a way to act it out to help yourselves and others understand it."

For more in-depth examples of activity overhauling and enhancing, refer to my book *The Communication Effect: How to Enhance Learning by Building Ideas and Bridging Information Gaps* (Zwiers, 2019b), which is this book's companion resource. It overhauls over 20 commonly used instructional activities with features of authentic communication.

ACTIVITY 5.4
Overhauling Activities

After looking at the sample activity overhaul process, which overhauls a think-pair-share, pick an activity that you commonly use and overhaul it with the five elements.

Sample Instructional Activity: Think-Pair-Share				
Clearly Builds Up an Idea or Argument	**Intentional Use of Clarifying and Supporting**	**Fill Information Gaps**	**Modeling and Scaffolding**	**Brain–Body**
Tell students that they share to help their partner build and listen to help themselves build up ideas (and it will help them on their products).	When listening, you have to ask at least one clarify and one support question.	Ask prompt that leverages different information from each partner; or give them different texts on similar topics.	Model how to use criteria to evaluate the strength of examples and evidence.	Have students come up with actions for one key term. Or they can write a chant that clarifies a term or idea for others.
Your Instructional Activity:				
Clearly Builds up an Idea or Argument	**Intentional Use of Clarifying and Supporting**	**Fill Information Gaps**	**Modeling and Scaffolding**	**Brain–Body**

ACTIVITY 5.5

Reflecting on How Overhauled Learning Fosters Pedagogical Justice

Cover up the following bullet points and answer this question: How do this chapter's overhauls to instruction foster pedagogical justice for multilingual students? You can jot down your thoughts here.

_____
_____
_____
_____
_____
_____
_____

When you are finished, compare your answer to the bullet points here. Circle the parts that overlap with what you wrote or thought about and underline any parts that you didn't have but think are important.

- The emphasis on a variety of products and performances provides multiple levels of challenge, success, and access to learning the content.

- Students know that they are gathering information for use in their idea-building and products-performances—not just for getting points on a quiz or test. Along the way, the teacher validates the uniqueness and creativity of students in their idea-building and work, fostering agency and confidence—even when students make surface errors using English.

- Lessons have plenty of processing, practicing, recycling, and reinforcing, which help multilingual students reinforce new language and content understandings.

- There is an emphasis on valuing students as critical and creative thinkers and preparing them for meeting future challenges in life.

- Students engage in many meaningful, positive, and relationship-building interactions with a wide range of peers.

- Instruction is adapted to respect and connect to multilingual students' interests, backgrounds, cultures, languages, and potentials. These are all treated as assets in the processes of learning through idea-building and communicating.

- Instruction weaves in an emphasis on personal growth as often as possible, emphasizing how much we care about students' character development rather than just seeing their deficits and treating them as test-takers.

Challenges

Much of what was covered in this and previous chapters is easier said than done, especially in settings where administrators are asking for fidelity to accumulation-focused curriculums. And yet, often the same administrators also ask for high-quality student engagement and interaction, which tend to be lacking in most curriculums. Yes, curriculums often insert some token interaction (e.g., "Turn and talk about the story") and engagement activities ("Thumbs up if you..."), but they often lack depth and coherence around big ideas, and many lack reasons for which students *want* to share with and listen to one another.

In short, there can be a lot of tension between faithfully following a one-size-prepares-all-for-tests curriculum and providing a unique group of unique students with engaging and interactive learning. If you are a teacher in a setting with this kind of tension, you can tell administrators that if they want cognitive engagement, classroom interaction, integrated language and content development, robust development of disciplinary concepts, and students' personal growth, then you will need to adapt the curriculum to meet the needs of your students.

This is especially true for your multilingual students. Most of the large, adopted curriculums were not written with multilingual students in mind. Some curriculums contain suggestions for multilingual students in the margins, which are mostly quick fixes to help students "access" the texts and tasks that were written for monolingual students. If we are to meet the unique needs of multilingual students, they need to *own* their learning.

Every lesson needs to help every student learn and grow as much as possible, wherever they are in reaching their many potentials. It is in this messy, "no way can one size fit all" instructional space where idea-building shines and personal growth thrives. Because every student has differently constructed ideas—which are always under construction—there is a lot to think and talk about, even if students' ideas differ in their construction or even if they don't fluently express it with perfect grammar and so-called "academic vocabulary."

CHAPTER IDEA

Here is one idea that you can build up from this chapter. If another idea was sparked for you, feel free to build it instead. Remember to add personal examples, definitions, questions, and insights as building blocks along with new blocks gathered from this chapter. Some sample blocks are provided.

IDEA STATEMENT: Everything we do in a lesson must help students build up and/or communicate their big ideas.		
		Curriculums don't always do this, so we need to overhaul them.
Students should enter class expecting to build up a new or existing idea.	I need to do a lot more art and movement to help students process the building blocks that they gather.	
	When multilingual students build and share their novel ideas, they feel agency.	

References

Danielson, C. (2009). *Implementing the framework for teaching in enhancing professional practice*. ASCD.

Hunter, M. (1984). Knowing, teaching, and supervising. In P. Hosford (Ed.), *Using what we know about reading* (pp. 169–203). ASCD.

Willis, J., & Willis, M. (2020). *Research-based strategies to ignite student learning: Insights from neuroscience and the classroom, revised and expanded edition*. ASCD.

Wood, D. J., Bruner, J. S., & Ross, G. (1976). The role of tutoring in problem solving. *Journal of Child Psychiatry and Psychology*, 17(2), 89–100.

Zeldin, T. (1998). *Conversation*. Harvill Press.

The System 6

> Two roads diverged in a wood, and I—
> I took the one less traveled by,
> And that has made all the difference.
>
> —Robert Frost

Moving from accumulation-based learning and its resulting pedagogical injustices to idea-building, growth, and pedagogical justice is a road that is less traveled by many districts. It is less traveled because valuing the diversity of students and their varying ideas is not what many settings have been doing well. It is also less traveled because it requires some major things from educational professionals:

- Extra time, work, and creativity
- Affirming and respecting student differences
- Trusting students and teachers
- Being open to less visible short-term results
- Being patient to see the long-term results
- More complex assessments

If changes such as the ones described in Chapters 2 through 5 are only happening in isolated pockets of a school or district, they will likely fizzle and fade away. You are probably familiar with this problem. The overhauls in the previous chapters require systemwide changes.

While it is hard to address *all* of the interlocking parts of a school system, here are five high-leverage dimensions of a typical system that we can overhaul to achieve pedagogical justice for multilingual students. Figure 6.1 shows a rough depiction of these dimensions and how they influence each other.

Notice that the arrows show the reciprocal influences that each dimension has on all other dimensions. After the description of each dimension, consider how the dimension influences and is influenced by the other four.

Figure 6.1   System Dimensions to Overhaul

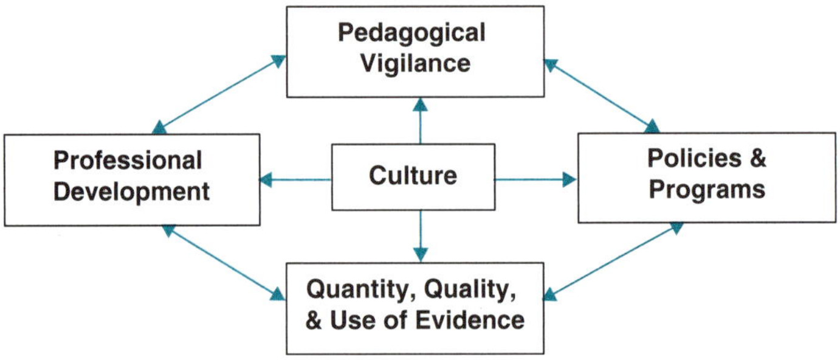

```
                    Pedagogical
                     Vigilance
                   ↗     ↑     ↘
                  ↙      ↓      ↘
        Professional ← Culture → Policies &
        Development  →         ← Programs
                  ↘      ↑      ↗
                   ↘     ↓     ↙
                    Quantity, Quality,
                    & Use of Evidence
```

Culture

Culture, in a nutshell, is what members of a certain group tend to do and think. It is the set of beliefs, values, communication patterns, attitudes, and activities that group members tend to share in order to collaboratively lead rich and productive lives. School (and district) culture encompasses what educators and students do and think in order to foster student learning and growth (Fullan, 2007). With respect to the overhaul work promoted in this book, culture includes what we do and think in schools to achieve pedagogical justice for every student.

For example, in one school a core belief is "*Every* student in every school is *highly* capable of (a) learning a wide range of complex ideas, academic skills, and ways of communicating; and (b) developing and growing in a wide range of dimensions needed for leading fulfilled and productive lives." Another district belief is "All ways of communicating and knowing are valuable for learning and relating to others." When all involved (admin, parents, teachers, students) share this belief, actions and progress follow.

We must foster a systemwide culture that assumes greatness in all students. This means looking for ways to mine and amplify the many gifts, talents, and funds of knowledge that our students have. It requires, as argued for in Chapter 4, getting to know our students well and building relationships with them. We have a responsibility to provide the very best of everything that we and our school have to offer, which includes forming a supportive community of learners over time.

A key aspect of classroom culture is how we treat each other during learning. This book's approach emphasizes strengthening several features of classroom culture that are typically lacking in accumulation-based classrooms. These include valuing relationships, communicating, collaborating, helping others feel that they belong, and listening to the voices of others.

Culture in educational settings is the most deep-seated and central of the system dimensions in this chapter. And it's the hardest to change. However, over time, it is possible to shift key aspects to improve learning and foster pedagogical justice. Several key aspects of school and classroom culture are expectations, communication, values, beliefs, behaviors, traditions, and routines (Shafer, 2018). Use Activity 6.1 to think about how to overhaul and improve these aspects.

ACTIVITY 6.1
Overhauling Your School Culture

The first column of Figure 6.2 contains aspects of school culture that you can develop as you work toward improving student learning, growth, and pedagogical justice. The middle column has ideas for what evidence you can look for in your setting.

Figure 6.2 Aspects and Evidence of Positive School and Classroom Culture

Cultural Aspect	Examples of Evidence	Possible Steps to Improve This in Your Setting
Expectations of students for what they can do and learn, how they think, how they can improve over time, and how they can grow	– Products and performances with high expectations of what students can do – Teachers exhibiting high expectations during lessons – Teachers trust students to work together, build up ideas, be creative, and communicate in various ways	
Expectations of teachers and administrators for professionalism, improvement over time, productive collaboration, and leadership	– Teachers respecting other teachers and administrators – Productive collaboration between teachers as well as between teachers and administrators – Trust between administrators and teachers – Push for growth as teachers and administrators support student learning and growth	
Communication between students, between students and teachers, with fellow workers, in meetings, and with parents	– Value all students, including those who you may think are not developing English "quickly enough" – Value communication between students and adults – Strive to clearly communicate with parents	

Figure 6.2 Aspects and Evidence of Positive School and Classroom Culture (Continued)

Cultural Aspect	Examples of Evidence	Possible Steps to Improve This in Your Setting
Values and beliefs (including agency, reaching potentials, use of formative assessment, and social-emotional growth)	– Teachers and students value student contributions and use of different languages – Adults and students believe all students can learn at high levels – All believe that idea-building, communication, and growth are more important than test scores – All value the uniqueness of people and their ideas	
Behaviors, traditions, and routines	– Students exhibit behaviors such as helping others build ideas and create products – Teachers listen to students and make adjustments to lessons – Teachers incorporate sufficient student-centered routines – Students have enough time within the lesson to collaborate – Use assessment that leads to helpful feedback – Teachers and administrators work together to improve instruction, assessment, and student growth	

Pedagogical Rights

Another aspect of culture that relates directly to pedagogical justice is our belief system around students' pedagogical rights. Many schools have not seriously looked at or considered the idea that students have pedagogical rights—so much focus has been on what students need to learn (e.g., standards) that the idea of students having rights seldom comes up. And yet, in glancing at some of the rights in Activity 6.2 you can see the potential power that they have to influence a culture of assets-based and idea-based learning in positive ways.

ACTIVITY 6.2
Supporting Students' Pedagogical Rights

Read each student right in Figure 6.3 and think about how evident or strong it is in your setting. If it needs strengthening, brainstorm ways to strengthen it and make changes in your setting so that the right is better realized and more evident. Then go through them and think about which are the top three to work on in your setting.

Figure 6.3 Strengthening Students' Pedagogical Rights

I Have the Right To…	Strong in Our Setting?	Ways to Strengthen This Right in Our Setting
Be engaged in learning		
Learn *useful* concepts and skills in every lesson		
Grow as much as possible in every lesson		
Choose how to show my learning (including the languages I use)		
Redo and revise my work		
Develop all my many gifts, potentials, and interests		
Be heard and valued by peers and teachers		
Be taught by teachers who are allowed to creatively teach		
Build up unique and valuable ideas		
Learn by talking with peers		
Learn from mistakes		

Policies and Programs

Districts have many policies and programs that affect the education of multilingual students. Some come down from the state, and some are tied to federal programs—and both types are hard to change. Others are at district and school levels. Policies and programs have a range of focuses: student placement, the language of instruction, assessment, grading, attendance, discipline, special education, and more.

Overhauling Policies

We must take a hard look at which policies are helping multilingual students and which are not. For example, a school might have a policy of placing multilingual students in a program that isolates them from monolingual students. This tracking puts them in classes where they learn language with others who have similar levels of English, yet it deprives students of the chance to interact with other students in the school, often keeping them from engaging with interesting content and students with varying proficiencies in English. The task is to figure out how policies like this one should be changed in order to best serve students over time. Are the policies helping students to develop and grow in the areas mentioned in Chapter 2? Are they supporting assessment and instructional practices outlined in Chapters 3 and 4? Do they empower teachers to engage in the overhauls of Chapter 5?

ACTIVITY 6.3
Overhauling Policies

After reading the example in the first row, pick one or more policies that impact multilingual students and fill in the chart. For the second and third columns of Figure 6.4, do not use test scores, but instead use other indicators and forms of evidence, some of which we covered in Chapter 3. If the effects in Column 3 outweigh the effects in Column 2, then change (or outright canceling) is needed. If the policy is harmful, then in Column 4 brainstorm ideas for changing the policy (if possible) in order to reduce its harmful effects and increase its positive effects. Finally, in Column 5 come up with ways in which you can know (evidence) if the changes are working for multilingual students.

Figure 6.4 Overhauling Policies

Policy	How It Helps Multilingual Students	How It Harms Multilingual Students	How to Change It (If Needed and Possible)	How We Will Know the Changes Are Working
Students are allowed to share evidence of their learning in English only.	It mostly doesn't, but some students might push themselves to learn more English.	Students don't have the right to draw from their full range of linguistic resources in their projects-performances. It diminishes opportunities for idea-building and growth and provides an inadequate picture of student learning and growth.	Students and teachers can co-create language-in-use policies based on the goals of the unit; focus on the quality of the idea and the communication of it.	We will see increased levels of student engagement, agency, and idea-building.

Overhauling Programs

Programs are often shaped by policy. Programs tend to include the sets of courses that you offer and require, along with the schedules and services that you provide to students and families. You can start by reflecting on the effectiveness of your current courses and schedules through the lens of the information in the last five chapters. For example, do students need an ELA (English language arts) class every day of every year? Do multilingual students need ELA and ELA-focused ELD (English language development) every day at the expense of taking other classes such as science, social studies, or art? Could students benefit as much or more from taking classes focused on starting a business, making ethical decisions, becoming authors of literature, engaging in design challenges, addressing environmental issues, making societal challenges, and so on? Would they use language more authentically in such courses? Would they learn more, think more, smile more, form more and better relationships, and have more agency if they engaged in more real-world situations? Would students benefit from being in a dual-language instruction setting?

ACTIVITY 6.4
Overhauling Programs

Pick several key programs and fill in the chart in Figure 6.5. For the second and third columns, do not use test scores, but instead use other indicators and forms of evidence, some of which we covered in Chapter 3. If the effects in Column 3 outweigh the effects in Column 2, then change (or outright canceling) is needed. In Column 4, brainstorm ideas for changing the program (if needed and if possible) to reduce its harmful effects and increase its positive effects. And in Column 5, come up with ways (evidence) in which you can know if the changes are working for multilingual students.

For example, you might have a set number of minutes each day that focuses on English language development. It is an extra page in the purchased curriculum guide and focuses on supporting the ELA lesson prior to it. It helps students with some of the language they will need, but it can be harmful because some lessons are boring and repeats of the content they have just had the previous period. A possible change is to find a stand-alone curriculum that is engaging and not just an "ELA support" class. A way to know if these changes are working is by asking teachers and students what they think about the new curriculum.

Figure 6.5 Overhauling Programs

Program	How It Helps Multilingual Students	How It Harms Multilingual Students	How to Change It (If Needed and Possible)	How We Will Know the Changes Are Working

EDUCATING NEWCOMERS

A common program question is "How do we meet the needs of newcomers in mainstream classrooms?" This can't be answered with a multiple-choice question, and there are no silver-bullet solutions. Not surprisingly, I recommend the ideas in this book, being patient, valuing home languages and cultures, and moving more toward instruction and assessment based on idea-building and growth in every subject.

Why? Accumulation-based teaching is one of the (perhaps *the*) worst approaches for newcomers. It forces students to memorize—in a new language, no less!—a wide range of disconnected skills, pieces of information, and parts of language, usually with the goal of being tested on them. English classes designated for newcomers often teach vocabulary and grammar in decontextualized and boring ways (e.g., "Circle the correct verb form in this sentence: The cat sit/sits on the chair."). The pace is quick, and there are few second chances or recycling of language.

By contrast, in idea-building and growth-based lessons, newcomers have many chances to use language with the goal of building up concepts and claims. Students collaborate and build relationships, despite differing ways of using first, second, and third languages. The focus is on productive communication, not memorizing content or correct grammar.

There are also scaffolds such as sentence frames and visuals, all of which are useful for building up and communicating ideas. Students are highly encouraged (and taught) to work hard to communicate with all other students. And there are many opportunities to do so each day. Newcomers are encouraged, when necessary and possible, to communicate in their primary language(s) to understand and build up ideas. Students help each other with final products and performances, which every student is able to do with success.

Teacher Professional Development

The teacher professional development (also called professional learning) dimension embodies ways to help teachers continue to develop and hone their skills within the Idea-Building Approach and for pedagogical justice for multilingual students.

I have heard people say that teaching isn't rocket science. They are right. Teaching is much more challenging than rocket science. This is because a rocket scientist doesn't have 25 running rockets all in one room, asking for different things all at once. Expert teachers are still learning after 30 years of teaching. And there are tens of thousands of books on teaching. Why? Teaching is the most important, complex, and challenging profession *of all*. Why? Each student is highly complex, growing, and changing by the day. Teachers have dozens of these highly complex people in their classrooms for hours on end.

Teachers must develop their expertise to tailor instruction and students' learning to their wide range of differing knowledge, motivations, interests, skills, identities, and ways of communicating (Carter Andrews & Richmond, 2019). At any given moment in time during a lesson, teaching includes assessing, managing behaviors, adjusting instruction, and caring—all while juggling things like interruptions, announcements, pencil sharpening, lost belongings, repeating directions, cleaning up, and so on. Teaching requires way more PD time and energy than what is offered each year, so we need to be highly selective and effective.

And for the many schools that are still mired down by accumulation-focused learning, it takes even more high-quality professional development, which often includes heavy convincing that change is needed to replace monolingual accumulation with multilingual idea-building across the disciplines.

Professional development efforts include analyzing findings from research studies, attending professional development sessions, participating in learning communities, instructional coaching, studying books, adopting new policies, meeting with consultants, and using web-based resources. Some of these professional learning efforts are effective, which means that they value student growth, agency, communication, and voice more than achievement measured by test scores. However, many instructional influencers, some subtly and some not so subtly, associate the effectiveness of their PD with test scores. They tacitly perpetuate memorization and accumulation, injustice, and biases that hinder learning and engagement in classrooms.

Figure 6.6 roughly shows how a system can strengthen professional development for the Idea-Building Approach. The main goal, at the top, is student learning and growth in all of their potentials. We gather evidence of that learning and growth and use it to inform instruction, assessment, and professional development. We need to

Figure 6.6 Improving Student Learning With Teacher Professional Development

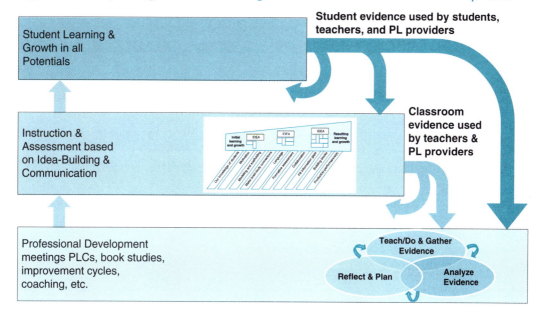

use students' learning and growth evidence (arrows on the right) to (a) help students reflect on how to improve their own learning, (b) help teachers reflect on how to adapt instruction, and (c) help PD leaders and PD efforts to improve professional development. Teachers use classroom-based evidence to inform and adapt their own instruction and assessment, while PD providers use it to improve PD.

In most cases, PD workshops are the most common approach for exposing teachers to new ideas, frameworks, models, and strategies. However, there is a substantial body of research (see work by Bruce Joyce, Linda Darling-Hammond, and Learning Forward) arguing that isolated workshops alone will not lead to enduring changes in practices. The two most promising approaches to PD implementation are professional learning communities (PLCs) and instructional coaching.

Professional Learning Communities

PLCs and their variations have been gaining momentum in the last two decades. They typically consist of regular meetings between similar-job educators who focus on improving teaching practices or addressing major challenges in their work. They usually bring in student work, anecdotes, or videos to analyze and reflect on as a team (Cochran-Smith, 2015). A team of third-grade teachers at a school, for example, might meet monthly to look at videos of student conversations to reflect on ways to improve prompts and to help students develop conversation skills.

PLCs vary quite a bit in content, process, and effectiveness. The more effective PLCs tend to choose a high-leverage focus or inquiry question to work on over time. It is common for PLCs to engage in inquiry cycles or plan-do-study-act (PDSA) cycles. While these can be effective, they are commonly used for more visible results in shorter time frames. I encourage PLCs to zoom out and think about how their collaborative work, evidence analysis, and reflections can help to overhaul teaching, learning, and assessment. The inquiry cycle might last one, two, three years, or more. And inquiries might focus on major overhaul components, such as these:

- How can we most effectively engage all students in building up ideas?
- How can we align instruction with what students need for their performances and products?
- How can we value student uses of their linguistic repertoires throughout learning and assessment?
- How can we value students' funds of knowledge and varied cultural practices?
- How can we adapt our current curriculum to focus on building up ideas?
- How can we foster students' purposeful idea-building every time they read?
- How can we make sure that we and our students focus on developing skills (analyzing, arguing, evaluating, summarizing, inferring, and comparing) in order to build up ideas or make decisions?
- How can we engage students in thinking and using language more than just the bare minimum?
- How can we adapt our instruction and curriculum to be more inclusive and culturally empowered?

- How can we develop teacher habits and mindsets that help them enhance all instruction and assessment with three features of authentic communication?

- How can we build stronger relationships with and between students?

- How can we most effectively assess the less visible yet highly important aspects of learning and growth?

- How can we empower students to grow into the amazing, unique, multilingual, and multicultural individuals they were born to be?

Instructional Coaching

Instructional coaching, just as its name implies, means more individualized support of the professional growth of teachers over time. Coaching can be done by instructional coaches, administrators, and fellow teachers. Entire books are devoted to coaching, so I will just focus on coaching for idea-building and communication in this section.

Here are some suggestions:

1. A coach and teacher collaborate to agree on an objective that includes defining what "success" looks like. For example, what does success look like in building and communicating the important idea(s) for the current unit of instruction?

2. They agree on what data will be collected—for example, classroom observations (or video observations), student work, and so on.

3. In most cases, coaching is built around inquiry cycles (like the bulleted PLC focus descriptions in the previous section).

4. Develop or borrow protocols that are designed to guide coaching conversations that focus on idea-building. For example, prepare look-fors and reflection questions that emphasize the suggestions in this book.

5. Different approaches to coaching vary in terms of how much explicit guidance (do this; do that; don't do this) a coach is expected to provide. Increasingly, I see a shift toward sharing more explicit guidance on instruction, albeit not in an overly directive way. Explicit modeling and co-teaching are also important topics.

6. In most of the literature, these cycles are enacted in fairly brief periods (6–8 weeks). You can suggest that PLCs focus more on the "big idea" goals, whereas coaches focus on more granular objectives in the interest of achieving the larger goal.

PD Piloting

Many successful approaches to systemwide change begin with a pilot group of teachers, which typically includes teachers who are most open to trying new things and changing the status quo for the better. The pilot group implements changes, tries new strategies, gathers lots of good data, and collaborates to reflect on it. Then the pilot gradually scales up. As new cohorts are added and stories of "success" get shared across the system, the chances of getting everybody on board increase. This is especially true of this type of overhaul work, which changes the *what* and *how* of learning in major ways.

ACTIVITY 6.5
Designing Professional Development

The most exciting, engaging, research-based, and effective professional development doesn't matter if it's focused on the wrong results for students. Use the ideas in previous chapters, along with Figure 6.6, to help you design a plan for professional development that helps your school(s) to engage in the overhauls described here. For example, you might design a multiyear PD effort that incorporates learning communities, coaching, book studies, lesson studies, PLCs, and more. Using a chart like Figure 6.7 can help. A sample chart with examples is provided.

Existing PD Focuses: Reading comprehension, writing

New PD Focuses: Idea-building, peer interaction, agency

Figure 6.7 Sample Professional Development Planning Chart

Existing PD Focuses: Reading comprehension, writing New PD Focuses: Idea-building, peer interaction, agency		
PD Strategies	**Year 1**	**Year 2**
PLCs	Monthly meetings, focused on idea-building in units and the role of reading comprehension in building ideas	Conversations focused on the overlap of idea-building and interaction
Coaching	Weekly individual sessions, focused on idea-building and interactions	Individualized support on idea-building and interactions
Instructional rounds	Instructional rounds on interaction and writing	Instructional rounds on interaction, reading, and idea-building
Staff meetings	Monthly, partly devoted to student agency and idea-building	Staff meetings focused on the overlap of student agency, interactions, and idea-building
Virtual book study	On culturally sustaining pedagogy	On social and emotional development

Quality, Quantity, and Use of Evidence

So far, this book has vehemently argued for reducing the time used for preparing students for yearly multiple-choice tests. Chapter 3 described alternative and more effective ways to see student learning and growth. This evidence can include numerical data from various kinds of assessments (rubrics, quizzes, and tests), but the more helpful types come from evidence such as observations, writing, projects, surveys, and interviews (Safir & Dugan, 2021). Chapter 3 describes these in more detail.

Start with teachers. Teachers are with their students many hours every week, have observed students on good and bad days, and have seen a wide range of work by each student. Teachers have had many interactions with each student, question–answer exchanges, and chances to analyze of their work over time. Work with colleagues to figure out what evidence you want and why. Chapter 2, for example, described several areas of learning and growth that we want to see, which means gathering evidence. Systemwide, figure out ways to keep track of important evidence. For example, one school keeps track of students' ideas over time in the students' binders. Students put idea-building visual organizers and argument balance scales in the back of each binder for each content area. Teachers review them at the semester and end of the year. One school even has short oral-defense interviews in which teachers ask students to describe their ideas in a short one-on-one conversation.

Second, if a school wants more tangible and helpful summative records of learning, they should use portfolios, performances, products, and projects. These are more real-world (even in primary grades) artifacts that not only show student learning more effectively but also motivate and foster more engagement in learning.

Third, we must move from thinking mainly about numerical data to thinking mainly about evidence of learning and growth, as described in Chapter 3. We already know that it's harder to design, harder to gather, and harder to interpret. But isn't it even harder to know that many multilingual students are frustrated and disengaged from learning because of our system's focus on attempting to quantify every little piece of learning? It's much harder to watch students drop out or graduate from K–12 schooling with less education and growth than what we know we could have offered.

Fourth, many schools need to overhaul how they use evidence. In many accumulation-focused settings, test scores rule the day and take up the most time; the data determine where to place students and what to emphasize in classrooms, which are usually ELA and math. But in settings that use better assessments and evidence of learning, educators analyze the strengths and needs of students.

In settings that focus on idea-building and growth, assessment evidence is used to help students grow (personally and socially), build up ideas (skills and content), and develop skills for building and communicating ideas. For example, a sixth-grade teacher observed a group of students discussing how to write museum descriptions of ancient Aztec artifacts. She noticed the strengths of using texts to help them include background information, but she also wanted them to come up with more interpretations—as archeologists would do—to include in the descriptions. She modeled this the next day and made a note to improve this even more in future similar projects.

Use Activity 6.6 to think about how to best use the evidence that you already gathered plus evidence that you will be gathering (perhaps as a result of this book). This includes evidence from other key parts of the school system.

ACTIVITY 6.6
Using Assessment Evidence

In this activity, you reflect on how you currently use assessment evidence in your setting and how you might change it to emphasize how to use it for idea-building and growth. I included sample responses in the initial rows of Figure 6.8.

Figure 6.8 Chart for Improving Uses of Evidence

Type of Evidence	How You Currently Use This (If at All)	How You Might Use This for Idea-Building and Personal Growth
Student writing	For grades and to inform mini-lessons on writing skills	To inform students on how the strength and clarity of their ideas can be improved; to encourage students to become writers to share their ideas
Paired student talk	Observe for content understanding	Observe for building blocks and uses of language for communicating the idea
Answering questions	Listen for accurate content	
Whole-class discussion	N/A	
Student products	Use rubric for grades	
Student performances	Use rubric for grades	
Student interviews		
State test scores		
Student idea visuals		
Teacher surveys		
PLC notes		
Videos of lessons		
Lesson observation notes		
Parent surveys		

Pedagogical Vigilance

Accumulation-based pedagogy has been around for a long time. It's what most parents, states, and schools are used to. It's easier to do, it's easier to measure, it's quieter, and it makes it easier to control students. And many teachers and leaders already lean into the "visibility," comparability, and countability of accumulation-based teaching. It will continue to hang around, ebb and flow, and influence instruction—especially when left unchecked.

We must therefore continue to be aware of the many supporters and promotors of accumulation pedagogy. These include testing companies, developers of teacher resources, so called "innovations," initiatives, PD focuses, consultants, curriculums, books, and any school- or districtwide emphases that influence teaching and learning. We must develop an ever-vigilant critical eye for analyzing the things that influencers offer in order to see if they are useful, can be adapted to be useful, or need to be set aside so something that is more useful can take its place ("useful" means that it helps to foster the suggestions outlined in this book).

First, be wary of lots of checkboxes, long lists of objectives, a focus on covering lots of standards, memorizing, and practicing skills just to practice them. Look for disconnected activities and lessons, test preparation activities, and lesson time spent practicing how to answer multiple-choice questions. Look for students doing the bare minimum and just "playing" school. Look for lots of short answers. Look for classrooms where just a few students want to answer teacher questions. Ask students *why* they are doing something and listen for answers such as "for participation points, we have to, it's in the lesson, there is a quiz on this tomorrow," and so on.

Many PD providers and education influencers are well-intentioned, but they are ignorant of the limited learning that results from focusing on memorizing disconnected and disengaging content for tests. They don't see the many other negatives that come from reducing student learning and growth down to numbers. Listen to what PD influencers say and write, especially when they tout results and positive outcomes based on yearly test scores or scores on multiple-choice assessments. If they claim to be research-based, look closely at where the research data comes from. How many studies? Who paid for the studies? Look at their claims and then consider the many variables that they don't mention that play large roles in student learning and growth. PD providers often want to quickly promote their ideas and methods as silver-bullet solutions, which they support with flashy test-score differences (e.g., "Our program increased student test scores 6.54% in just eight weeks!").

Second, take a close look at the PD books that are currently used in your setting. Many provide lists of teaching practices or principles. Such resources can be very popular, and the authors can have cultlike followings. This is often due to the perception that these products seem to make teaching easier, cleaner, and less complex. But as you have seen in the previous chapters and know from experience, effective instruction is hard, messy, and highly complex. A book with a few dozen silver-bullet strategies is likely aiming at the age-old, low-hanging fruit of helping students memorize things and improve skills for tests to get more points than the year before.

If you have one of these books, take a close look at these practices. Do they view students as the following:

(a) Obedient recipients and regurgitators of knowledge or (b) critical thinkers who can create and use knowledge?

(a) Objects and products or (b) subjects and producers?

(a) Skill practicers or (b) skill users?

(a) Compliant workers or (b) creative designers?

(a) Generically similar or (b) wonderfully diverse?

(a) Short-answer givers and choosers or (b) big-idea builders?

If the answers to these questions lean toward (a), then be wary.

Third, some resources provide lists of teaching practices that come from meta-research studies. These are studies that have gathered hundreds of studies and looked for common practices that show success. Be wary of three things in meta-studies: (a) what the authors of the meta-studies and the studies being analyzed consider to be "successful" and "effective"; (b) the statistical methods used in the meta-analyses; and (c) conclusions that reduce hundreds of studies (and the learning of thousands of diverse students) down to a single number (e.g., effect size) that tells teachers how to teach.

Fourth, there are books about education that make it onto bestseller lists. These are often written by authors with second- and thirdhand knowledge of education. They tend to pick controversial topics (e.g., reading instruction, knowledge deficits, etc.) and find examples of newsworthy challenges or "shocking gaps" in—you guessed it—student test scores. Most of these books use test-score data to argue that students aren't learning enough, teachers aren't teaching enough, and schools aren't good enough. Educators and other writers (e.g., researchers, professors, consultants, administrators, and journalists) who have not spent lots of time with real students in real schools tend to depend on downloadable scores, statistics, and calls for accountability to shore up their ideas.

Fifth, curriculums often promote accumulation. Most of them do their best to pick interesting texts and topics, but a lot of their energies end up focusing on covering standards and preparing for tests. The notion that students are agents in the building of disciplinary ideas and that they can use different building blocks from their diverse experiences, school, and other students just doesn't fit very well in a test-based paradigm (see Chapter 1).

Sixth, sift out the practices that put the teacher too much at the center with too much control, giving little student choice. Watch out for too much teacher talk. For example, more than five minutes of teacher talk without a chance for students to stop listening and do something with what they just heard is likely teacher-centered and overly controlled.

Seventh, remember that accumulation-based learning and pedagogical injustice go hand in hand. Listen to what students say about themselves as learners. Ask students who aren't engaged in learning why they aren't engaged. Take a close look at the assessments that you are using and analyze them for linguistic, cultural, or other biases. Analyze them for validity.

Eighth, there have been many one-dimensional school reform and improvement efforts. They tend to focus on just one aspect of education, touting it as *the* answer. For example, some efforts have focused on formative assessment, others on project-based learning, others on culturally responsive teaching, RTI (Response to Intervention), dual-language education, differentiation, cooperative learning, social-emotional learning (SEL), and so on. Most of these are helpful (many aspects of them are even suggested in the previous chapters), but they are much more effective and endure when they are implemented systemwide and over time.

Ninth, clarify the long-term focus of any major program, initiative, project, and so on. Does it lead toward idea-building and growth or toward accumulation? Many programs and trends (e.g., RTI, culturally responsive teaching, personalized learning, and mindfulness) have solid foundations. But be wary of any that associate their effectiveness with yearly test scores. We must make a clean break from the tests and the "learning" that they influence. Yes, students will take the tests, but (as you are likely tired of reading by now) we must not limit or corrupt our teaching as a result of test results or by what they (or test-score interpreters) think we need to do for students.

Tenth, don't let any grade levels escape notice. In primary grades, there might be a focus on phonics, anti-phonics, or rote math learning. These grade levels aren't always state-tested, but a range of other assessments varying in quality are given. Many focus on accuracy, which is important, but why? Accuracy in reading (decoding) is meant to help students comprehend texts. And why do they read texts? For tests? No. To spark and build up new understandings and ideas. This also applies to AP classes in high school. Students will be better prepared for the discipline if they build up ideas as robustly as possible.

ACTIVITY 6.7
Evaluate How Accumulation-Focused Your Setting Is

Use the chart in Figure 6.9 to roughly rate to what degree your setting answers these questions. Each question explains what receives a high rating. The higher the rating, the more your shade the corresponding bar. If you end up with lots of shading, it is likely time to discuss ways to incorporate the suggestions in this and related resources on instructional change.

Figure 6.9 Questions for Rating Accumulation-Based Learning in Your Setting

Questions	Rating
Ask students why they are doing an activity. If they answer, "For points," or "Because we have to," or "To prepare for a test or quiz," or something like that, then they get a high rating (more shading).	
Observe students to see how much they are just doing the bare minimum when they use language. If there is a lot of bare minimum, then they get a high rating.	
To what extent are students tested with boring assessments such as quizzes, tests, and essays? If the classroom uses a lot of these, then give it a high rating.	
Ask teachers what they think successful learning looks like. If they mention scores, grades, or counting up of anything, then give it a high rating.	
Listen to educator discussions of learning and if terms like "success," "gaps," "achievement," and "performance" are attached to test scores, then give them a high rating.	

Strengthening Pedagogical Justice Systemwide

A big part of developing positive and effective schools is strengthening the six dimensions of pedagogical justice—while at the same time eliminating the five root causes of pedagogical injustices (see Chapter 1). These are ongoing processes. Like a garden, without constant upkeep the system tends to "regress toward the mean" of accumulation-based learning, lack of trust in students, suppressing their voices, limiting their creativity, assimilation, and focusing on their deficits. We must therefore point every part of the system toward strengthening the dimensions of pedagogical justice. Just one or two of them will not make a lasting difference. Activity 6.8 can help you think about which dimensions to start with.

ACTIVITY 6.8
Systemically Strengthening Pedagogical Justice

For each of the six dimensions of pedagogical justice in the first column of Figure 6.10 reflect on how well it is fostered or not by each of your system's dimensions in Columns 2 through 6. For example, you can start with the first row and move to the right, thinking about how your classroom culture fosters students' agency and voice or not. If you think it's not enough, brainstorm ways to make it happen in each column. You can also go down the columns asking, for example, how your policies and programs foster each one of the dimensions on the left. Some examples are included for each column.

Figure 6.10 Chart for Systemwide Strengthening of Pedagogical Justice

	\multicolumn{5}{c	}{System Dimensions}
	Classroom Culture	Policies and Programs	Professional Development	Use of Evidence	Pedagogical Vigilance
Agency and voice			PD on agency and voice		
Engaging challenges					Survey students on engagement and challenge
Meaningful interactions	Make interactions an hourly norm				
Idea-building			Make this a focus of PD		
Assessment for learning				Analyze evidence for idea-building	
Critical and creative thinking		Adopt policies that strengthen these			

Again, as in a garden, pedagogical injustices and their roots act like weeds. They keep popping up from various participants and components in the system—and we need to address and reduce their influences as soon as possible (refer to Chapter 1 for a refresher on the pedagogical injustices).

Try answering some or all of these questions about injustices in your setting:

- How does our system promote or reduce unjust placement of students in tracks, remedial classes, and special programs that label and isolate them?

- How does our system promote or reduce students' feelings that they don't belong in school?

- How does our system promote or reduce students' lack of motivation?

- How does our system promote or reduce the mindset that learning means filling one's head with stuff for quizzes and tests?

- How does our system promote or reduce the injustice of separating students from their potentials?

If any of your answers lean toward promoting injustices, work with colleagues to come up with ways to address the problem. If, for example, the system focuses on test scores and ignores the strengths, languages, and aspirations of students, then you can think about strategies for getting to know students' strengths, validate them, and communicate their value to the students themselves *and* the community.

ACTIVITY 6.9
Prioritizing and Planning

Achieving pedagogical justice takes time, organization, prioritizing, and planning. Consider the school level. Start with the 12 elements of the Idea-Based Learning and Growth Approach outlined in Chapter 4. I put them into Figure 6.11. Think about which areas need the most overhauling in your setting (rank them, if you want), the teacher–classroom observation evidence and student evidence you want to see after a certain period of time, and the things you need to do to develop the area. You can begin on this page, but I recommend coming up with a similar chart in digital form. I included sample responses to get you thinking. You can use them and/or come up with your own.

After filling in a chart like this, you can zoom in on your top priorities and flesh out the types of evidence you will be looking for, ways to use it, and the specifics of the steps you plan to take.

Much of this overhaul work will start in classrooms as teachers try out idea-building strategies and assessments. Each setting will be different with respect to who and how these changes start and spread. The main variable is people. Teachers, coaches, leaders, and parents will have different opinions on if and how to implement significant changes such as those recommended in this book. In your setting, you might be able to get started in several classrooms at the unit level. Yet several coaches and one assistant principal at the site are on board and have started to work at the PLC and coaching levels. At meetings, they highlight idea-building practices, videos of student interactions, and students' products and performances—with an extra emphasis on showing the abilities and strengths of multilingual students.

Figure 6.11 Sample System Priority and Planning Chart

Element	Teacher + Classroom Evidence (by Date)	Student Evidence to Analyze	Steps for Developing This
1. Focus learning on idea-building	All teachers come up with effective ideas for half of their units	For idea-based units, idea-building visuals	Use part of PLC meetings to share and work on ideas for current units
2. Design engaging products and performances	All teachers come up with effective ideas for half of their units	Students do extra work on their products	Meet with other teachers to brainstorm these
3. Fill information gaps	At least once a day, students are given different texts before sharing them with each other	Students orally share more second and third sentences	Share activity ideas with each other in PLCs

(Continued)

Figure 6.11 Sample System Priority and Planning Chart (Continued)

Element	Teacher + Classroom Evidence (by Date)	Student Evidence to Analyze	Steps for Developing This
4. Use building blocks	Visuals on walls and comments by teachers related to the use of information and skills to build up ideas	Students share work and refer to blocks helping them build up ideas	Bring in student work to teacher meetings (PLCs) to analyze
5. Know students	Use of student languages and interests in curriculum	Student surveys and interviews	Strategize how to get to know students better every week
6. Define results	Results that incorporate idea-building, growth, and communication	Students push themselves to work hard on high-quality products-performances	Meet with the team to outline ideas, skills needed, and growth goals
7. Formative assessment	Teacher provides feedback on idea-building, especially clarifying and supporting	Students make changes in response to teacher feedback and self-reflection	Agree in PLCs to gather and analyze formative evidence of idea-building
8. Collaboration	Teacher models speaking skills and sets up activities that support student talk	Students talking with each other for at least a quarter of a lesson to build up ideas	Coaches, admin, or other teachers observe for quantity and quality of lessons
9. Modeling-scaffolding	Teacher models twice a lesson (sometimes whole class and others small group)	Students use scaffolds less and less in a lesson and over a unit	Analyze lessons to prioritize modeling needs (reading, conversing, etc.)
10. Brain–body	At least one activity per lesson incorporates movement, music, drama, and creativity	Students engage in two or more brain–body activities during a lesson	Teachers share brain–body strategies in staff meetings

Figure 6.11 Sample System Priority and Planning Chart (Continued)

Element	Teacher + Classroom Evidence (by Date)	Student Evidence to Analyze	Steps for Developing This
11. Motivation	Teachers incorporate motivating hooks, questions, topics, activities, and assessments	Students share that they are motivated to come to school, talk more, finish their work, and build ideas	Ask students what motivates them to learn and make adjustments to curriculums
12. Language	Teacher pushes students to use increasingly clear language (e.g., sentence frames, vocabulary) to authentically communicate	Students push themselves and each other to use language to clarify ideas and building blocks	Challenge students to use two or more sentences when answering questions

Obstacles

I realize that many teachers, curriculum designers, and schools do not have ample latitude to change what they are doing. This can be especially true in school systems that have been labeled "low-performing" based on standardized test scores. These schools, many of which have large populations of multilingual students, often have required curriculums, pacing guides, and tests to be used with high fidelity. Some even have different "state intervention" categories.

My first suggestion is that district leaders should allow, encourage, and support teachers in choosing and changing what and how they teach to meet the needs of their students. Leaders must value the wisdom and skills of teachers, who know their students and their strengths.

If leadership is not supportive of these changes, it isn't hopeless. Elements of the Idea-Building Approach can be applied to and strengthened in most mandated curriculums (see Chapters 4 and 5). For example, a teacher can choose an important concept in a unit to build up (see examples in Appendix C). The teacher can insert an engaging product or performance to use alongside the mandated assessments. The teacher can then weave in the use of brain–body strategies, collaborative activities, and language modeling to strengthen the learning. Over time, the teacher can increasingly highlight the importance of building up and communicating ideas. Throughout the unit, the teacher can get to know students, value their unique talents and perspectives, and help them to grow into the great people they were destined to be.

Teachers at a school site can work together to gather rich data on the learning and growth of multilingual students (see Chapter 3) and share it with other teachers and leaders. Teachers can share their own insights and reflections on student progress, student motivation, feelings of agency, and social belonging. Teachers can share if and why they like teaching more than when they were focused on test preparation.

Regarding tests, students can and will still take them. Large state tests do tend to be harmful on multiple levels and will hopefully be replaced or eliminated someday, but for now, we can minimize their damage by focusing classroom time on effective learning and growth. We have an *educational* "Hippocratic Oath" to not harm or hinder the education of all students. This means that we have the responsibility to do all that we can to provide the most effective education possible to every student.

Another obstacle is comparing education to other fields where countability is more effective. Education is often compared to medicine, industry (factories), sports, and game shows, but education is unique. It is a field focused on human learning and growth of young people. It is the building of ideas within the brain, all of which contribute not only to the humanization of the individual but to the society that the individuals make up.

Messaging

A vital aspect of overhauling is being convinced that this is the right way to go. If you are convinced, the next step is to figure out how to convince key decision-makers in your setting (e.g., district and school leaders) that it is worth it to engage in this transformation. Remember that many educators and other decision-makers have never ventured very far beyond accumulation-based learning. They can't imagine education without focusing on comparing students and accountability. You need to communicate that the risks of making these changes are far less damaging than the harms students face in the current system, no matter where their score land on the spreadsheet.

Interview students who have been engaging in idea-based learning and growth. Record the interviews and share clips. Gather examples of student products and performances. Gather statements from teachers about how this work has changed their teaching and inspired them. One of my favorite things to hear from teachers is, "This is why I got into teaching!" If you are a district decision-maker, work with your team to figure out how to communicate this work to the community and to parents.

You can use student quotes such as this one from a fourth grader in a district engaged in this overhaul work: "I feel my communication skills have grown a lot. I've been hearing lots of students build their ideas, and then I add on to mine. It will help us a lot in the future, I think."

Communicate that the highest priorities are idea-based learning, personal growth, authentic assessment for learning, language development, valuing students' diverse linguistic and cultural strengths, and pedagogical justice. With these enormously important dimensions occupying our efforts, there will be little time for focusing on tests. And that's a good thing.

An Adventure (Vision)

This work is a bit like a high-seas adventure into uncharted waters. You have heard the saying, "Ships are much safer in the harbor, but that's not what they are built for." Education is like these ships. We have been playing it safe in the harbor of accumulation-based learning for too long. But we still aren't getting very far, circling the shallow and boring harbor.

For our multilingual students in particular, shallow and disengaged learning isn't "safe" at all. It wastes their precious time and limits their opportunities because too many decision-makers (a) don't think we can "take the risk" that a major overhaul might lower their test scores; (b) have low expectations and don't think students can handle building up complex ideas; (c) want to make sure that multilingual students stay on "their side" of the bell curve of academic success; and/or (d) don't care enough about pedagogical justice.

We must remember that this overhaul work focuses on closing two big gaps, neither of which has anything to do with test scores. The first is the gap between what our education system is doing for students and what it should be doing. It is the gap between the many pedagogical injustices that students currently endure and achieving pedagogical justice. The other is the gap between who students are right now, whose potentials and individualities are being stunted by schooling, and the amazing people they were born to be. We owe it to our students to take some risks, leave the harbor, and head toward brighter futures. And for students and their futures, the *true* stakes are too high to keep them trapped in lagoons of inch-deep learning year after year.

ACTIVITY 6.10
Closing Important Gaps

In addition to the gaps described in the chapter text, it behooves us to think about other important gaps to close, which are not focused on test-score differences. These are gaps that have resulted from the pedagogical injustices outlined in Chapter 1 and that continue today. They are gaps that schools (a) tend to cause and (b) can and must help to close. Figure 6.12 briefly describes them and provides a space for each type of gap in which you can apply some of the ideas in this book and related resources in order to help close them in your setting if you think the gap exists for one or more students.

There are more "gaps" like these, many of which are highlighted in this and previous chapters. Feel free add to this chart as needed. If you are not sure, I encourage you to ask students and find out if and how much these gaps exist and then work together to close them. These are much more important areas to address than test-score differences.

Figure 6.12 Important Gaps That Schools Can and Should Close

Type of Gap	Description	Ways to Close It (If You Think the Gap Exists in Your Setting)
Agency gap	This is the gap between how empowered in learning and personal growth students currently feel and the higher levels of agency they should be feeling.	
Belonging gap	This is the gap between how welcome, accepted, and encouraged students currently feel and the higher levels of belonging they should be feeling.	
Engagement gap	This is the gap between how engaged in learning and growth students currently feel and the higher levels of engagement they should be feeling.	
Relationship gap	This is the gap between how strong students currently feel their relationships in school are (with both adults and peers) and how they should be feeling about their relationships.	

(Continued)

Figure 6.12 Important Gaps That Schools Can and Should Close (Continued)

Type of Gap	Description	Ways to Close It (If You Think the Gap Exists in Your Setting)
Authentic assessment gap	This is the gap between the student learning that is currently assessed and what students have actually learned.	
Creativity gap	This is the gap between how much students are encouraged and allowed to be creative in their learning and assessment and the levels of creativity that should be happening during learning.	
Identity gap	This is the gap between how students currently feel about how their multilingual and multicultural identities are valued and fostered in school and how much and how well they should be valued and fostered.	

Consider these words by Maxine Greene:

Our classrooms ought to be nurturing and thoughtful and just all at once; they ought to pulsate with multiple conceptions of what it is to be human and alive. They ought to resound with the voices of articulate young people in dialogues always incomplete because there is always more to be discovered and more to be said. (1995, p. 43)

Most likely you have said, "This is going to take a while," more than once while reading these chapters and doing the activities. Undoing decades of accumulation-based instruction and assessment takes time. Undoing many years of not valuing the personal growth, diverse backgrounds, and immense potentials of students takes time. This all requires a lot of trial and error, convincing key people, waiting for some people to retire, and ongoing professional reflection. It requires actively weaving together the things in this and previous chapters, all while engaging in long-term cyclical analyses of evidence showing you what works for your students in your setting.

We must approach the work with patient urgency. The overhaul suggestions described in this book will take years, and the results may take even longer to see. Test scores might go up or down. We must stay the course and do what is right for students, instruction-wise, assessment-wise, and growth-wise. That's the patient part. The urgent part is that the current teach-to-the-test education is doing serious damage to the learning and growth of multilingual students—and many other students as well. We need to start now.

The Idea-Building Approach doesn't require the abandoning of curriculums, standards, tests, or grades. In many settings, it does require major restructuring, prioritizing, and overhauling of instruction and assessment. In schools that engage in the work described in this book, test scores go up, go down, and stay the same. But in the eyes of most students, the yearly test scores don't matter at all. What matters to students is relationships, feeling a sense of belonging, being valued and respected, feeling a sense of agency, feeling success in learning, building lasting ideas, and being able to voice their thoughts and feelings in a safe and collaborative environment. When we neglect these things, learning and growth suffer—especially for students whose languages, learning styles, and backgrounds don't align with accumulation-based instruction.

It's time to have some serious high-level discussions about education and its role. As Tyack and Cuban argue, "School reform is also a prime arena for debating the shape of the future of the society. Such debate is the broad civic and moral enterprise in which all citizens are stakeholders" (1995, p. 136). Schools can be powerful places for humanizing and equipping our students for having great lives and improving the world.

If, after all this overhaul work, we think that we are missing out on the information and learning that comes from accumulation-based instruction and multiple-choice assessments, then we can go back to emphasizing it. It won't be hard to change back. But for now, if you are convinced of the value of idea-building and personal growth as engines for powerful learning of multilingual students, then join those of us who have already begun the journey. As you take the steps to overhaul your system for pedagogical justice, you will see the true power that teachers and schools have to help all students reach their many potentials and achieve pedagogical justice.

It's time.

CHAPTER IDEA

Here is a final big idea that you can build up from this chapter. If another idea was sparked for you, feel free to build it up instead of this one. Remember to add personal examples, definitions, questions, and insights as building blocks along with new blocks gathered from this chapter. Some sample blocks are provided which you can keep or not.

IDEA STATEMENT: Changing the system is vital for overhauling education for pedagogical justice.			
		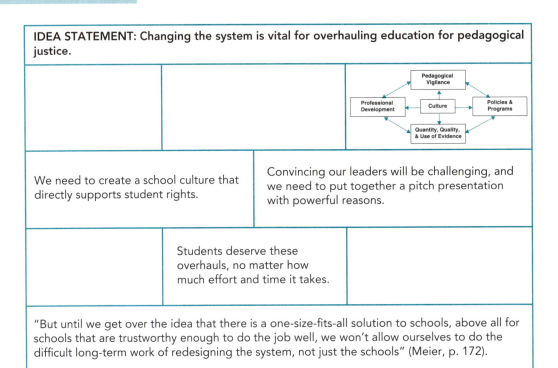	
We need to create a school culture that directly supports student rights.	Convincing our leaders will be challenging, and we need to put together a pitch presentation with powerful reasons.		
	Students deserve these overhauls, no matter how much effort and time it takes.		
"But until we get over the idea that there is a one-size-fits-all solution to schools, above all for schools that are trustworthy enough to do the job well, we won't allow ourselves to do the difficult long-term work of redesigning the system, not just the schools" (Meier, p. 172).			

References

Carter Andrews, D. J., & Richmond, G. (2019). Professional development for equity: What constitutes powerful professional learning? *Journal of Teacher Education*, 70(5), 408–409.

Cochran-Smith, M. (2015). Teacher communities for equity. *Kappa Delta Pi Record*, 51, 109–113.

Fullan, M. (2007). *The NEW meaning of educational change*. Teachers College Press.

Greene, M. (1995). *Releasing the imagination: Essays on education, the arts, and social change*. Jossey-Bass.

Safir, S., & Dugan, J. (2021). *Street data: A next-generation model for equity, pedagogy, and school transformation*. Corwin.

Shafer, L. (2018). What makes a good school culture? https://www.gse.harvard.edu/news/uk/18/07/what-makes-good-school-culture

Tyack, D., & Cuban, L. (1995). *Tinkering toward Utopia: A century of public school reform*. Harvard University Press.

APPENDIX A

Summary Chart

Here are many of the key building blocks from the previous chapters that you can use to overhaul education for multilingual students in your setting.

Pedagogical Justice Dimensions	Pedagogical Injustices	Instruction and Assessment Priorities	Idea-Building Approach Elements
• Agency and voice • Engaging challenges • Idea-building • Meaningful interactions • Assessment for learning • Critical and creative thinking	• Placement • Belonging • Lack of motivation • Mindsets about learning • Separation (*Root causes*: Lack of trust, learning is countable, dehumanization, students as objects, and bias)	• Big ideas • Idea-building skills • Collaborative argumentation • Language and communication skills • Personal growth (positive self-perception, perseverance, social skills, and character traits)	• Know students • Clarifying results • Idea-building • Building blocks • Fill info gaps • Collaboration • Products–performances • Motivation and intrigue • Language • Brain–body • Modeling–scaffolding • Formative assessment

(Continued)

225

(Continued)

Idea-Building Lesson Features		
Prepping	**Gathering**	**Processing**
• Clarifying expectations • Hooks (motivation–intrigue) • Connections and reviews • Pre-assessing knowledge, interests, and abilities • Providing background knowledge and language • Teacher modeling for idea-building	• Experiences • Fieldwork and service • Case studies • Collaboration • Nonwritten texts • Technology/AI • Written texts	• Movement • Hands-on, sensory, music • Story-fy • Visuals • Projects • Collaborative processing • Writing • Scaffolding
Idea-Communicating Lesson Features		
Modeling	**Practicing**	**Workshopping**
• How to design or make • How to speak or perform • To use language • Analyzing models	• Whole class • Small group • Individuals • Use feedback	• Features and traits to highlight • Strategic groups • One-on-one work • Tools and materials

Examples of Overhauled Units

APPENDIX B

The abridged unit examples in this appendix are meant to help you to further answer the question, What does all this (i.e., the overhauls suggested in the chapters and Appendix A) look like in *my* setting?

Each sample unit provides lesson summaries along with numbered descriptions of instructional activities that support the vision of this book's approach focused on idea-building and student personal growth. As you read each example, think about not only how they align with the 12 elements of the Idea-Building Approach in Chapter 4 but also how they foster the six dimensions of pedagogical justice in Chapter 1. Also, note that lessons and units will vary in length from these samples. For example, one lesson might span across multiple days. In addition, the lessons are not complete. When they are planned for a real classroom, they include extra activities, mini-lessons, and teacher strategies (e.g., modeling, scaffolding, questioning, language development). And you will see some aspects of communicating ideas in idea-building lessons and vice versa. For example, writing is a powerful way to process new building blocks.

With respect to explicit (obvious) development of language for multilingual students, you will not see an abundance of vocabulary activities, grammar exercises, sentence frames, or other language practice strategies. This is because, as described in this book's chapters, students learn more language when they are using it in authentic ways to communicate receptively, productively, and interactively (i.e., when they don't realize they are learning it). Add extra language practice work if you think it is helpful for communication and idea-building, but don't sacrifice student engagement and agency by overdoing language instruction out of context.

These units are mostly meant to help teachers across content area courses who have a mix of multilingual and monolingual students. They can also be used to create units for "unmixed" classes such as English language development, academic literacy, and intervention programs. Yet ideally and eventually, most unmixed courses will be unnecessary as a result of having *all* courses use strong idea-building instruction that provides rich learning and language use for *all* students.

Lastly, as you read through these sample units consider how they might help schools to achieve pedagogical justice. None of the unit topics or essential questions explicitly focus on typical justice topics (e.g., discrimination, immigration, segregation, civil rights, etc.). This was intentional because I want to emphasize the importance and power of (a) weaving justice-thinking into a wide range of subjects and units, (b) strengthening instruction with culturally and linguistically leveraged practices, and (c) immersing all students in idea-building that is engaging, socially constructed, and agency-fostering. We want the instruction and assessment in every class—not just the content itself—to foster pedagogical justice.

Second-Grade Math

Objectives
(Key standards that focus the unit's content and inform ideas. But be ready to add and notice other objectives that students will develop during the unit to build up ideas, communicate them, and grow.) • Understand that in adding or subtracting three-digit numbers, one adds or subtracts hundreds and hundreds, tens and tens, ones and ones; and sometimes it is necessary to compose or decompose tens or hundreds. (2.NBT.B.7) • Explain why subtraction strategies work, using place value and the properties of operations

(Continued)

Essential Question (EQ)
"What is subtraction, and how is it useful?"
Draft Big Idea to Build
Subtraction means to take one amount from another amount.
Product-Performance
In pairs, co-design a poster that the teacher can use to teach next year's second graders what subtraction is. Present your poster, using hand motions and objects when possible, to peers in the other second-grade classroom to build up their ideas about subtraction.
Idea-Building Lessons
1. Do a store simulation. Give money to some students who buy items at your store. Give them correct and incorrect changes. Present the essential question (EQ). Explain product-performance. Start filling in the *Idea-Building Visual*.[1]
2. Show a slide show of objects that reduce (cookie jar, elevator, gasoline, time in car, money, water level). As a class and in pairs, come up with subtraction questions for each picture. Solve them in pairs.
3. Model a poster project based on questions from the day before: "Who in the world needs to subtract?" Give each student a different problem and have two students give math talks in front of the class. Then others give mini-math talks in small groups—always with a focus on sharing examples and solution methods, making connections between them, and using all of these to build up the big idea.
4. Model co-solving subtraction problems with objects and base ten blocks. Give several problems to students to solve with the blocks. Have students make up new problems for each other. Encourage students to think of problem examples using items from home that others might not have. Pair-share with this prompt: What is subtraction?
5. Students practice solving problems with base ten blocks. Use the problems as examples in *Idea-Building Visual*.[1] Work on math agency in triads and ask students, "What can we say to ourselves and to others to remember our math powers?" Gather answers on a poster.
6. Do movement math (students stand and some sit; hold up and hide fingers). Pairs come up with their own problems to trade with another pair (using movement, objects, and/or base ten blocks). In pairs, develop an explanation of subtraction to a

(Continued)

(Continued)

> Martian who arrives and has only ever done addition with numbers.
> 7. Model translating blocks into numbers and using regrouping. Watch the video on regrouping. In triads, students develop a draft explanation of regrouping.
> 8. Model regrouping with blocks and on paper. When talking, explain every block and pencil movement. Students practice saying encouraging things to fellow students.
> 9. Students do several regrouping problems in groups or individually and practice explaining regrouping in *Stronger and Clearer Pairs*.[2] Use lots of problems as examples in explanations.
> 10. Students imagine themselves in different jobs and come up with subtraction problems for those jobs. Observe and select some student-created problems for the rest of the class to do. Some students teach them up front (as in a math talk).

Idea-Communicating Lessons

1. Model a sample product (poster) and presentation. The class co-crafts a checklist of what makes it effective. Students pair up and brainstorm poster ideas, remembering to use unique situations and objects that grab others' interests.
2. Students draft their posters using problems from school and ones they created. They choose one to solve in different ways and then make connections between the solution methods.
3. Model presenting a poster (including key terms to use, tone of voice, and asking questions). Students practice in small groups.
4. Students give presentations to each other in different groups (of six). Each pair teaches the other four and gives them a unique problem to solve.
5. Students finish presentations. Students engage in a whole-class discussion and use student-created sample problems to build up final ideas in the visual. Give students a unit quiz.

Assessment

- Ongoing observation of problem-solving, interactions, and product creation
- Final product-presentation
- Self-reflection on math powers and math identity
- Quiz on subtraction (problem-solving and written description of what it is, including regrouping)

[1]Idea-Building Visual

1. This is a visual organizer that helps students build up their big ideas with building blocks that tend to consist of clarifications and evidential supports. Yet students can also include questions,

images, quotations, personal examples, or anything else that helps them to build up the idea.

2. This book tends to use the wall format, but you can use a range of organizers such as semantic maps, outlines, flowcharts, fishbone diagrams, and so on.

3. This visual is meant to help students keep track and prioritize (bigger blocks are more important) the things they are learning during a unit. Ideally, however, the idea and its blocks go beyond the unit and keep building throughout life.

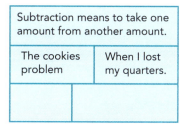

²Stronger and Clearer Pairs

1. Put students in facing lines, standing up.

2. Prompt for an original response; ask an essential question that engages students in idea-building.

3. In three timed pair-shares in a row (e.g., Partner A gets a minute, then Partner B; standing up in facing lines is best), students answer questions; in each successive pair-share, they borrow and use the language, ideas, and evidence of current and previous partners. Ideas get...

   - Stronger (often longer) with better supporting evidence and examples; and
   - Clearer with more precise terms and linked, organized, complete sentences.

4. Listeners need to help talkers communicate as strongly and clearly as possible, asking clarification and support questions and offering information, if needed (What about ...?) if the talker pauses.

5. After the sharing, students add to their idea-building visuals.

Third-Grade English Language Arts

Objectives
• Explain the author's purpose and message within a text (Grade 3 TEKS) • Determine a theme or central idea and explain how it is supported by key details (NYSED NG-ELA-Gr3)
Essential Question (EQ)
"Why is it important to have friendships with people who are different from us?" (Based on the novel *Because of Winn-Dixie* by Kate DiCamillo)
Draft Big Idea to Build
Life is much richer with friends who are different from us. (Also allow students to come up with a different idea or theme about friendship, relationships, or community)
Product-Performance
A public service video or podcast communicating the big idea about life to a certain audience, including a student-written short story or poem and an explanation of how it also builds up the idea.
Idea-Building Lessons
1. Introduce that one purpose of novels is to build up themes for improving our lives. Show an idea-building visual. Present the EQ, the draft-idea statement, and start filling in the visual. Do an initial book-walk to make predictions on how it will help to build up the idea. 2. Read the first pages aloud and have pairs discuss why the character and setting are important. Predict the plot in pairs. 3. Students read in pairs, putting summary and prediction/inference sticky notes every two pages. Pose possible themes in quad groups. 4. Students switch partners and share sticky notes. Give a short explanation of inferences and their value for idea-building. Have students practice (as authentically as possible) validating and encouraging partner ideas. 5. Model hand motion chant for character, setting, conflict, rising action, resolution, and theme. Brainstorm current possible themes based on the EQ. Read aloud and have students just listen (eyes closed) to visualize what is happening. Then have them draw the most important image they saw and share it with a partner. 6. Pick students to lead a literature chant. Introduce an idea-building visual, read aloud, and put new sticky notes on the visual. 7. Students engage in small-group reading and discussions. Students ask questions to clarify and support, focused on building the idea, and put them out in the middle for you to see.

(Continued)

8. Model gathering building blocks from the text, from previous texts, and from our own lives (which are often the most interesting and remembered blocks of all). Continue small-group reading and discussions, but this time students also have two "personal" cards to remind them to share (at their comfort level) examples from home and community to add to their own and others' ideas (and to create interesting information gaps to fill with authentic oral language). Also encourage multilingual students to use and teach words and expressions in their home languages when possible.
9. Model reading complex sentences in a novel and model keeping track of key parts of the plot. Students read silently and take notes. Students prepare a one-minute "elevator speech" in pairs on a big idea (partner asks questions to clarify and support to help talker reach a minute, if needed).
10. Pairs use idea-building visuals in a "mixer" activity in which they quickly meet with six different partners to get and give any building blocks that others have and don't have. Remind students to build up the strongest and clearest idea possible. Remind students to be active and interested listeners, valuing partner comments.

Idea-Communicating Lessons

1. The teacher models several effective podcasts, and the class co-creates a checklist for quality. Pairs work on the first draft of the podcast.
2. Students work on podcasts. Remind them to use evidence from the novel, other stories, and their own lives. They share it with another pair for feedback. Students make adjustments and present the podcast in small groups. Record them.
3. Model writing a poem (with a What and How organizer) and a short story (with a story map) that communicates the big idea. Brainstorm poem and story topics and encourage students to bring up topics from their own lives. Provide additional topic choices if needed. After choosing, pairs start filling in the organizer.
4. Pairs *Co-Craft Literature*[3] (a short story, children's book, or poem). Encourage the use of home language(s), cultural resources, and backgrounds in this work.
5. Students present a draft of the work in triads as clearly and strongly as possible to communicate the big idea and explain how the work supports the big idea.

Assessment

- Ongoing observation of interactions and collaboration
- Podcasts and stories or poems, along with their presentations
- Peer and self-assessment reviews, including questions on agency, perseverance, and character
- Strength and clarity of ideas on the idea-building visual

[3]Co-Craft Literature (Short Story, Children's Book, or Poem)

1. Students use big ideas to brainstorm possible settings, characters, character changes, and problems that can help to communicate the big idea.

2. Students draft the story (can use a story map). Encourage them to incorporate first languages, along with interesting parts related to their homes, cultures, and backgrounds. Remind them that they are filling information gaps with the story and with the parts of the story. The more unique, the better.

3. If a children's book, have them sketch out the illustrations.

4. After a first draft, have them meet with another pair who reads it and provides feedback related to any additional information that is needed, figurative language that would add some color, and so on.

5. Students write a final-ish draft to share with a larger group.

Fourth-Grade Science

Objectives
• Construct an argument that plants and animals have internal and external structures that function to support survival, growth, behavior, and reproduction (e.g., thorns, stems, roots, colored petals, heart, stomach, lung, brain, and skin). Each structure has specific functions within its associated system. (NGSS.4-LS1-1) • Learn and use terms: *camouflage, wings, claws, heart, gills, beak, survive, reproduce, prey, predator, carbon,* and *photosynthesis*
Essential Question (EQ)
What physical features keep plants and animals alive?
Draft Big Idea to Build
Plants and animals have internal and external features that help them survive.
Product-Performance
• Pick one interesting plant and one interesting animal and then create a poster and interview about their survival to present to others. For example, "So, Kelp, what keeps you alive? Well, Platypus, I have roots to that stick to rocks so I don't drift away or float to the surface." • Create a chant or song based on the podcast and/or interview.

APPENDIX B: EXAMPLES OF OVERHAULED UNITS 235

(Continued)

Idea-Building Lessons

1. Introduce the topic with an animal video, present the EQ, and describe the products they will create. Add, "What about plants? Do they have internal and external features that help them stay alive?" Have students draw a plant and animal they know well, with room for writing names of features inside and outside, with arrows. Present *Idea-Building Visual*.[1]
2. Students go outside and observe plants and animals and come up with questions about what features help them survive. Model a drama and song. Have students work in pairs to add a verse. Add to idea visual.
3. Conduct a class discussion with many images on internal features, using hand motions for some features. Stop at each image and have pairs use new vocabulary to answer the question, What internal features help this stay alive? Fill in the idea visual.
4. Conduct a class discussion with many images on external features, using hand motions for some features. Stop at each image and have pairs use new vocabulary to answer the question, What external features help this stay alive?
5. Use the *Info Gap Cards*[4] activity with two sets (one set of four plant cards, one set of four animal cards). Pair up with the other type to share what was learned (new building blocks). Remind students to thank partners and tell them what will be useful to their idea-building.
6. Use triad collaboration (give triads different extreme environments, such as the deep sea, Mars, and Death Valley) to brainstorm internal and external features needed by plants and animals. Come up with one new plant and animal that would survive in these places. Draw the animal and plant and write an explanation of features and their rationale.
7. Read aloud about dinosaur extinction and mammal survival while students draw pictures for their notes. Share in pairs to explain how their visual notes add building blocks to the big idea. Model first lines of *Role-Based Improv*[5] conversations and have students continue the improv in pairs (one playing a dinosaur and one a mammal).
8. Present a slide show on interesting plants and animals. Then pairs choose two to focus on. Model how to gather information and take notes to build up the idea about features. Give a mini-lesson on evaluating internet sources; pairs pick two sites to evaluate, then share with another pair.
9. Each partner researches features of their plant or animals, then shares with the partner. Students then engage in an *Enhanced Whole-Class Discussion*[6] on the purposes of features (to hide, to escape, to stay warm, to find food, to digest food, to pump

(Continued)

(Continued)

blood, etc.) with hand and body motions that you and they make up.

10. Hold an *Enhanced Whole-Class Discussion*[6] to answer the EQ. Students write a quick (timed) draft letter to the principal answering the EQ with the writing prompt: The principal found a rock, a dead fly, and a robot vacuum cleaner—and wondered why they weren't alive. Students peer edit for clarity and strength and use of new vocabulary. Students fill in self-reflection exit ticket on student agency, social skills, and character development.

Idea-Communicating Lessons

1. Model sample posters and interviews (with hand motions) and highlight new vocabulary. Co-develop rubrics to strengthen and clarify all three products and presentations. Students start working on posters and interviews.
2. Model use of hand motions and visuals to help audiences learn from the poster; model using key vocabulary for presenting. Students work on posters and interviews, and they practice interview presentations in groups of four (using the rubric for feedback and revision).
3. Students give their interview presentations in groups of eight as others take notes and provide feedback. Record these. Students fill in and turn in positive comment slips ("_[name]_ really helped me to ..." or "I really liked how _[name]_...") and read some aloud to the class.
4. Model chant with motions based on features from a plant or animal. Students create a chant about features as well, using new vocabulary and highlighting their choices. Practice it with another pair for feedback.
5. Students give presentations and use them to build up the big-idea visual and prepare for the final podcast.

Assessment

- Ongoing observation of interactions and product creation
- Use of the co-created checklist with the interviews, posters, and chants
- Strength and clarity on the idea-building visual
- Interviews and self-assessment reviews with questions about agency and social skills

[4]Info Gap Cards

1. Each person in a group of four gets a different card.
2. Students read their cards and try to remember the information. Sample card:

> **Cuttlefish**
>
> **Habitat:** Coral reefs
>
> **Diet:** crabs, shrimp
>
> **Dangers:** sharks, barracuda, seals, dolphins,
>
> **Features:** Use polarized light to communicate; tentacles to grab prey; change color to camouflage; hear infrasonic sounds of prey and sounds of predators; use jet propulsion to escape, sometimes use ink clouds to escape.

3. Students pair up and decide who will ask all the questions first (sample questions: What are you? What features keep you alive? How have you adapted to survive?).

4. When a student is the asker, the student should also ask questions to clarify and support—especially if the talker doesn't say enough.

5. Each student meets with all three group partners. Each time, students read the card less, talk more, act out features, and have more fun.

6. The group discusses and writes down their stronger ideas using the four examples from the four cards in the group.

[5]Role-Based Improv

1. Pick a text that has characters with different things to share with one another (different perspectives, opinions, stories, motivations, traits, etc.).

2. Tell students the prompt (e.g., "Mammal sees a ball of fire heading toward them and warns Dinosaur, but Dinosaur isn't concerned").

3. Assign roles for each pair (e.g., mammal and dinosaur).

4. Students read (or listen to) the text with the prompt in mind, thinking about their roles and taking notes on what they will say.

5. Have students review their notes and put them onto one note card, with key words and not in complete sentences.

6. Students converse with their roles in mind. They should ask questions to clarify and support (e.g., What do you mean by warm-blooded?).

⁶Enhanced Whole-Class Discussion

1. To prepare for discussion, practice the hand motions for clarity and support and remind students that they are sharing and listening to build up the idea.

2. Ask an idea-building initial prompt (What features help us, other animals, and plants stay alive?) and don't let them raise their hands. Have them think, jot down notes, draw, and then share their thoughts with a partner.

3. Ask, "Who would like to share something they heard from a partner that they didn't know before?"

4. After a student offers to share, ask, "What can we say and ask our colleague to value what they said and to clarify and strengthen the idea and/or building blocks for it? Remember that one goal is to end up with an idea that is as strong and clear as possible. The other goal is to depend on me as little as possible."

5. Optionally, take notes on a large idea-building visual.

6. Every three to four minutes have students turn and share something (that helps to build up the idea) with a partner.

7. You can also use cards or hand motions to prompt for clarification or support if students need them.

Fifth-Grade U.S. History

Objectives
• Describe how geography and climate influenced the way various pre-colonization Indigenous peoples of North America lived (CA-HIS-SS 5.1). Describe their varied customs and folklore traditions. • NYS-SSF.5.1c Examine and compare elements of culture, including customs, beliefs, values, languages, and patterns of organization.
Essential Question (EQ)
How does culture emerge and add meaning to a group of people?

APPENDIX B: EXAMPLES OF OVERHAULED UNITS   239

(Continued)

Draft Big Idea to Build
Elements of culture stem from human creativity in meeting needs for meaning in a geographical setting.

Product-Performance
Choose two Indigenous people groups from different North American regions: West Coast, Plains, Southwest, Northeast, Midwest, and Caribbean. Create a videocast using examples from these two groups to answer the EQ.

Idea-Building Lessons

1. Introduce the EQ and reflect on the map of Indigenous groups before Europeans arrived. Describe product-performance they will create. Introduce culture as deep—not just heroes, holidays, and food. Begin whole-class *Idea-Building Visual*.[1] Assign a written reflection on how students want to personally grow in the next month.
2. Have students rotate to different stations that each have artifacts and images. They answer these questions: What is culture? Why is it important? Why does it emerge? Why did this cultural object or ritual get created? Start a word wall with key terms that will be used for building. Come up with hand motions to remember some of the terms.
3. Students engage in group work on the top four mysterious ancient objects in North America. In groups of eight, each pair gets an object (image) to infer its cultural significance and origins. Then pairs share with the others in the group.
4. Make *Enhanced Gallery Walk*[7] posters on the influence of geography on past Indigenous cultures.
5. In groups, listen to songs from different tribes and interpret translations. Small groups build up the importance of music, then and now. They add to their big ideas. Remind students to share and add music from their own backgrounds. Help them add words to the word wall and idea visual. Have an write-and-share ("I really liked how . . .") session in which they share encouraging comments with each other.
6. Students watch short videos and/or read articles on different groups for more idea-building blocks. Pairs choose two people groups for their project and start their research on one group's culture.
7. Model reading skills of determining importance and summarizing. Pairs continue to research the first group. Each partner individually studies different texts and images and then they pair-share. Both add to the idea visual.
8. Model interpreting evidence like an archeologist. Pairs interpret evidence and artifacts as they study their second group's

(Continued)

(Continued)

> resources. They meet with another pair to share findings, using new words and hand motions for them.
> 9. Model how to compare and finalize notes from both people groups; students do a *Stronger and Clearer Pairs*[2] (if you have three pairs who chose the same people group) to learn from others. Discuss discovered commonalities. Add to idea-building visual.
> 10. Students read and watch Indigenous people sharing aspects of their culture. Do a *Role-Based Improv*[5] conversation between two members of the two groups (What part of your culture do you think is important? Why? How do you think it started? Are there any aspects of other cultures that you think your group could benefit from? Why?). Meet in groups to fill in new words on the word wall and new blocks on the idea visual.

Idea-Communicating Lessons

1. Model how to synthesize information from previous lessons to compose a script and curate images/videos for a screencast (video of narrated slide presentation of an idea). Co-craft a checklist for quality based on ways to communicate the idea clearly and strongly. Students start working on the script and slides.
2. Students work on script and images, music, or video to be included. Model speaking and using transitions, pauses, tone, and stress when reading the script. Students practice reading aloud, advancing slides, and playing video. Students do an "encouraging comments write-and-share (I really liked how...)."
3. Students practice in small groups for peer feedback using the checklists. Students do final polishing in preparation for recording.
4. Model how to record and edit screencasts. Students record and edit them.
5. Watch several screencasts with checklists; validate learning from them. Hold a class discussion to answer the EQ and other assessment questions. Students engage in paired writing (each writes a sentence after the other on one piece of paper) answering, "How can we and the world learn and improve from these groups' cultures? and What are aspects that compare and contrast with a current culture that you know well?"

Assessment

- Ongoing observation of reading, oral interactions, and giving feedback
- Hand motion quiz for key terms
- Final evaluations of screencasts using the co-created checklist
- Final paired writing to show the answer to several questions
- Self-assessment survey on personal growth

[7]Enhanced Gallery Walk

1. Groups of three or four create a poster with key information that will help audiences build up their ideas.

2. Before presenting their posters, students practice what they will say with the same group members who ask questions to clarify and support that the eventual audience might ask in order to help the presenter(s) prepare.

3. Have one member stay at their poster to explain it and teach the concept to others, while the other group members go around and become mini-audiences for the other groups' mini-presentations. Listeners take notes or fill in an organizer.

4. During the gallery walk presentations, have listeners validate throughout and after with comments such as this: "Wow, that's interesting! Great job! I really liked how you ... Keep ... in your next presentation. Thank you! I felt like you really cared that we learn this stuff."

5. Afterward, they add to their idea-building visuals.

Sixth-Grade Math

Objectives
• Use reasoning about rate to solve real-world and mathematical problems. • Understand the concept of a unit rate a/b associated with a ratio $a:b$ with b is not equal to 0, and use rate language in the context of a ratio relationship. • Solve unit rate problems including those involving unit pricing and constant speed. (CC.6.RP.3)
Essential Question (EQ)
"What is rate, and is it useful in life?"
Draft Big Idea to Build
Rate means a comparison between two related numbers that have different units, and it is useful in many ways.
Product-Performance
Make a pitch to investors/donors for a business/project you are starting. Prepare visuals, a one-page summary, projected profits or

(Continued)

(Continued)

positive changes, and reasons to invest/donate. Use at least five different rates during the presentation. Create a podcast on what a rate is and how it is useful in life.

Idea-Building Lessons

1. Start with *Active Drama Launch Problem*[8] and images (e.g., "The medicine for a remote island town is used up at a rate of 15 bottles per day. It's stormy, but you need to fly your seaplane"—show images of production lines, graphs, cars, planes, etc.). Students answer a brief survey and engage in short discussion on math confidence and identity.
2. Introduce the concept of rate and the challenge to find out as many ways to use rates in life as possible. Students do a resting and post-run-in-place heartrate comparison. Time a student drawing stars on the front board, and then ask, "How long will it take her to draw 500 stars?" Do written sample problems in pairs. Start the *Idea-Building Visual*.[1]
3. Students do an *Info Gap Cards–Math*[9] activity. (Each member in the group of four has a different rate problem about space. Each student explains the problem and solution methods and they have a final chat about what a rate is.)
4. The teacher models a pitch to fund a space program (e.g., put a human on Mars), including rates that astronauts have to use in problem form. Triads come up with another program to donate to (e.g., deep sea station, sea turtle conservation).
5. Students continue their triad work to flesh out their "donate to us" pitch, which includes related rate problems, and then give the draft pitch to another triad who solves the problems (and vice versa). All six then add to their idea visual. Do an "encouraging comment write-and-share (It really helped me when [name] . . .)".
6. Triads meet with different triads to give a final pitch for investments or donations. Some triads present their pitches to the class and present their "top" rate problems for the class to solve, with multiple methods and representations.
7. Present a model business idea that has rates and unit costs in it (e.g., chocolate factory) and students solve sample problems from each with multiple methods and representations.
8. Present another business that has rates and unit costs in it (sporting equipment rentals) and sample problems from each, with multiple methods and representations.
9. Present another business that has rates and unit costs in it (e.g., a circus) and sample problems from it, with multiple methods and representations. *Do Stronger and Clearer Pairs*[2] on the EQ. Share how others helped you build up your idea and made you feel good about your math and learning.

(Continued)

10. Model a pitch to donors/investors (the students), such as, "You all have a million dollars and will decide whether or not to donate or invest in my idea." Communicate with rates (i.e., don't just give rate problems), and then ask students what a rate is (pair-share). Have them do calculations and ask you rate questions as if it were their real money.
Idea-Communicating Lessons
1. Co-create a checklist for a good pitch. The class brainstorms business or nonprofit project ideas (the teacher provides choices). Work with a partner to come up with a business or project idea. Then create possible rates to communicate and rate problems involved in both the funding and the work. 2. Partners research costs and create market research surveys for classmates. Analyze and use these numbers in the pitch. The teacher collects sample problems from pairs for the class to do. 3. Partners write the script of their pitch and prepare the slides, images, objects, and so on. Model persuasive language and get the audience involved. 4. Pairs present pitches in groups of eight; each has $1 million to invest; they should ask questions about their roles. 5. Finish up pitch presentations; do a final class discussion to answer the EQ with references to examples from pitches and other real-world rates. Finally, each student prepares a written script for a podcast that answers the EQ. Model how to be animated when recording a podcast.
Assessment
• Ongoing observation of problem-solving, oral interactions, and giving feedback • Final pitches using the co-created checklist • Final podcasts and written scripts • Class discussion and final short-answer test • Self-reflection on math identity, agency, belonging, and character traits

[8]Active Drama Launch Problem

1. Tell a math-rich story (with images, if possible) in which you act out (and students act, too) certain actions and events in the story.

2. Stop, at times, for students to come up with possible math questions (e.g., How long does it take to fill up the tank?).

3. The first read includes the acting out of what is happening.

4. The second read can be students drawing, taking notes, writing down numbers, and asking additional questions.

Sample Active Drama Launch Problem: *The medicine for a remote town is used up at a rate of 15 bottles per day. It's stormy, but you need to fly your seaplane with enough medicine for 10 days. You need to hurry. Worse weather is coming. You fill up the plane's 40-gallon fuel tank at a rate of three gallons every five minutes. After loading the medicine, you start the engine, do your safety checks, head into the wind, and take off (act this out). Now you are flying. It's bumpy. The headwind is slowing you down. Your airspeed dial says you are going 120 miles per hour (mph), but your ground speed is only 80 mph. You burn fuel at 10 gallons per hour. The town is 150 miles away. You are wondering if you will make it there and back.*

[9]Info Gap Cards (Math)

1. Prepare four different problems on the same topic (e.g., rate) and give one to each in a group of four (A, B, C, D).

2. Each student solves their problem silently using two different methods.

3. A pairs with B, and C pairs with D to share. They cover up the problem, share what it said, and show how they solved it. The listener often asks, "Why did you do that?"

4. They share with the other two partners in the same way.

5. All four meet to share similarities across problems and to build up the idea (e.g., about rate), adding to their big-idea visuals.

Seventh-Grade English Language Arts

Objectives

- Support claim(s) with logical reasoning and relevant evidence, using accurate, credible sources and demonstrating an understanding of the topic or text. (LAFS.7.W.1.1.b)
- Organize the claim(s) with clear reasons and evidence clearly; clarify relationships among claim(s) and reasons by using words, phrases,

APPENDIX B: EXAMPLES OF OVERHAULED UNITS 245

(Continued)

and clauses to create cohesion; provide a concluding statement. (CC.1.4.7.J)
Essential Question (EQ)
How do we make the best choices in arguments and controversial issues?
Draft Big Idea to Build
We build up both sides of an argument as strongly and clearly as possible before we decide which side weighs more.
Product-Performance
After building up both sides of an issue and choosing which one is heavier, prepare a presentation to government officials to explain your chosen side of a technology-focused controversy. Prepare an opinion article for the local paper or a letter to leaders in the tech industry or government.
Idea-Building Lessons
1. Present the sample controversy (e.g., Should we pause the development of artificial intelligence [AI] for six months?) Ask students to think of their initial opinions—and then tell them to park these initial opinions in the back of their minds. Present the EQ. Show the *Argument Balance Scale*[10] and tell students they will collaboratively build up *both* sides of the issue as well as possible *before* they decide. Introduce performance and products. Read aloud a two-sided article on AI and ask students what to listen for and what to do with the information. 2. Model the building up of both sides on the balance scale (e.g., on a large scale on the wall) with the topic of pausing AI or not. Watch a short video on AI and have students take notes to build up either side. Model building with clarify and support blocks. 3. Read aloud the first half of a recent article on AI from a news source. Students take notes to build up either side of the issue, and they "ask the author" clarification and support questions. Then partners read the rest of the article aloud to each other. Stop them at times to summarize. Students then share possible building blocks for the whole-class scale. 4. Give four minutes to study the large balance scale visual; then cover it and have students do a *Pro-Con Activity*[11] with two successive partners. Model and explain how loaded language is commonly used in arguments. Students read different articles with

(Continued)

(Continued)

an eye on loaded language. They add any new blocks to the balance scale visual.

5. Do a whole-class discussion of modeling how to evaluate which side of the (AI issue) scale weighs more. Talk about the differing values that we all have. Have triads decide on the heavier side of the AI issue. Have students write an quick "ticket out the door" answering a question each on agency, perseverance, and working well with others.
6. Introduce two new, related issues: (1) Is the internet making us smarter? (2) Is social media good or bad for society? Give half the class one issue and half the class the other, and facilitate a whole-class discussion on what they will do to answer it. Start with, "What do we do with our initial opinion? Yes, we PARK IT way back in our minds!"
7. Model evaluating the credibility of sources on the internet. Have students, in pairs, start researching their issue, looking for "blocks" for each side and deciding how "heavy" or "strong" they are, depending on its content and the credibility of the source. Students meet with another same-topic pair to share and add to their visuals.
8. Do a two-person jigsaw reading of A and B articles, and model collaborative argument conversations, with emphasis on asking clarify and support questions. Use hand motions for clarification, support, and evaluation. Practice conversing with different partner using a *Pro-Con*[11] on their topic. Model language for describing pros and cons ("one advantage of . . ." or "a negative aspect of. . .").
9. Students do final research for building both sides of the argument. In pairs, decide (they don't need to agree) which side is heavier. Get in same-topic groups of six (to share the strongest evidence on each side and fill in any information missed. Model language for concession ("Even though this evidence ..., we think that...").
10. Students engage in *Opinion Continuum Lines*[12] with same-topic groups. Add to visuals. Find a new partner to talk about which side they chose and why.

Idea-Communicating Lessons

1. Model a presentation on the AI issue. Co-craft a checklist for quality. Have students prioritize building blocks and start to plan their presentations, which will include visuals and movement. Remind students to be careful with loaded and emotion-based language.
2. Students work on presentations in pairs. (But each student needs to make a balance scale to practice the next day.) One partner practices the presentation, while the other uses a checklist for feedback. Then they switch.
3. Pair Issue 1 students with Issue 2 students to practice presentations. Model with a volunteer and model providing feedback with lots of

(Continued)

positivity. The listener uses a checklist to ask questions and provide feedback.

4. In four groups, students present to other-issue students (not same as the previous day) and record each presentation. The small audience provides feedback and turns in notes to the teacher.
5. Go over the model AI opinion article. Highlight clarity and strength in each paragraph. Students start writing articles or letters on their opinions of the issue they presented.

Assessment

- Ongoing observation of visual (scale) development, oral interactions, and giving feedback
- Final evaluations of argument presentations using the co-created checklist
- Clarity and strength of article or letter
- Self-evaluations and reflections on confidence, helping others, social skills, and persistence

[10]Argument Balance Scale

1. Model putting the question or issue with two opposing sides to build up in the middle of the crossbar. (There is also a 3D version you can cut from cardstock paper, on which you put evidence cards of different sizes.)

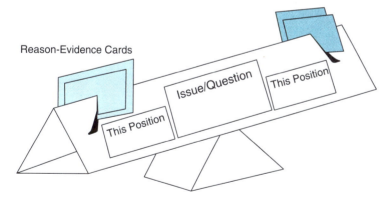

2. Pair up students and have both students start building up one side. They put reasons, evidence, and examples in the margin next to that side.

3. Then students collaborate to choose the heaviest evidence or reason and put it in the largest box. Then they add other boxes.

4. Students do steps 2 and 3 for the opposing side.

5. Optionally, they find potential "holes" or weaknesses and put them at the end of the arrows.

6. Students find a different partner and share what they have on each side. They add or subtract boxes or box sizing on each side, depending on what they hear.

7. They evaluate and compare the "total weight" of both sides to decide which side is heavier. It's OK to disagree, knowing that we all value reasons and evidence differently.

8. Students ask partners which side they think is heavier and share their justifications.

11 Pro-Con Activity

1. In pairs, one student is the director and the other is the talker. The talker can choose the topic, or you can give them the topic.

2. Optionally, beforehand you and/or students can create Pro-Con charts with one- or two-word reminders for three or more pros and three or more cons.

3. The director then says the topic and "Pro," and the talker describes one pro with two or more connected sentences (e.g., An advantage of AI is that it can remind people to take medicine. This can save a lot of lives of people who forget a lot. For example, ...").

4. If the talker says only one sentence, the director should ask a clarification or support question.

5. When the talker finishes with each two-or-more-sentence description of a pro or con, the director says the opposite (e.g., "Con!"), and the talker must start the next description with one of these three transitions: *On the other hand*, *However*, or *Then again*—along with the hand motion of starting with one forearm across the chest, palm down, then lifting it in a 180° arc, pivoting at the elbow.

6. If the talker uses "But..." or no transition, the director says, "Don't forget the transition."

7. Repeat four more times (two more pros and two more cons).

[12]Opinion Continuum Lines

1. This is a variation of *Stronger and Clearer Pairs*[2] in which students use a continuum strip to keep track of where their current opinion is on an issue. Here is a sample:

Should we pause AI for 6 months?				
Yes				No

2. Give students a strip of paper and have them write the question at the top and YES and NO on opposite sides.

3. Give them a sticky note with their name or "me" on it and have them put the sticky note on the continuum where their opinion currently lands. Tell them to be ready to move the note after they talk with each partner.

4. Have students line up facing A and B lines. Line A shares current opinion on the issue, explaining why. Line B partners ask for clarification or support questions if needed.

5. Line B partners share with A.

6. Both partners consider what they heard and change their sticky note positions on the continuum if their opinion changed at all.

7. The person at one end of Line B moves down to the other end, and all Bs shift to the next Line A partner to repeat the process (starting with Line B, this time).

Eighth-Grade Science

Objectives
• Construct and interpret graphical displays of data to describe the relationships of kinetic energy to the mass of an object and to the speed of an object. (MS-PS3-1)

(Continued)

(Continued)

- Construct, use, and present arguments to support the claim that when the kinetic energy of an object changes, energy is transferred to or from the object. (MS-PS3-5)

Essential Question (EQ)

How does energy transfer from one form to another?

Draft Big Idea to Build

Different forms of energy transform from and into one another.

Product-Performance

Design a lab that shows that energy can transfer into different forms and vice versa for an audience of sixth graders. Gather data and explain your design (e.g., your data gathering process and how you kept variables constant) and conclusions. Then propose a new way to harness energy from nature.

Idea-Building Lessons

1. Start with an engaging video on collisions in space to hook attention and prompt student questions. Outline experiments and performances that students will create. Introduce the EQ, the big idea, and the idea-building visual.
2. Each student tosses an object in the air and catches it. They share with partners to answer: What are all the energy forms in the activity you just did?. Students read the chapter section on potential and kinetic energy. Students meet with new partner to answer: Look around. What types of energy do you see? Add to idea visual.
3. Students do an En*hanced Jigsaw*[13] on energy in sports. Model language to use for sharing.
4. Students share sports energy transformations in home groups. They add to their idea-building visuals. They read additional articles about friction and entropy. Lead a class brainstorm on other transformations in life (chemical, heat, light, and spring).
5. Read aloud the first part of an article on other forms of energy and their transformations. Students do an *Info Gap Card*[4] activity on types of energy and transformations (I am chemical energy. I am. . .). Add blocks to idea visuals.
6. A-B partners read different articles on harnessing energy from waves and tides. They describe energy transformations to each other. They add to their visuals and do a *Pro-Con*[11] on either energy source. Have a quick check-in (using hand signals) on agency and skills for collaborating with others.
7. Students start a poster that shows energy transformations to go with their argument-based article-letter arguing for or against funding the source. They start writing letters (or podcast scripts).

(Continued)

8. Students finish drafts of articles-letters-scripts for funding energy sources. They engage in peer feedback partnerships for clarity and strength of claim. They do a *Stronger and Clearer Pairs*[2] that answers the EQ.
9. Give two different sets of materials (cars on ramps and rocks on seesaws) to triads; they experiment with them, changing variables, asking lots of what-if questions, and talking about energy transformations.
10. Model interpreting and creating graphical displays of data showing the relationship between the two types of energy in the labs. Model using target terms for experimenting and making conclusions. Have students talk about designing a lab with their materials. They add to their idea visuals.

Idea-Communicating Lessons

1. Co-develop rubrics for lab presentations. In pairs, students start designing the lab (using either cars or rocks) to show and describe four different types of energy transformations. Have a class discussion on and model controlling and changing variables.
2. Students continue to collaborate to finalize labs on transformations. Highlight language to use in their presentations. Students engage in *3rd Observer-Coach Conversations*[14] prompted by the EQ. Third observers share with the class the positive conversation behaviors and helpful ideas of their two conversers.
3. Model body language, being animated, and getting the audience involved. Students practice lab presentations with opposite lab groups. Students get and give feedback. They add notes on transformations from other groups' labs to their idea visuals.
4. Students give final presentations in new groups of six (video-record these); others take notes and ask clarification and support questions.
5. Show several recordings of presentations to help build up their idea visuals. Plan a day to share with sixth graders, if feasible. Facilitate an *Enhanced Whole-Class Discussion*[6] to answer the EQ. Students engage in self-reflection on identity as learners, confidence, and perseverance.

Assessment

- Ongoing observation of visuals, oral interactions, and giving each other feedback
- Observe presentations and video recordings for areas of the checklist
- Evaluate clarity and strength of argument-based letters
- Student survey on self-perception, agency, and perseverance

[13]Enhanced Jigsaw

1. Remind students of the big idea that the jigsaw will help them build up.

2. Each same-text group reads about a certain topic (a sport) and comes up with building blocks (types of energy and their transformations).

3. Students take notes and practice sharing with the same-text group, which asks questions to clarify and support.

4. Students get into home groups to share. They act out motions when appropriate. When listening, each student in the home group must ask a clarification or support question.

[14]3rd Observer-Coach Conversations

1. In 3rd Observer-Coach Triads, A and B will converse, and C will observe and coach.

2. Model and/or remind students of key skills for conversing, such as clarifying, supporting, and back-channeling.

3. Ask the prompt, which should leverage different information (building blocks) from different students. Before talking, all three write down an idea to build, as well as several building blocks.

4. A and B listen to all three ideas posed and choose one to build up. (If an argument, they park their initial opinions way back in their minds and choose one side to build up first.)

5. A and B then share their building blocks with one another, especially the ones that the other doesn't have. They ask each other clarifying questions (What does . . . mean? How?) and support questions (Can you give an example of . . . ? Why . . . ?).

6. The student observer listens and takes notes on their visual, using sticky notes and symbols, when possible. When there is a lull, the observer can pass a note or verbally interject to keep the conversation between A and B going. Near the end, if C has any building blocks not discussed yet, C can offer them to A and B.

7. C goes over the final notes and visuals to show how much clearer and stronger their idea is from conversing. A and B can do some

reflection to talk about conversation skills that were strong and what to work on for next time.

10th-Grade History

Objective
• Evaluate the impacts of the Industrial Revolution (IR), including population growth and the migration of workers from rural areas to new industrial cities, the emergence of a large middle class, the growing inequity in wealth distribution, the environmental impact of industrialization, and the working and living conditions. (MA.CF.WHII.T2)
Essential Question (EQ)
Was the IR (1750–1850) more positive or negative?
Draft Big Idea to Build
The IR was more positive for some people and more negative for others, yet overall it was more positive/negative.
Product-Performance
Students will create a video or screencast that builds up both sides of the issue and then (after pausing to allow the watchers to decide) explains their chosen side with clarity in describing the values used. The video or screencast will contain different types of building blocks (primary sources, perspectives from diverse people, etc.) and will connect to current needs and tech revolutions, AI, and so on.
Idea-Building Lessons
1. Review major historian questions: Is this (topic, event, idea, and person) significant, and why? How did life change or not change? What were its causes and effects? What perspectives did people back then (and now) have on this? What can we learn from it? Are our sources sufficient and credible? Give an overview of historical revolutions (agriculture, artistic, military). Show a video on IR in England. Present the EQ. Do not share the draft idea yet. Show the *Argument Balance Scale*.[10]
2. Students do an *Info Gap Cards*[4] activity on causes of IR (economic, political, social, and tech-energy factors) and have an *Enhanced Whole-Class Discussion*[6] on why it started at that time and why in England (and why not other places?). Discuss why historians care about different types of causes. Pairs fill in the left side of the *Causes–Effects Organizer*[15] and have pairs change partners to explain the causes and their influences.

(Continued)

(Continued)

3. Tell students that now they will focus on the IR's effects and they will evaluate these effects for various groups of people and for history overall to answer the EQ. Have an *Enhanced Whole-Class Discussion*[6] using images to predict the effects of the IR. After discussing them, put them on large notes on each side of the whole-class *Argument Balance Scale*.[10] Read the first article on IR's effects. Students evaluate credibility and clarify the author's purpose.

4. Students watch the video again and take notes on the effects this time, keeping in mind different people's categories (children, women, middle class, wealthy). Students read the second article and take notes. Have triads conduct conversations on effects for each side of the argument and how big their blocks are and why.

5. Students do an *Enhanced Jigsaw*[13] with primary sources (official documents and letters) about the impact of the IR. Model how to interpret the documents to serve their purposes. They add to personal balance scale visuals.

6. Students engage in an *Enhanced Gallery Walk*[7] with primary sources (diaries and personal stories about the impact of the IR on them). Have students discuss challenges of perspective and empathy when studying history. For example, students can talk about how much "weight" the positive or negative experience of a person (child factory worker) is weighted against that of the middle class and wealthy—many of whom wrote down the history of the IR. If there is time, discuss the saying, "History is written by the winners." Students add to their personal balance scale visuals.

7. Have students in groups of four write four role cards to help you prepare a *Role-Based Improv*[5] activity for next year. They come up with bullet points for a role (e.g., child factory worker) on what the person does, why, how they feel, how life is different than before the IR, and the like. Then students in the group trade cards and try out the activity. They add to the whole-class balance scale visual and personal visuals.

8. Ask how many students are leaning toward a side as of now—then remind them to PARK their leanings in the back of their minds. Hold a guided-class reflection on whether or not they have built up both sides as strongly and clearly as possible yet. Ask, "If not, what other blocks (clarifications, evidence, sources, quotations, etc.) do we need to help us decide?" Students do a *Pro-Con Activity*[11] on IR with each pro and con description using three or more sentences. Students offer five shout-outs ("I really liked how/what [name]...").

9. Students do final research for strengthening both sides. Model collaborative argumentation conversation in which both students build up both sides and then decide which is heavier *after* building up both sides *as much as possible*. Remind students to qualify the positives and negatives for people categories and clarify how to

(Continued)

compare them. Students practice with a partner using their notes. Then they find a different partner and converse without notes. It is OK to choose different sides, but they need to explain how values play a role.

10. Students find two new partners and have a *3rd Observer-Coach Conversation*[14] on the topic. Observers share the positive behaviors, skills, and content that they observed. Collect observers' notes. Students meet in different triads to share current developed opinions as a one-minute elevator speech and get feedback. Tell them this will help them with their products and presentations. Finish with validations and appreciations.

Idea-Communicating Lessons

1. Show a model of a screencast and a presentation of it. Co-develop rubrics for screencasts and presentations. Students with similar opinions pair up to start working on their script and visuals for slides. Remind students to include references and links in the notes. The last few slides focus on "Why does this matter?" to make connections to modern needs and revolutions. Observe for strengths and needs.
2. Students work on scripts and slides. Remind them that all of what they do is meant to clearly communicate to others the importance of looking at the past's major turning points and how they can inform us now. Model language (put it on the wall) that will be helpful in the screencasts and presentations. Students do an idea-trading mingle at the end of class to share and get ideas (they write down names to give others credit).
3. Students put slides together, finalize them, and record the screencast (pairs can alternate talking) in a quiet place. They show it to another pair who gives feedback using the rubric. Students improve the screencast based on feedback and re-record at school or at home.
4. Create groups of six that don't include students' screencast partners from previous lessons. Try to mix students with differing opinions. Video-record with a phone. The five students observing use the rubric to take notes and provide feedback. Collect these for assessment. Pairs regroup to share the feedback they received and make adjustments to the product and presentation.
5. Hold a final *Enhanced Socratic Seminar*[16] to see if the class can agree to a side. Start by reminding students to be open to changing their opinion if the seminar brings up new evidence and reasons—even though the opinion is on their screencast and so near and dear to them. Give students an *Opinion Continuum*[12] with a sticky note on it that says "me" or "my current opinion." At times during the seminar, have students move their note left or right and explain to a partner why.

(Continued)

(Continued)

Assessment
• Observer-coach notes • Observations of argument-based academic conversations • Video screencasts and any scripts written for them • Presentations in small groups • Short-answer test on the content • Self-evaluations on social interactions and self-efficacy in building up both sides

[15]Causes–Effects Organizer

1. Put an event, idea, condition, or person in the center (e.g., IR). If more than three, use sticky notes.

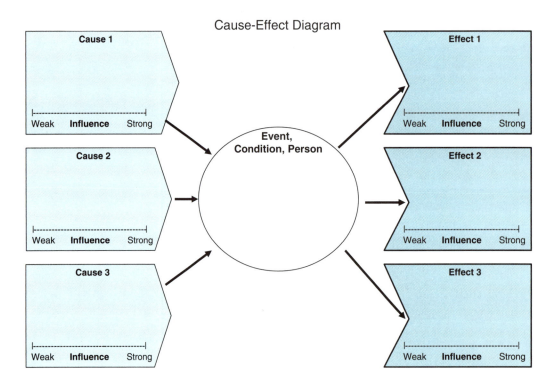

Cause-Effect Diagram

2. As students study it, they look for causes and effects to put in the shapes on the left and right.

3. They also put why they think it is a cause or an effect in the shape (e.g., advances in energy uses were a highly influential cause of the IR because . . .).

4. Pairs or groups can also decide how influential the cause was by putting (and justifying) an *X* between Weak and Strong in each shape.

5. Similarly for effects, students decide how influential the event/idea/condition/person was in bringing about the effect.

[16]Enhanced Socratic Seminar

1. Remind students that the seminar is not a debate to win, but rather it is a powerful chance to collectively develop important ideas and push our thinking.

2. Put students in inner and outer circles. (I often recommend multiple smaller Socratic seminars [e.g., four students in each circle]. They are hard to manage all at once, but each student gets to talk a lot more.) The outer-circle students ("copilots") sit behind their inner-circle "pilots," take notes, and pass notes at times to their pilots. Stop at times to have pilots talk with their copilots to reflect on what else needs to be discussed. Pilots and copilots switch seats halfway through the seminar.

3. Once or twice, have inner-circle pilots turn to chat in pairs while the outer-circle copilots pair up to talk to other copilots.

4. When someone shares a thought that could use some support or clarification (e.g., just one sentence), pause for all to think about a clarification or support question to ask. Copilots can write them down and pass them to pilots.

Examples of Big Idea Statements

APPENDIX C

Here are some examples of big idea statements that you can use with your students. Refer to Chapters 2 and 4 for more information on how to use these. And remember that some ideas are bigger than others. You might have students build up a big idea at the unit level while simultaneously building up a larger yearlong or lifelong idea about how the discipline works. As you look at these lists, you can roughly categorize them into "unit level" or "year-life level" ideas. Do the same with the ideas that you teach that are not on these lists. For example, you might have a unit-level idea about changes brought on by the Gold Rush and a yearlong idea about the push-and-pull factors of migration.

Many of the idea statements are useful for collaborative argumentation. In the most obvious ones, I inserted the opposing side in parentheses.

History

- Bigger isn't always better when it comes to ancient civilizations.
- People migrate when their circumstances change.
- All migrations involve push-and-pull factors.

259

- People in the past thought and felt very differently than what we assume.
- Past historical events impact us today.
- History repeats itself.
- A war can help us understand humankind.
- All history is biased.
- History has silenced millions of voices.
- The Gold Rush transformed California's economy and population.
- Historical photos, objects, and documents can help us understand the past.
- We can learn a lot of history by talking to our parents and grandparents.
- History paints a picture of who we are.
- We can belong to more than one culture.
- Ancient people needed to be highly creative to survive.
- Museums, archives, and galleries are highly important.
- Changes in agricultural practices allowed civilizations to emerge.
- A great leader serves and inspires.
- News programs play biased roles in influencing democracy.
- The "Great Migration" influenced the development of humans in key ways.
- We can't ever be sure of what happened in our past.
- Conflict and change keep causing each other.
- Some things don't change.
- We can use archeological evidence to learn how they lived their daily lives.
- The meeting and merging of cultures can have both positive and negative results.
- The ability to control fire was crucial for human civilization.
- The printing press (or wheel, telephone, light bulb, computer) was the most important invention of all time.

Science

- Understanding physical science helps us understand the world.
- Climate change is negatively affecting pollinators.
- All animals have adaptations to help them survive.
- When a thing gets hotter, its molecules are moving faster and have more kinetic energy.
- Clouds help us predict the weather.
- The sun is so bright compared to the other stars because it is much closer to Earth.
- The water you drink is millions of years old.
- How are sound waves and light waves similar in their effect on life?
- Weather patterns in a given region determine what people grow as their food source.
- What we think of as heat is really energy.
- We can't live without the sun.
- Being healthy means our emotions and physical well-being are balanced.
- As more animals go extinct, so will humans.
- Light is made of waves and particles.
- We use rocks in many different ways.
- Human curiosity leads to new understandings about the universe.
- The automotive industry should make research and funding for electric cars a priority.
- When the sun makes long and short shadows, it is Earth, not the sun, that moves.
- Our understanding of the environment affects how we use it.
- Environmental sustainability requires changes in how we live and work.
- Technology affects the environment.
- Biodiversity is vital for us and the world.

- Governments must play a key role in sustaining the environment.
- We must invest in renewable energy resources.
- Each citizen has responsibilities to the environment.
- An environmental crisis consists of three factors.
- We are heading toward a "silent spring."
- Nothing we do is "carbon neutral."
- Vaccines give antibodies a sampling of a disease so they can prepare to fight it.
- Living things have certain features.
- The earth is like a huge organism.
- Science is about observing, hypothesizing, experimenting, and explaining.
- All matter is made of atoms.
- Antibiotics have changed history.

Social Studies, Civics, and Government

- Social media provides a platform for people to present themselves and their lives in a certain light.
- Citizens have responsibilities to others.
- Culture is how people think, act, believe, and get along.
- Being free means having choices.
- People produce, distribute, and consume goods in an economy.
- Natural disasters affect humans in many different ways.
- Homes vary depending on available resources and climate.
- Other perspectives help us evaluate the world.
- Utopia is impossible.
- Understanding others' perspectives helps us understand ourselves.
- People rely on one another to meet their needs.
- Power almost always leads to oppression.
- Everyone in the world is part of our family.

APPENDIX C: EXAMPLES OF BIG IDEA STATEMENTS

- The benefits of technological progress are (not) worth it.
- The causes and effects of history often repeat themselves.
- A society depends on four essential qualities to thrive.
- Freedom is internal and external.
- Government plays a large role in our freedom.
- Governments should (not) limit individual rights and freedoms for the common good.
- The government should (not) dictate which books should be allowed in the classroom.
- We should (not) lower the voting age.
- Citizens should follow rules for several reasons.
- It's important to consider and respect others' perspectives.
- Several things would happen without a government.
- Some people are more "free" than others.
- An ideal society, or utopia, isn't possible.
- An ideal society would have several qualities and ideals.
- Oppression has several root causes.
- Learning about other cultures teaches us about our own.
- Current politicians need to learn from previous leaders.
- We can—and must—change the world.
- Where you live in the world affects your way of life.
- Communities change over time politically, socially, and economically.
- People explore, migrate, or emigrate for varying political, social, and economic reasons.
- Culture is a way of life of a group of people who share similar beliefs and customs.
- Culture is both a unifying and divisive force in human relations and history.
- When cultures meet, there is an exchange/clash that has intentional and unintentional consequences.

- Goods/services and natural/human/capital resources impact daily life.
- People's lives are different based on the time frame in which they live.
- Artifacts are representative of culture and its values.
- Geography influences needs, culture, opportunities, choices, interests, and skills.
- There is a relationship between the consumption and conservation of natural resources.
- Knowledge of the past helps us understand the present and make decisions about the future.
- Interdependence can lead to some freedoms and independence as well as community and cooperation.
- All civilizations have certain structures or systems.
- Living in a society impacts the freedoms and choices of different individuals in different ways.
- Utopia is (isn't) possible.

Math

- You can find the product of two numbers by breaking them into smaller multiplication problems and combining the partial products.
- If I know how to multiply, I know how to divide.
- The needs of our planet and the needs of the consumer affect our package design.
- The bigger the denominator, the smaller the fraction.
- Fractions and decimals represent parts of a whole.
- Tables help to graph a parabola.
- The slope of a line shows the rate of change.
- Fractions can be written as decimals and vice versa.
- All polygons have an area and perimeter.
- Multiplication is repeated addition.
- If the slopes of two lines are equal, the lines are parallel.

APPENDIX C: EXAMPLES OF BIG IDEA STATEMENTS

- Understanding percentages helps to find the best deals when shopping.
- Linear functions can be represented in various forms.
- What you do to one side of an equation you must do to the other side of the equation.
- On a graph, x and y represent different things. This information is combined to make new pieces of information or idea.
- The sum of all angles in a triangle equals 180.
- A number's place tells us how many ones, tens, and hundreds there are.
- Division is finding how many times one number fits into another number.
- The angles in a triangle always add up to 180 degrees.
- Numbers can be added in any order.
- If a number is outside the parenthesis, you multiply everything in the parenthesis by that number.
- Multiplying polynomials is like multiplying multidigit numbers.
- A quadratic equation can model a projectile motion.
- In a fraction, the numerator is how many parts you have, and the denominator is how many parts the whole is divided up into.
- A reflection of a point over an axis is the same distance from the axis as the original point.
- Numbers can be decomposed.
- We can create math problems just by looking around.
- Math can improve the world.
- Math is a vital tool for communication.
- Throughout math and life, it's important to look for patterns.
- Math can help to eliminate poverty.

Personal Growth and Life

- Nature affects our emotions.

- Life does not proceed in a straight line; it grows in a zigzag pattern.
- We understand the world better when we learn about other perspectives.
- Life is short—seize the day.
- Best friends are loyal until the end.
- The quest for beauty is (not) worth it.
- Nature (nurture) has more influence on human development.
- A good ending never justifies unethical or harmful means.
- We have many different values and beliefs, which are shaped by many different influences.
- The media plays a large role in shaping our thoughts.
- We must not let others define who we are.
- I am a mosaic of all my experiences, conversations, thoughts, and feelings. How well does my family know me?
- One of the best ways to be happy is to help others.
- One of the greatest traits of all is to make others feel important and loved.
- It's important to take care of my body.
- You are what you eat.
- Friendship grows from shared interests, commitment, and time together.
- Don't judge a book by its cover.
- Social media has a negative (positive) influence on society.
- I can learn or improve at anything with enough support, patience, and time.
- It's important to understand and learn from other perspectives.
- Relationships with others influence who we are.
- Success is not just getting good grades or making lots of money.
- Being a team member means being cooperative, respecting each other, and working with others.
- I want others to describe me as . . . .

- Family can have positive and negative influences on us.
- We can learn a lot from older people.
- We must value and celebrate uniqueness.
- We should always try our hardest to do our best work.
- It's important to be happy with yourself while also pushing yourself to grow.
- Character is what you do and think when others aren't watching you.

Literature and Language

- Character changes can teach us how to be better.
- Literature can be windows into understanding lives in different places and times.
- Stories have problems or challenges to overcome.
- Fables, folktales, and myths are universal literary forms that reflect human cultures and values.
- Literature and film can serve as vehicles for social change.
- Language has power.
- There is a world inside every word.
- Stories teach us how others think and feel—even if they are half a world away or lived a thousand years ago.
- Reading literature is about what happens to us as we enter into the plot alongside authors and their characters.
- We all have stories to tell.
- Letters make sounds, which make words, which make sentences, which make meaning.
- What and why we read influences how we read.
- Communication is the most important skill of all.
- All stories are biased.
- Literature has changed (for the better, for worse) over time.
- Science fiction breaks a lot of rules to stretch our minds.
- Figurative language fills literature with life and color.

- We need to improve at objective and collaborative argumentation.
- Some literature topics are timeless and universal.
- Being multilingual multiplies life meanings.
- We need to evaluate what we read.
- We must try to be as clear as possible whenever we communicate.
- Writing is not just for others.

Visual and Performing Arts

- Music inspires people.
- Patterns can be recognized in music.
- Culture shapes music, and music shapes culture.
- We need art to survive.
- Music communicates powerful messages.
- Throughout history, art has been used to bring about major changes.
- Pictures paint a thousand words—or more.
- Dance is the only way to communicate certain messages.
- All of us are artists and need to "do" art every day.
- Creativity is coming up with a new way to communicate.
- Acting can improve life.
- Different forms of art should be used for different audiences.
- Painting (or drama, dance, jazz) should be more valued in our society.
- Art brings people together.
- Historical art helps us understand the lives of people in the past.
- Art can be used to manipulate people.

Examples of Products, Projects, and Performances

APPENDIX D

Here are some examples of products, projects, and performances that motivate idea-building and provide a way for students to communicate their ideas to others.

Math

- Create and write directions to a math card or board game.
- Design something (e.g., a one-person high-speed vehicle) and make a scale model of it.
- Create a blueprint for a new house or building.
- Plan a vacation or party and its budget.
- Create a poster to explain an important math idea to younger students.
- Be a funder and choose between proposals from two different entrepreneurs.
- Design a playground or park.
- Create a presentation on whether postsecondary education is "worth it," based on potential future earnings.

- Create a business plan and proposal to present to a funder.
- Design, do, and gather data from polls, surveys, and elections.
- Write a mathematically coded message.
- Create a poster for a math fair.
- Write an article helping readers to decide which home improvement loan to choose.
- Design a theme park and a budget to run it.
- Propose a policy change at your school or in your community using statistics as evidence.
- Create a game about real life with bills, earnings, taxes, or the like.
- Make a diagram that compares animal populations of different areas.

Science

- Build and explain a scale model of a scientific process or relationships.
- Design an experiment that tests a hypothesis that is based on an observed phenomenon.
- Prepare a science fair presentation that surprises attendees.
- Write an article that argues for making major changes that help the environment.
- Prepare a lab presentation for younger students on a science concept.
- Co-craft a drama in which you act out a science idea.
- Come up with a song that explains a scientific phenomenon.
- Create a short story from the perspective of a ___ that teaches an idea.
- Present research to hypothesize the answer to a current big question in science.
- Write a researched story about living a year on another planet or under the sea or something similar.
- Write an article that clarifies and corrects a major misconception about the world, health, weather, or something similar.

- Study case studies of environmental disasters and extinctions to write up a set of warning signs and recommendations.

History

- Present research on an ongoing question that historians still have.
- Create a realistic journal from a historical person.
- Design a children's book that shows an event, its causes, and how people felt before, during, and after it happened.
- Write an article that clarifies misconceptions about a famous event or person.
- Create a drama/skit that depicts a historical event and write an explanation of its significance.
- Write a believable account from a person whose voice is typically not listened to or has been underrepresented in historical sources.
- Interview a family member or neighbor about their history and views of human progress during their lifetime.
- Prepare a museum exhibit (choose what to display, how to display, and short explanations of the objects).
- Prepare a short guide or presentation on "How to Be a Historian."
- Collaborate in pairs—one from the perspective of an artist and one from the perspective of a historian—to write a speech on the value and accuracy of a work of art that depicts a historical event or person.
- Create a hypothetical "texting-based" conversation between two historical people during an event.

English Language Arts

- Write an argumentation article for an online news site or magazine.
- Research several poems and write a how-to guide for becoming a poet.
- Convert a short story into a script for a short drama.
- Find a theme in a story and argue why it should be a theme to work on for the entire school (and give suggestions for working on it).

- Write a short story, children's book, or poem on an important theme or topic.
- Create a work of visual art focused on communicating an idea and write an explanation of it.
- Identify needs at school and in the community and work as a class to be a group of artists and authors who start a local "renaissance" that highlights needs and ways to solve them.
- Build up both sides of an argument about using certain works of literature in school and prepare a presentation to the school board.
- Write a book review for a school or local publication.
- Write an article arguing for the value of reading novels.
- Write a journal from the perspective of a character in a story.
- Start a school newspaper or magazine focused on a certain topic or idea.

Index

Academic capital, 22
Academic learning, 15, 22, 43, 69
Academic vocabulary, 52, 66, 183
Accumulation-based learning, 1,
    30 (figure), 209
  teaching, 28–29
  tests, 26–28
Achievement, 4, 22, 31, 44, 82–83
Active drama launch problem, 243–244
Adventure, 218
Agency and voice, 9–10
Argumentation, 51–52
Argument balance scale, 51
    (figure), 247–248
Assessment information, 100
Authentic assessment, 14

Bias, 33–34
Big ideas, 47–59
  argument questions from topics,
      55 (figure)
  essential question, 54 (figure)
Big ideas quality, 86–87
Big idea statements, 49, 54 (figure), 56
    (figure), 59 (figure), 120–121
  civics, 262–264
  government, 262–264
  history, 259–260
  literature and language, 267–268
  math, 264–265
  personal growth and life, 265–267
  science, 261–262
  social studies, 262–264
  visual and performing arts, 268
Bourdieu, P., 22
Boyd, M., 13

Brain–body connections, 137–138
Building blocks, 125–127
Building ideas, 32, 61–65, 135, 153, 180

Causes–effects organizer, 256–257
Civics, 262–264
Claim-based big ideas, 47
Classroom, assessing the overall ideas,
    110–111
Co-craft literature, 234–236
Collaboration, 134–136
Collaborative assessments, 110
The Communication Effect, 3
Computer programs, 4
Concept-based ideas, 47
Content knowledge, 60–61
Conversations, 97–98
Cultural capital, 22
Cultures, 143–144, 186–188,
    188 (figure)–189 (figure)
Curriculums, 25

Data dives, 22
Decisions making, 61–65
Deep knowledge, 12
Dehumanization of students, 32–33
Designing and analyzing assessments,
    students in, 110–111
Design products/performances,
    122–124
Disconnectedness, 27

Eighth-grade science, 249–251
Elder, L., 16
English language arts (ELA), 25,
    271–272

273

English language development (ELD), 19
English-speaking students, 2
Enhanced gallery walk, 241
Enhanced Jigsaw, 252–253
Enhanced socratic seminar, 257
Enhanced whole-class discussion, 238–240

Factory model, 24
Fill information gaps, 127–129
Formative assessment, 94–96
Formatively assess, 138–140, 140 (figure)–142 (figure)
Framework, 12
Freire's banking model, 24
Future vision, 76

Humanizing, 32, 217, 221
    learning, 44–45

Idea-Based Learning and Growth approach, 3
Idea-building approach, 3, 12–13. *See also* Building ideas
    english language arts, 271–272
    history, 271
    lessons, 172–173
    math, 269–270
    science, 270–271
    visual, 230–231
Idea-communicating lesson, 177 (figure)
Info gap cards, 236–238
Initiation-response-evaluation (IRE), 24
Initiation-response-feedback (IRF), 24
Instruction
    building blocks, 155–156
    challenges, 183
    developing language(s), 178
    fostering growth, 179–180
    gathering, 162–166
    idea-building lessons, 172–173
    idea-communicating lesson, 177 (figure)
    modeling, 173–174
    organization, 156–157
    overhauled units foster pedagogical justice, 157–158
    overhauling activities, 180–181, 181 (figure)
    overhauling curriculums, 149–150, 151 (figure)–152 (figure)
    overhauling lessons, 158–159
    overhauling units, 153–155
    practicing, 174–175
    prepping, 159–162
    processing, 167–173
    purposeful questions and answers, 157
    workshopping, 176
Instructional coaching, 199–200
Item bias, 27–28

Languages, 88–89, 136–137, 143–144
    communication skills, 66–67, 67 (figure)–68 (figure)
    developing, 178
    literature, 267–268
Learning, 82–83, 84 (figure)–85 (figure)
    assessment, 14–15, 82–83, 84 (figure), 85 (figure), 90–91
    evidence charts, 101–104, 102 (figure), 103 (figure)
    interviews, 96–97
    neat and clean, 29
Linguistically/culturally enhanced assessment, 109–110
Linguistic capital, 22
Literature, 267–268
Little wiggle room, 28–29

Mainstream, 34
Meaningful interactions, 13–14
Meaningful learning, 37
Memorization, 34
Messaging, 217
Meta-idea, 52
Modelling, 133–134
Monolingual students, 2
Motivation, 129–133
Multilingual-multicultural standards, 46
Multilingual students, 1–2, 4
Multiple-choice, 26–27

Negative impact, 28
Network of understanding, 12
Nystrand, M., 13

INDEX

Opinion continuum lines, 249
Overhauling activities, 180–181,
    181 (figure)
Overhauling assessment
  achievement, 82–83
  assessment information, 100
  big ideas quality, 86–87
  classroom, assessing the overall ideas,
    110–111
  collaborative assessments, 110
  conversations, 97–98
  designing and analyzing assessments,
    students in, 110–111
  formative assessment, 94–96
  language, 88–89
  learning, 82–83, 84 (figure), 85 (figure)
  learning assessment, 90–91, 106–109,
    107 (figure), 108 (figure)
  learning evidence charts, 101–104,
    102 (figure), 103 (figure)
  learning interviews, 96–97
  linguistically and culturally enhanced
    assessment, 109–110
  pedagogical justice, 113–114
  personal growth assessment, 111–113
  portfolios, 100–101
  products-performances, 91–92,
    93 (figure), 94 (figure)
  purpose of, 79–82
  skills, 88
  student self-assessment, 100
  tests and quizzes for, 98–99
  unit progress chart, 105
Overhauling curriculums, 149–150,
    151 (figure), 152 (figure)
Overhauling lessons, 158–159
Overhauling policies, 191, 192 (figure)
Overhauling programs, 193, 194 (figure)
Overhauling units, 153–155
  examples of, 227–228

Paul, R., 16
Pedagogical injustices, 30 (figure)
  accumulation-based learning approach,
    25 (figure)
  belonging, 19–20
  indicators of, 23
  lack of motivation, 20
  main cause of, 24–26, 24 (figure)
  mindsets about learning, 21

placement, 19
purpose of education in mind, 37–38
root causes, 29–36
separation, 21–23
teaching, 28–29
tests, 26–28
Pedagogical justice, 2, 3, 113–114
  agency and voice, 9–10
  critical and creative thinking, 16–18
  dimensions of, 8–9, 8 (figure)
  engaging challenges, 10–12
  foundations of, 74–75, 75 (figure)
  idea-building, 12–13
  learning assessment, 14–15
  meaningful interactions, 13–14
  purpose of education in mind, 37–38
  systemwide, 210, 211–212
Pedagogical rights, 189–190, 190 (figure)
Pedagogical vigilance, 205–208
Pedagogy
  authentic communication, 145–146
  big-idea statement, 120–122
  brain–body connections, 137–138
  building blocks, 125–127
  collaboration, 134–136
  cultures and languages, 143–144
  design products and performances,
    122–124
  fill information gaps, 127–129
  formatively assess, 138–140,
    140 (figure), 142 (figure)
  idea-building approach, 118–119,
    118 (figure)
  language, 136–137
  modelling, 133–134
  motivation, 129–133
  results outline, 119–122
  scaffolding, 133–134
Personal growth
  assessment, 111–113
  ideas for, 69–73, 71 (figure), 73 (figure)
Planning, 213, 213 (figure),
    215 (figure)
Portfolios, 100–101
Prepping, 159–162
Prioritizing, 213, 213 (figure), 215 (figure)
Processing, 167–173
Pro-con activity, 248–249
Products-performances, 91–92, 93 (figure),
    94 (figure)

Professional development piloting,
  200–201, 201 (figure)
Professional learning communities (PLCs),
  25, 197–199

Quality, 28, 202–203
Quantity, 202–203

Revisable assessments, 15
Root causes
  accumulation-based learning, 30 (figure)
  bias, 33–34
  dehumanization of students, 32–33
  ignorance, 34–36
  lack of trust, 30–31
  learning is countable, 31–32
  pedagogical injustices, 30 (figure)
Rubin, D., 13

Sample idea-building visual, 48 (figure)
Scaffolding, 133–134
Schema understanding, 12
Science, 261–262, 270–271
Second-grade math, 228–230
Seventh-grade english language
  arts, 244–247
Sixth-grade math, 241–243
Social capital, 22
Social growth, 15
Social studies, 262–264
Standard English, 46
Stronger and clearer pairs, 231–234
Students, 43–44
  argument questions from topics, 55
    (figure)
  building ideas, 61–62
  build up ideas skills, 63 (figure), 65
    (figure)
  content knowledge, 60–61
  future vision, 76
  ideas, 58, 58 (figure)
  language and communication skills,
    66–67, 67 (figure), 68 (figure)
  pedagogical justice, foundations of,
    74–75, 75 (figure)
  personal growth, ideas for, 69–70, 71
    (figure), 73 (figure)
  product/performance, 59, 59 (figure)
  standard, 56, 56 (figure)

texts, 57
Student self-assessment, 100
Summary chart, 225–226
System, overhauling
  accumulation-based learning, 209
  adventure, 218
  culture, 186–188, 188 (figure),
    189 (figure)
  gaps, 219–221, 219 (figure),
    220 (figure)
  instructional coaching, 199–200
  messaging, 217
  obstacles, 216–217
  overhauling policies, 191, 192 (figure)
  overhauling programs, 193, 194 (figure)
  pedagogical justice systemwide, 210,
    211–212
  pedagogical rights, 189–190,
    190 (figure)
  pedagogical vigilance, 205–208
  prioritizing and planning, 213, 213
    (figure), 215 (figure)
  professional development piloting,
    200–201, 201 (figure)
  professional learning communities,
    197–199
  quality, 202–203
  quantity, 202–203
  teacher professional development,
    195–197, 197 (figure)
  use of evidence, 202–203, 204 (figure)
  vision, 218

Teacher-centered classroom, 24
Teacher professional development,
  195–197, 197 (figure)
Test-prep teaching, 21
10th-Grade History, 253–256
Transmission learning, 24
Tricks without treats, 26

Unit progress chart, 105
Use of evidence, 202–203, 204 (figure)

Validity, 27
Vision, 76, 218
Visual and performing arts, 268

Workshopping, 176

Helping educators make the greatest impact

CORWIN HAS ONE MISSION: to enhance education through intentional professional learning.

We build long-term relationships with our authors, educators, clients, and associations who partner with us to develop and continuously improve the best evidence-based practices that establish and support lifelong learning.

Continue Learning

Improve instruction and foster pedagogical justice by collaborating with me to

- Design and use classroom observation tools that focus on communication, idea building, student agency, and language development
- Improve the effectiveness of professional learning teams
- Deepen assessment practices to leverage the strengths of multilingual students

This work is comprehensive and requires iterative implementation and reflection cycles over time. But with the right support and time, you can make change.

To work with me, please email jazwiers@usfca.edu